POSITION OF WOMEN IN THE DOMAIN OF LAW

- Acknowledgement -

Ya Devi sarve Bhutshu Shktirupen Sansthita
Namstasye Namastaye Namo Namah!

With great devotion and inspiration I devote this thesis to my spiritual Divine mother H. H. Shree Mataji Nirmala Devi who has not only a source of inspiration to me in writing this thesis, but who has been a virtual fountain of energy & knowledge in every walks of life to me. It will not be an exaggeration to mention here that, this thesis has been written herein is a result of divine inspiration on my humble self. It is as though a written transcription of her own thoughts as I understood. she is creator of this work.!

Firstly, I wish to express my humble gratitude to the Hon'ble Bombay High Court. As the permission of the Hon'ble H.igh Court of judicature at Bombay, to write this piece was the first milestone for the starting of this journey. I also express my gratitude to my Hon'ble The Principle District and Sessions Judges at Amravati, Buldana, & Pune who accommodated me for this work.

I want to express my deep gratitude to my parents Adv. B.G. Deshpande & Sou. Pratibha Deshpande, who have influenced me to choose this path of knowledge. My father has bestowed upon me the knowledge of noble heritage of legal acumen. I had the pleasure to work with him during the initial days of my legal career. And this has guided and inspired me through all these days. My mother has given me the moral fund of ethics and energy to face all the situations & fluctuations in life.

Secondly, I would like to express my great gratitude to my revered guide Dr. B.S. Bharaswadkar. By his valuable guidance and co-operation only, I can prepare this thesis. Otherwise, this work would not have been seen the dawn of presentation.

It will be a matter of ingratitude; if I would not mention my Late father-in-law Shri Nanasaheb Bhedi who was a fountain of inspiration to me in domain of knowledge. He was not only proud of me being well educated but all of his daughter in-laws . He is who gave me Doctorate degree before actually I get it.

I may also add the great regards to my mother-in-law Smt. Nalini Bhedi as she silently helped me through her constant co-operation on the domestic front. For this work when I used to sit constantly, I always observed a sense of proud & satisfaction on her face. she liked to study hard.

My brother Prof. Dr. Satish Deshpande, gave me constant support and encouragement by his non-intervening attitude. So he taught me to be self reliant. Since my post-graduation I gave him lot of trouble, but I had not seen the sign of anger or hesitation till date to help me, whenever required by his sincerity and hard work.

I have no words to express my gratitude for my beloved sister-in-law Dr. Padma Deshpande. Her innocence, hospitality, pleasant and submissive nature won not only my heart but the thread of this thesis. She is an ideal woman to me; she acquired position in the heart and not only on paper.

All my parental and in-laws relatives, of course were very kindly & positively helpful to me during writing this literary piece Had it not been for their blessings; I would not be able to complete this work. My Sister Adv Neelima Gokhale, brother Adv. Sanjeev Deshpande,. Enlightened me on legal aspects...

The last but not the least is my better half – my husband – Mr. Kiran Bhedi and my beloved son Tejas Bhedi who were deprived of the great deal of my time and attention towards them. Without their immense contribution this work would be dead letter. I have no hesitation to mention here that my husband is instrumental for taking this work. Otherwise, I was hesitant because of my liabilities at work place & home. But he is a very ardent follower of hard work, discipline, enthusiastic, encouraging, energetic & constant inspiration for achieving this goal. He gave me active & dynamic help during preparation of this treatise. Being a management person and workaholic, he never disturbed me and by others during this work or any other official work.. He is the instrument of my entire career. He always encouraged me to be on the height of academic field and feel proud of my career activities. Therefore, I get a strong back up and moral support from him to achieve the equal position from him being women as envisaged in domain of law.

INDEX

POSITION OF WOMEN IN THE DOMAIN OF LAW (GENDER AND LAW)

CHAPTER - I

INTRODUCTION

HISTORICAL POSITITON OF WOMEN IN THE DOMAIN OF LAW

POSITION OF WOMEN IN THE DOMAIN OF LAW

OBJECTIVES: -

The main objective in undertaking this research is to throw light at the place of women in the entire scheme of universal atmosphere by delving deep into the ocean of scriptures history and the entire universal structure.

Law, though apparently is a branch of many sciences and philosophies, this branch has also a special touch of universality regulating the entire conduct of human life. In its narrow sense, Law may deal with day to day civic life, but in its comprehensive sense it has very much to do with the entire gamut of human civilization.

There is common but a mistake belief that women generally occupy a secondary position in the Indian culture and philosophy. However, if we just have a superficial look in some of the pages of our history India has produced great women seers and philosophers like Garegyi and Maitreyi whose deep knowledge in its most comprehensive connotation was beyond doubt. They not only possessed knowledge about Secular things and matters but human life and the very purpose of our entire existences. They were as though were the incarnation of the spirit of the goddess of creation known as Mahakali, Mahalaxmi and Mahasarswati. The very fact that, we were worshippers of the goddess of universe itself shows the very high culture from which we perceived the female being.

Our ancient seers had described the all pervading and pure power and prowess of the entire female being in a memorable verse in the following words: -

यत्र नार्यस्तु पुज्यन्ते, रमन्ते तत्र देवता : ।।

(Gods and goddess dwelled where women are worshiped)

This, the very source of universal existence admittedly being vested in female being. It logically follows that, this strength is to be more precise in a Sanskrit word **"SHAKTI"** which is exhibited in various forms of secular and other objects.

It is pleasant paradox that the very source human existence should be subjected to human laws in our day-to-day life. But even in that sphere, the softer sex has played a distinct role and has made immense contribution even with regards to worthy matters and administration of authority. It will not be an exaggeration to say that women have played significant role in law givers and low makers. They have ruled as queens and have also laid down certain rules and regulations by way of religious dicta. The celebrated seers like Gargeya and Maitreya have not only laid down spiritual dictums but have also acted as judges in between two philosophers advancing contradictory religious theories and philosophers. In an intellectual wrestling (if it can be so called) between Shankaracharya and Mandan Mishra one of them at least played the role of an umpire as through and one imagine the inherent structure of this women bestowed with such a great and rare honour.

Even if we come to a relatively modern period (from the mystical era) we find able women like Ahilyabi Holkar wearing a royal rob and administering Justice and conducting

other royal affairs. Such examples though rare are not less in number. It was Jijabai not only inspired Shri Chhatrapati Shivaji to fight for freedom, but also guided and actively participated though indirectly in the conduct of Shri Chhatrapati's administration.

Even recently Rani Laxmibai and Rani Durgavati have also valiantly and brilliantly conducted themselves in the military as well as civil affairs with equal strength. They placed the double role of law makers and law givers. They were a law unto themselves in an elevated and noble sense on social front Savitribai Phule his maiden march. Not only in war, in administration of justice and other fields but in the field of preaching and establishing peace and coexistence all over the world women have played a very significant role. By a happy coincidence it was India's Mrs. Vijayalaxmi Pandit who was the first president of the UNO general assembly formed after the devastating Second World War.

Till, today there are many women legislators, Prime Ministers, Chief Ministers and other dignitaries occupied position all over the world. Mrs. Sarojini Naidu, Vijaya Raje Shinde, Mrs. Indira Gandhi are some such glorious example. Women have also played important role as distinguished judges in High Courts and Supreme Court Mrs. Sujata Mahohar, Mrs. Fatima can be cited as such examples. Kiran Bedi is an ideal example for those specially who are the inspired women officers for and others in general. She has created heaven in prison. She is the first women officer, who win the Maggassys Award.

The object of this thesis is ultimately to present a synthesis of all these conflicting struggles and attempts made by the softer sex to enrich the treasure of civilization culture and almost all spheres of human life with particular reference to the branch of law in its widest connotation. This is ultimately with a view to remove an inferiority complex amongst the female community all over in our country, whose voice has been suppressed in a medial period due to some volcanic political events in some parts of the world. However because of the amidst attempt of women education by Maharshi Dhondo Keshav Karve and other social activist female get education platform and learn and express them self. It is also aimed at presenting a full picture of the contribution and position of women in the domain of law with a view to cut to size the superiority complex amongst some despotic thinkers obvious of the latent and patent abilities of the female sex.

HYPOTHESIS: -

A brief account of position of women in olden days shows that, women have achieved highest echelon in all spheres of life. The question is, whether they achieved such position due to glorious Indian culture or with the help of their instinct traits. It is said that, the civilization of the country is known by the attitude of the society towards women. How the society looks at the women.

Of late, status of women is burning issue. At a glance one can see that, numbers of legislations are passed to uplift the position of women as to achieve their equal status with men. Whether the legal provisions reflects as social reality. The answer is there is a paradox in female laws and social reality. Instead of discussing this aspect at length at this juncture, I think it proper to understand the basic legal provisions relating to women.

Constitution of India : -

Art 14 of the constitution of Indian envisaged the basic rote in which further voyage of equality proceeds; Art 14 of the Indian constitution contemplates.

"The State shall not deny to any person equality before law or the equal protection of the laws within the territory of Indian."

Art 15 of the constitution of India has shown the specific path on which the principles of equality must be followed. Art 15 runs as follows " the state shall not discriminate against any citizen on grounds only of religion, race, caste, sex, place of birth or any of them."

As such there is a legal prohibition to discriminate between men & women only on account of their sex. Art 16 provides for equality of opportunity in matters of public employment. Art 16 (4) give ample powers to state to make any special provision for reservation of appointments or posts in favour of any backward class of citizens, which in the opinion of state is not adequately represented in the services under the state.

Art – 21 of the constitution of India contemplates, "No person shall be deprived of his life or personal liberty except according to procedure established by law".

Of late, our Hon'ble Supreme Court & Hon'ble High Court are giving multifaceted shape to this article as to encompass the widest meaning of Art 21 as right to live which includes right to have medical aid, right to education, right to gender equality.

In its recent judgment[1] their Lordships Dr. A.S. Anand & V.N.Khare, while dealing with the Art 21 & 14 constitution of Indian held that.

Each incident of sexual harassment at the place of work results in violation of fundamental right to gender equality and the right to life & liberty. The two most precious fundamental rights guaranteed are of

---

[1] AIR 1999 SC 625

sufficient amplitude to encompass all facets of gender equalities including prevention of sexual harassment and abuse. Their Lordships further held.

The sexual harassment of female at the place of work is incompatible with the dignity & honor of a female and needs to be eliminated and there can be no compromise with such violation admits of no debate.

The principles laid down by their Lordships clearly indicate the position of women in domain of law.

Apart from constitutional enshrined provisions, many references can be given of the ordinary legislations relating to women. For example 598A, 304B, 376 A, B, C, 494 of IPC.

Amongst all these provisions sections 498A IPC has become more debatable in regard to its bias use by the female.

However, in view of decision of our Bombay High Court in Balkrishna Moghe[2] case reported, Their Lordships Justice

---

[2] 1998 (3) MLJ 331

A.V.Sawant & J. Chandrashekhar Das held that,

"Section 498A is valid piece of legislation having regard to the social evil that was sought to be remedial, classification of the husband and his relatives as a separate class under section 498A of IPC is not discriminatory and there is no violation of the guarantee enshrined under Art 14 of constitution.

Further while giving its finding on the definition of cruelty. There is valid nexus between section 498A & the object sought to be achieved".

The Hon'ble Bombay High Court & the Hon'ble Supreme Court have thus considered the status of women in domain of law.

The innovative amendment like in section 114 A of Indian Evidence Act in regard to presumption as to absence of consent in certain prosecutions for rape has been added in Indian evidence Act.

As such, one can site number of illustrations as to show how the legislature, executive & judiciary have acknowledge the position of women in domain of law.

One more example I would like to refer here which though is last but not the least, is the recent amendment of Maharastra State in Section 29 of Hindu Succession Act[3] which was incorporated in Hindu Succession Act on 22 June 1994 as Section 29 A, 29 B & 29 C.

By way of this Maharastra Amendment, the daughter are made coparcener as like male in regard to all the rights & obligations which a male coparcener have under the Hindu law. The said Maharastra Amendment has made classification between the female those married before 22 June 1994 & female married or going to be married after 22 June 1994.

This piece of legislation has brought the female at per with male in some proprietary rights. These provisions confer on the daughter a status of a coparcener. The object and reasons for passing this Act state, the constitutional mandate of equality between men and women the pernicious system of

[3] Mayne's Hindu Law 19th edition

dowry existing due to the existence of coparenery system and to remove the inequality and to destroy the breeding around of dowry. These provisions have the effect of conquering the exclusive and last vestige of a citadel of the males by females (though not all) and demolishing the monopoly of the males to own joint Hindu family property by capturing a seat for themselves equal to and along with their male associates. The ancient age monopoly has been broken & given a pride of place along with her father & brother & other male members of the coparcenary. Thus constitutional mandate of equality of sex is carried out by this legislative stroke, which demonstrates place & position of women in domain law.

All these legislations no doubt give protection to women world. But the question is, whether these legislations could control the burning issue of the female world in regard to their status.

By this thesis, I wish to analysis the position of women as **"SHAKTI"** as it was in golden ancient days and the identity crisis of the women now a days with special reference to their legal rights by virtue of various innovative legislations favouring women, as an attempt to make them on par with men. By this research, I also wish to conclude that position of women is the inseparable part of the society & consequently of law. Therefore, position of women is interwoven in the domain of law.

Law is nothing but a moral and legal sanction of the society for the purpose of generating security and discipline amongst people. I wish to conclude that, in those days moral rules (unwritten) were so strong, so women could show their position in the administration of law, irrespective of their education and written rules.

However, in the present days due to changed scenario of society, more and more women legislations are made as to provide them this armor for protecting and exhibiting their position from all the devices of society. And thus, the position of women in domain of law with special reference to Indian culture is as significant as it was in ancient days and their position is quiet different that than of men.

The Judicial voyage shows that, the Hon'ble Supreme Court has recognized the Hon'ble and special status of women in society. Consequently to consider that delicate and vital position of women in the society, Law makers have give special considerations to women legislations which is the utmost need of the society as to show the graphic civilization of the Indian Society with the help of law. So, I wish to show by this thesis whether position of women can be assessed and uplifted successfully with the help of law much less in the domain of law. And I feel it was up grated it will be through divine law.

CHAPTER II

Position of Women in Scriptures & Vedic and Post Mahabharata Period.

Position of Women in Scriptures & Vedic Period.

According to Brihadaranyaka Upanishad[4], man is completed by the equal halves of man & women like halves of a shell completing the whole shell ardhavrigalamiva. The women fill up the void in men's lives-not only as equal partners but infinitely more superior to them in their inherent & special rights as mothers.

If god made man in His own image then the Mother of god made woman as the reflection of the Holy Spirit. The Mother Universe bestowed in her womb the primordial Truth, which could never be vanished. It is eternal, pure, resilient, all pervading.

A befitting praise to the Devi in the Devi Mahatma status, "all forms of knowledge are aspects of thee, and all women in the universe are thy form".

[4] Great Women of India by Yogi Mahajan

In the scheme of creation man & woman were born as equals, complementary to each other, as the two wheels of chariot. There are two types of wheels rotating because they are similar yet are not similar. In Indian marriage the question of competition or equality is not considered.

This consciousness follows from the archetype Purusha & Prakriti. Pursha, the male principle of the universe, yang, is the external witness of the Play of prakruti, the female principle of universe, yin, which spontaneously creates all material reality. Parvati is Shiva's Shakti necessary for involving him in creation. Shiva is described as sky, Parvati as the earth, Shiva is subject Parvati is object. Shiva is ocean Parvati the sea. Shiva is a sun, Parvati the light. The two are actually one different aspects of the ultimate reality.

Ardha Natnareshwara concept in India illustrates that show the man & woman are complement to each other. Though they have different roles to play each is the component of other & incomplete without the other.

Position of women in Vedic era :

From the Rig-Vedic age women were partners with men in all spheres. Women studied both the physical & metaphysical knowledge & become great scholars, seers & teachers. When Yajnavalkya wanted to divide his property between his two wives Katyayani & Maitrey, the latter elicited to accept saying, what should I do with all the worldly wealth through which I cannot gain immortality?

The "Ramayana" places the mother in the highest position. In "Kishkindha kanda" of Ramayana, states that the wife is the self of the man. In "Ayodhya kanda" the mother is enjoined to be honored as much as the father.

In "Mahabharata period", women were well versed not only in philosophy but also in all branches of knowledge. They enjoyed equal rights with men in all respects. The great ascetics Sulbha roamed from place to place in search of truth. Even Raja Janaka respected Sulbha's knowledge & drew inspiration from her. Harivansha wife of Prabhasa attained the highest perfection in Yaga & expanded the Brahma Vidya.

Arundhati wife of great sage, Vasistha who equaled her husband in knowledge and intellect.

Gargeyi, Maithreyi, & Sulabha are famous for their spiritual debates. In several mantras it is said that, women of this country have given its man folk valor, spiritual illumination, piety, & intellectual brilliance.

A woman's dharma was held above her family attachments. Dharma rested on the foundation of a women's strength of character. Heroic queens Kunti & Draupadi were exemplary characters & paragons of virtue, sacrifice & righteousness. Draupadi's fiery words to her defeated son were an example of her fortitude.

All these philosophers, saint or poet though were learned remains absorbed in her own work & can not even think of self assertion or self advertisement. Even Shri Mataji Nirmala Devi explains that, "A women should stay in the background and a man in the fore front. She should help him in the forefront. She should help him in the background for she is current of his power.

She must remain within her moryadas i.e. the norms and boundaries of social conduct, which lend her dignity honour & protection. Her greatness lies in the service to others & through being the mother of great children. You cannot create flower. But least you can nature innocent lines & cast the mould of her statesmen & patriots.

As we know lord Ram is known as Kausalya's Ram, Krishna is known as Yashoda's Krishna, A great king Chhatrapati Shivaji Maharaja is the great output of Jijamata. Sita is held as ideal wife & great mother of Lava & Kusha. Gandharai is known for her impartiality. Kunti great mother of Pandava's & she upholds Dharma. Draupadi's arguments about Dharma in Kuruabha are also famous.

In fact the great wars in Ramayana & Maharashtra were fought to uphold the dignity of women. In famous "Vidhura Neeti" Vidhura stresses that women should be specifically looked after because they are worthy of being worshiped.

Position of Women in Post Mahabharata Period till foreign invasions :

The goddess earth is the great mother, we worship her as Bharat Mata the land of the Indian subcontinent mother worship inspired the freedom struggle. During freedom struggle Bharat Mata had to be liberated from foreign yoke. The great Bengali Poet Bankimchandra stirred the soul of the Indian masses in his inspiring hymn "Vande Mantaram" (hail to thee my mother).

In post Maharashtra period there was certain shift in attitudes & recreations of women because of well spread trade, wealth for centuries together, leisure & Peace. Music & dance became very popular which has brought some looseness in morals. Some puranas describe women as fickle minded, frivolous, untruthful. The great stress was given on physical purity & chastity which slowly led to the preference of marriage in early age.

Buddism gave much stress on sanyasa so viewing women as incarnation of evil trying to men was considered. Upnayana ceremony became formal without vedic mantras marriage ceremony also Slowly equated to Panama. Therefore the Vedic education was slowly got devised to women. And so, the intellectual advancement & status suffered a set back in principle. But in actual practice women continued to share the earlier respect & achievements in social life.

There are galaxies of poetesses in the 7th century. Lick poetess Vijaynka was ranked as a peer of Kalidas in vaidharbhi style of composition. Kshanavati an astronomer & Lilawati a mathematician were very famous. Many women excelled in temple, architecture, philosophical debates, warfare, trade & industry, administration etc. child marriage did not take roots as prevalent practice women were not punished for adultery. A woman was allowed to remarry in case of unheard for long period of her husband or his death, importance or outcaste etc.

Sati & Devadasi practices started. Devadasi system started for entertaining deity by unmarried girls on festive occasions in temples with their songs. There was slight appreciation of the practice of a women becoming a sati out of intense love, devotion & attachment to her husband. There are a lot of examples of widely respected widows like Prabhavati Devi of Vakataka dynasty, Mayanalla Devi of Gujarat, Karpura Devi of Aimer. Sonless widows inherited the property of their husbands.

Changing Social Scenario due to foreign invasion[5] :

India had to face invasion by Arab, Afghan, Pathan, Turk, Mughal & Europeans who were not mere barbarians but also flag bearers of definite ideologies, which they compelled upon us. We tried to protect our cherished values by rigidifying the customs needs at that time and codifying religious injunctions, which ultimately got codified as laws. These invasions lead to increase in child marriages and a decline in women's education through home education was wide spread.

[5] Ancient women in India

The spirit of sacrifice of Indian women is beyond record. Each tale of sacrifice is more breath taking than the other. So many lives have been sacrificed at the alter of Bharat Mata. Mother India that even soil of Bharat is worthy of worship. Nobility in women does not depend upon race, cast & creed but upon ideals. It is the outcome of their dharmic way of life.

For example, Dhatri Panna Dasi of Mewar gave sacrifice of her won son for saving life of Udaising second son of Maharana Sanga. She placed her own son in the cradle in place of Udaising & Ranbir murdered him considering as Udaising.

Queen Chinnammaji was a woman of such extraordinary administrative skill & genius that her husband entrusted the reins of government to her hands. She gave shelter to Shivaji's son Rajaram. She repulsed the Moghal army & totally routed it. Aurangjeb was impressed by her valor she also defeated Mysore army.

Ahilyabai Holkar a great devotee of siva, while performing daily routine she would always militate & may & thus receive tremendous inner strength & guidance to face mounting challenges of life. Ahilya showed rare administrative ability & the Peshwa, the ruler gave her complete charge of the state. She was a very kind & humane person, well known for justice but if required she could rule with an iron hand.

Rani Chennamma queen of Kittur was the first ruler to defy & overcome the mighty British Empire. After death of Raja Mallaraja Desai the little state prepared under her benevolent rule. In he rule women & children were always respected & sheltered. Thus is a maryada (code) strictly adhered to in Indian culture. In fierce battle with British Rani was imprisoned & she died after 5 years.

The Ruins of the ancient palaces of India tell tales of unbelievable honour, beauty & sacrifice of Rani Laxmi Bai of Jhansi. Each stone of the Kjamso fort is a monument to glory. Indian historians paid rich tribute to their Queen saying that, even the soil of Jhansi is sanctified by the Heroic sacrifice of the martyrs. She bravely defended the fort of

Jhansi against British but compelled to make dramatic escape through British ranks. She joined powerful commander Tatya Tope. She fought valiantly until a bullet hit her & she fell to ground. The British commander general Rose was so struck by her superhuman force that he saluted her fallen body saying.

"We may have won the battle but the glory goes to Jhansi Ki Rani" Jijabai, the mother of Shivaji was the most outstanding Queen of Maharashtra. In a conflict between her husband & father, well verse in the duties of a married woman the determined Jijabai had the fortitude to stand by her husband. Jijabai brought up Shivaji on the foundation of Dharma. She taught him to regard women in high esteem. Jijabai was a great social reformer & was ahead of her time.

Queen Tarabai-wife of Rajaram bravely led Maratha forces, moving from fort to fort & displaying a rare military genius. She is a tigress Queen who by dint of her courage did not allow Aurangjeb to impose Moghal rule in Deccan.

Rani Padmini, Queen of Chittor possesses the power o perpetually & to save her honor, she burnt herself in ceremony of Jauhar. Allaudin Khilji, Muslim ruler, wanted to possess her after seeing her exquisite beauty & threatened to besiege he palace. So Queen Padmini's soldiers launched surprise attack on sultan but finally overpowered them. When Queen did not see signal of victory she assembled the women in the fort & addressed them saying- "let our honor is defiled by these barbaric men let those among you who desire, to perform Jauhar enter into the fire. "Then offering prayer to goddess Jagadamba, they peacefully gave up their souls in the fire to vindicate their honor.

Women Freedom Fighter :

Sarojini Naidu is affectionately known as the Nightingale of Bengal. A poetess turned freedom fighter. She so believed that "until & unless we raise the fallen women in this country & make their voice heard, India's salvation would remain a distant freedom. A Cambridge graduate, she championed the cause of women emancipation & succeeded in getting the resolution passed for women's franchise. She charged Indian youth with "give me liberty or death. She was first governor of U.P. independence.

Kamala Devi Chattopadhya-during the civil Disobedience movement 1930 openly prepared salt & sold it even in the high court premises. When she was taken to court for trial she invited the magistrate to buy salt & asked him to resign & join the movement. She started selling salt in the courtroom for this she was jailed for six months. The woman of war became the artisan's messiah after independence. She received Padma Bhushan Award.

Cornelia Karuna Salve was a very active, dynamic & serve child. She was determined & became the first woman graduate in Mathematics Honors from Fergus on college under the tutelage of the great mathematician. Rangler Paranjape she even studied law. She was a principle of St. urasula's High School Nagpur. Out of Rs. 125 monthly salary she surrendered Rs. 100 as management refused to take it she gave it away to charity. Her husband Barrister Shri P.K. Salve & she herself with their patriotic zeal found vent in the meeting with Mahatma Gandhi. There after every Saturday Cornelia would go to clean the colonies of untouchables Harijans. She took part in Chitnis Park meeting. For which she was arrested but later released because she had little children to look after.

Shri Mataji Nirmala Devi- in 1942 the principle of Nirmala's college reported Cornelia about her underground activities in the freedom struggle & how she had led a procession boldly facing the British soldiers. Tears of admiration filled Cornelia's eyes & she said, " I am a very proud of mother to have such a brave girl" she had complete trust in her daughter, knowing that one day she was destined to transform the world when she was pregnant with her, she had a great desire to see a lion in the open. Shri Nirmala Devi is not only the freedom fighter but also much more than it as she gives spiritual realization to thousands of seekers of truth.

Position of women in 19th century :

Till the beginning of 19th century the bad practices of sati, Kulinism, purdah were limited to few castes in few areas, but the picture appears to be very bleak. The emancipation of women & liberation movements started & gave a different direction to the understanding and lives of women. British pointed India in bad shape. They have praise for Indian women in beginning; in order to loot us they had to destroy the social fabric system of education trade etc. woman was increasingly considered merely as an object of enjoyment. The McCauley's education system aimed at cutting the very roots of our culture did have some effects on the social structure.

It is necessary to take reference of the first lady lawyer of India specially when the subject is about of position of women in domain of law.

Cornelia Sorabji[6] (1866-1954) was a pioneer woman lawyer of India whose formative with the high noon of the British Empire. She occupies a

---

[6] **Academic Books – Cornelia Sorabji – India's Pioneer Woman Lawyer** - http;//www.oup.co.in

significant place in Indian history a crucial role in trying to open up th legal profession to women much before they were to plead before the courts of law. This detailed biography uses rich and hitherto unused a remarkable individual who has remained neglected in studies on India's transition to also in the historiography of women and gender.

A Parsee and daughter of a convert to Christianity, Sorabji was the first woman to study the second Indian woman barrister, and among the early Indian women to practice at the Court. She was also appointed to a senior office under the British Indian government interests of the purdahnashins, the women in purdah who owned property accomplishments, she failed to develop a critique of the Empire, and by opposing I politics in the Gandhian era, she placed herself on the wrong side of history.

With considerable skill and insightful analysis, the author has succeeded in dissent Sorabji from the established stereotypes in nationalist of feminists studies. She also life to the complexities of gender issues in colonial India, and raises questions about it her life from the perspective of emancipatory politics of gender.

The foreign rule in India saw a sudden shift in the way of life of women, Except for a few examples of great women, the period of independence struggle & the post independence period did not see much of improvements in the conditions of the common woman. In the present day scenario in India, though quite a lot of contributions to the nation building are earning from women they are being locked upon as mere commodities & their beauty consciousness has been exploited in various ways.

United Nations commissions on the Status of Women :

United Nations established a body in 1946 to monitor the situation of women & to promote women's rights. The commission's work has been instrumental in bringing to light all the areas in which women are denied equality with men. These efforts for the advancement of woman have resulted in several declarations & conventions of which the convention on the elimination of all forms of Discrimination against women is the central & most comprehensive document.

Indian constitutions and gender equality

The preamble of our constitution, which is key to open minds of makers, enshrined the principle of gender equality. Part 3 fundamental Rights & Duties part 4 directive principles not only grants equality to women but also empowers the state to adopt measures of positive discrimination in favour of women.

CHAPER III

POSITION OF WOMEN AS ENVISAGED IN THE CONSTITUTION OF INDIA

WOMEN AND CONSTITUTIONAL LAW :-

"Women constitute half the world population, perform nearly two -thirds of works hours, and receive one - tenth of the world's income and own less than one - hundredth percent of word's property."[7]

Half of the Indian populations too are women. Women have always been discriminated against and have suffered and are suffering discrimination in silence. Self - sacrifice and self - denial are their nobility and fortitude and yet they have been subjected to all inequities, indignities, inequality and discrimination.[8]

- Justice K. Rama Swamy

The Indian constitution adopted by the constituent Assembly on 26th November, 1949 is a comprehensive document enshrining various principles of justice, liberty, equality and fraternity. These objectives specified in the preamble and elsewhere form part of basic structure of the Indian constitution. The

[7] A Report of the United Nations, 1980

[8] Madhu Kishwar Vs. State of Bihar (1996) 5 SCC 148.)

fundamental law of the land assures the dignity of the individuals irrespective of their sex, community or place of birth.

With regard to the women, the constitution contains many negative and positive provisions, which go a long way in securing gender justice.

While incorporating these provisions, the framers of the constitution were well conscious of the unequal treatment meted out to the fairer sex, from the time immemorial. The history of suppression of women in India is since long and the same has been responsible for including certain general as well as specific provisions for upliftment of the status of women. The rights guaranteed to the women are on par with the rights of men and in some cases the women have been allowed to enjoy the benefit of certain special provisions.

The general provisions relating to the equal rights available to them are, the right to vote and other political rights; the fundamental rights contained in part III of the Constitution and the directive principles etc.

The preamble to the Indian Constitution contains various goals including "The Equality Of Status and Opportunity" to all the citizens. This particular goal has been incorporated to give equal rights to the women and men in terms of the status as well as opportunity. It has been the basis for many legislations like the modern Hindu laws which aim at giving equal status and rights to the women.

Even though, all the fundamental rights contained in part III, Articles 12 to 35 are applicable to all the citizens irrespective of sex, certain fundamental rights contain specific and positive provisions to protect the rights of women.

Part III of the Constitution of India

Fundamental Rights and Duties

RELEVANT ARTICLES OF THE CONSTITUTION OF INDIA RELATING TO GENDER EQUALITY -

Article 14 : Equality Before Law :-

The state shall not deny to any person equality before the law or the equal protection of the laws within the territory of India.

Article 15 : Prohibition Of Discrimination Of Grounds Of Religion, Race, Caste, Sex Or Place Of Birth :-

The state shall not discriminate against any citizen on grounds only of religion, race, caste, sex, place of birth or any of them.

No citizen shall, on grounds only of religion, race, caste, sex, place of birth or any of them. Be subject to any disability, liability, restriction or condition with regard to –
Access to shops, public restaurants, hotels and places of public entertainment : or
These of wells, tanks, bathing ghats, roads and places of public resort maintain wholly or partly out of state funds or dedicated to the use of general public.

Nothing in this article shall prevent the state from making any special provision for women and children.

(4)[9] Nothing in this article or in clause (2) of Article 29 shall prevent the state from making any special provision for the advancement of any socially and educationally backward

[9] Added by the constitution (first Amendment) Act, 1951, Section 2. – Introduction to the Constitution of India by D.D. Basu Eighteenth Edition

classes of citizens or for the scheduled castes and the scheduled tribes.)

Article 15 (3) of the Constitution specifically provides that the Prohibition of discrimination on grounds of religion, race, caste, sex or place of birth as contained in Article 15, shall not prevent the state from making any special provisions for women and children. In other words, the state is empowered to make any such provisions and it shall not be violative of Articles 15. Article 15 (1) prohibits gender discrimination. Article 15 (3) lifts that rigor and permits the state to positively discriminate in favour of women to make special provisions, to ameliorate their social economic and political justice and accords them parity.

Clause (3) of Article 15, which permits special provisions for women and children, has been widely resorted to, by the State , and the courts have always upheld the validity of the special measures in legislation or executive orders favouring women. These provisions could be seen in the sphere of criminal law, Labour and Industrial laws, Service law and criminal procedure etc.

Article 15 (3) embodies one of the two exceptions to the prohibition contained in clauses (1) and (2) of Article 15. It empowers the state to make special provisions for women and children. This particular advantage has been conferred on the women because the framers of the constitution were well aware of the unequal treatment meted out to women in India from the time immemorial. The other reason for making special provisions for them is their physical structure and the performance of maternal functions, which place them at a disadvantage in the struggle for subsistence.[10]

Hon'ble the Supreme Court has upheld the constitutional validity of proviso to section 31 (1) (1) of the Andhra Pradesh cooperative societies Act, 1964 and of the Rules 22 © and 22 A (3) (a) framed there

---

[10] Muller vs. Oregon, 52 L.ED. 551 as Quoted in J.N. Pandey, Constitutional Law of India, 26th Edn. 1994 at P. 100.

under relying upon the mandate of Article 15 clause 3.

The proviso read with the said rules provided for nomination of two women members by the Registrar to the managing committee of the cooperative societies with a right to vote and to take part in the meetings of the committee. The court upheld the validity of these provisions on the ground that Article 15 (3) of the constitution permitted the making of special provisions for women.[11]

Thus it would be no violation of Article 15 if institutions were set up by the state exclusively for women or places reserved for them at public entertainments or in public conveyances. The reservations made for women in educational institutions and public employments are protected by Article 15 (3). The following few cases may be helpful in understanding the concept of protective discrimination in favour of women.

In Yousuf Abdul Aziz Vs State of Bombay.[12]

---

[11] T. Sudhakar Reddy vs. Govt. of A.P. 1993 Supp (4) SCC 480.

[12]. AIR , 1954 SC 321

The validity of section 497, Indian Penal Code, which punishes only the male counterpart in the offence of adultery and exempts the women from punishments was challenged as violative of Art 14 and 15 (1) of the constitution. The petitioner contended that even though the women may be equally guilty as an abettor, only the man was punished, which violates the right to equality on the ground of sex. The Supreme Court upheld the validity of the provision on the ground that the classification was not based on the ground of sex alone. The Court obviously relied upon the mandate of Article 15 (3) to uphold this provision.

Similarly, in Saumitri Vishnu vs. Union of India[13] the petitioner challenged the validity of section 497, Indian penal code on the ground that it violates Articles 14 and 21, because this provision recognizes only the husband of the adulteress as the aggrieved party and not the wife of the adulterer. It was contended that section 497 is a flagrant instance of' gender discrimination' and 'male

[13] AIR 1985 SC 1618.

chauvinism[14]. The Supreme Court held that the law does not violate either Art 14 or 15, on the ground that the offence will be committed only by a man. The Supreme Court obviously followed the ratio of Yousuf Abdul Aziz vs. State of Bombay, as declared by a constitutional Bench.

In Revathi vs. Union of India[2]. The Supreme Court held that section 198 (2) of Criminal procedure code which gives the husband of adulteress the right to prosecute that adulterer but does not give the wife of the adulterer the similar right, is not discriminatory following the aforementioned Judgment.

Article 16 : Equality Of Opportunity In Matters Of Public Employment :-

There shall be equality of opportunity for all citizens in matters relating to employment or appointment to any office under the State.

No citizen shall, on grounds only of religion, race caste, sex descent, place of birth, residence or any of them, be ineligible for, or discriminated against in respect of any employment or office under the State.

---

[14]. AIR 1988 SC 835

Nothing in this article shall prevent Parliament from making any law prescribing, in regard to a class or classes of employment or appointment to an office [15](under the Government of, or any local or other authority within, a State or Union territory, any requirement as to residence within that state or Union territory) prior to such employment or appointment.

Nothing in this article shall prevent the State from making any provision for the reservation of appointments or posts in favour of any backward class of citizens which, in the opinion of the State, is not adequately represented in the services under the state.

Article 16(4-A)[16] : Nothing in this article shall prevent the state from making any provision for reservation in matters of promotion of any class on classes of posts in the services under the state in favour of scheduled castes and the scheduled Tribes

---

[15] Subs. by the constitution (Seventh Amendment) Act, Section 29 and sch. for" under any state specified in the first schedule or any local or other authority within its territory, any requirement as to residence within that State."

[16] Ins. by the constitution (Seventy –Seventh Amendment) Act. 1995-Constitutionla Law of India by Dr. J. N. Pandey.

which, in the opinion of the State are not adequately represented in the services under the state).

Nothing in this article shall affect the operation of any law which provides that the incumbent of an office in connection with the affairs of any religious of denominational institution or any member of governing body thereof shall be a person professing a particular religion or belonging to a particular denomination.

Article 21 : Protection Of Life And Personal Liberty :-

No person shall be deprived of his life or personal liberty except according to procedure established by law.

Article 23 : Prohibition Of Traffic In Human Beings And Forced Labour :-

Traffic in human beings and beggar and other similar forms of forced labour are prohibited and any contravention of this provision shall be an offence punishable in accordance with law.

Nothing in this article shall prevent the State from imposing compulsory service for public purposes, and imposing such service the state shall not make any discrimination on grounds only of religion, race caste or class or any of them.

Article 24 : Prohibition Of Employment Of Children In Factories, etc. :-

No Child below the age of fourteen years shall be employed to work in any factory or mine or engaged in any other hazardous employment.

Article 25 : Freedom Of Conscience And Free Profession, Practice And Propagation Of Religion :-

Subject to public order, morality and health and to the other provisions of this part, all persons are equally entitled to freedom of conscience and the right freely to profess, practice and propagate religion.

Nothing in this article shall affect the operation of any existing law or prevent the state from making any law – Regulating or restricting any economic, financial, political or other secular activity which may be associated with religious practice :

Providing for social welfare and reform or the throwing open of Hindu religious institution of a public character to all classes and sections of Hindus.

Explanation I :-

The wearing and carrying of Kirpans shall be deemed to be included in the profession of the Sikh religion.

Explanation II :-

In sub-clause (b) of clause 92) the reference to Hindus shall be construed as including a reference to persons professing the Sikh, Jaina or Buddhist religion and the reference to Buddhist religion and the reference to Hindu religious institution shall be construed accordingly.

Part IV of the Constitution of the India Certain Directive Principles Of Policy To Be Followed By The State :-

Article 39 : The State shall, in particular, direct its policy towards securing – That the citizens, men and women equally, have the right to an adequate means of livelihood :

That the ownership and control of the material resources of the community are so distributed as best to sub-serve the common good.

That the operation of the economic system does not result in the concentration of wealth and means of production to the common detriment :

That there is equal pay for pay fro equal work for both men and women :

That the health and strength of workers, men and women, and the tender age of children are not abused and that citizens are not forced by economic necessity to enter avocations unsuited to their age or strength :

[17](f) That children are given opportunities and facilities to develop in a healthy manner and in conditions of freedom and dignity and that childhood and youth are protected against exploitation and against moral and material abandonment).

Article 39 (A)[18] Equal Justice And Free Legal aid :-

[17] Subs. by the constitution (forty – Second Amendment Act, 1976 Section 7(w.e.f. 3-1-1977)

[18] Ins by the constitution (forty – fourth Amendment) Act 1976 Scc 8 (w.e.f. 3.1.1977).

The state shall secure that the operation of the legal system promotes Justice, on a basis of equal opportunity, and shall, in particular, provide free legal aid, by suitable legislation or schemes or in any other way, to ensure that opportunities for securing justice are not denied to any citizen by reason of economic or other disabilities).

Article 42 : Provisions For Just And Humane Conditions Of Work And Maternity Relief :-

The state shall make provision for securing an humane conditions of work and for maternity relief.

Article 44 : Uniform Civil Code For The Citizens :-

The state shall endeavour to secure to the citizens a uniform civil code throughout the territory of Indian.

Article 51(A) : Fundamental Duties :-

It shall be the duty of every citizen of India :-

(e) To promote harmony and the spirit of common brotherhood amongst all the people of India transcending religious, linguistic and regional or sectional diversities: to renounce practices derogatory to the dignity of women :

JUDICIAL EXPLORATION- (Menaka's Case):-

The apex court has laid foundation in momentous Menaka Gandhi Vs. Rani Jethmalani's case[19]. It was held that, "life under Art 21 does not mean mere animal existence but right to live with basic human dignity."

This judgment has become the starting point for expansion of the horizons of art.21. In 1980's Supreme Court played a vital role making clear the problems of oppressed and depressed class like women, children, labour, prisoners etc. The press, NGO's social workers helped it in the process and the rigid rule of locus standi was relaxed. Which resulted in easy access to justice by way of public interest litigation. It is a innovative judicial process for direct access to the supreme court. The Supreme Court has also given recognition to international covenants and declaration in United Nations.

THE PANCHAYATS[20]

Article 243(D) : Reservation Of Seats :-

(1) Seats shall be reserved for a the Scheduled castes : and the Scheduled Tribes. The number of seats so reserved shall be, as

[19] AIR 1978 SC 619

[20] The constitution 73rd Amendment Act 1992.

nearly as may be, the same proportion to the total number of seats to be filled by direct election in that panchayat as the population of the scheduled castes in that panchayat area or of the scheduled Tribes in that panchayat area bears to the total population of that area and such seats may be allotted by rotation to different constituencies in a panchayat.

(2) Not less than one – third of the total number of seats reserved under clause (1) shall be reserved for women belonging to the scheduled castes or, as the case may be the scheduled Tribes.

(3) Not less than one – third (including the number of seats reserved for women belonging to the scheduled castes and the scheduled Tribes) of the total number of seats to be filled by direct election in every Panchayat shall be reserved for women and such seats may be allotted by rotation to different constituencies in a Panchayat.

(4) The offices of the chairpersons in the panchayats at the village or any other level shall be reserved for the scheduled castes, the scheduled Tribes and women in such manner

as the legislature of a state may by law, provide :

Provided that the number of offices of chairpersons reserved for the scheduled castes and the scheduled Tribes in the panchayats at each levies in any state shall bear, as nearly as may be, the same proportion to the total number of such offices in the panchayats at each level the population of the scheduled castes in the state or of the scheduled Tribes in the state bears to the total population of the state :

Provided further that not less than one – third of the total number of offices of chairpersons in the panchayats at each level shall be reserved for women:

Provided also that the number of offices reserved under this clause shall be allotted by rotation to different panchayats at each level.

(5) The reservation of seats under clauses (1) and (2) and the reservation of offices of chairpersons (other than the reservation for women) under clause (4) shall cease to have effect on the expiration of the period specified in Article 334.

(6) Nothing in this part shall prevent the legislature of a state from making any provision for reservation of seats in any panchayat or offices of chairpersons in the panchayats at any level in favour of backward class of citizens.

THE MUNICIPALITIES[21]

Article 243 T : Reservation Of Seats :-

Seats shall be reserved for the scheduled castes and the scheduled Tribes in every Municipality and the number of seats so reserved shall bear, as nearly as may be, the same proportion to the total number of seats to be filled by direct election in that municipality as the population of the scheduled castes in the Municipal area or of the scheduled Tribes in the Municipal area bears to the total population of that area and such seats may be allotted by rotation to different constituencies in a Municipality.

Not less than one – third of the total number of seats reserved under clause (1) shall be reserved for women belonging to the scheduled castes or as the case may be, the scheduled Tribes.

Not less than one – third (including the number of seats reserved for women belonging to the scheduled castes and the scheduled Tribes of the total number of seats to be filled by direct election in every

---

[21] Inserted by constitution Seventy Fourth Amendment, Act 1992 Section

Municipality shall be reserved for women and such seats may be allotted by rotation to different constituencies in a Municipality.

The offices of chairpersons in the Municipalities shall be reserved for the scheduled castes, the scheduled Tribes and women in such manners as the Legislature of a state may, by law, provide.

The reservation of seats under clauses (1) and (2) and the reservation of offices of Chairpersons (other than the reservation for women) under clause (4) shall cease to have effect on the expiration of the period specified in Article 334.

Nothing in this part shall prevent the Legislature of a state from making nay provision for seats in any Municipality or offices of chairpersons in the Municipalities in favour of backward class of citizens.

In Air India vs. Nargesh Mirza[22] , The Supreme Court struck down the Air India regulations relating to retirement and pregnancy bar on services of Air hostesses as unconstitutional on the ground that the

[22] 1981 (4) SCC 335

conditions laid down therein were entirely unreasonable and arbitrary. The impugned Regulation 46 provided that an air hostess would retire from the service of corporation upon attaining the age of 35 years or on marriage, if it took place within 4 years of service or on first pregnancy, whichever occurred earlier. Under Rule 47, the Managing Director was vested with absolute discretion to extend the age of retirement prescribed at 45 years. Both these regulations were struck down as violative of Article 14 which prohibits unreasonableness and arbi4rariness.

RESERVATION FOR WOMEN IN ELECTIONS :

Provisions providing for reservations of seats for women in local bodies or in educational institutions are valid, the Supreme Court has held in the case of Government of A.P. Vs. P.B. Vijay Kumar[23] That the reservation to an extent of 30% made in the State services by Andhra Pradesh Government to women candidates is valid,

[23] AIR 1995 SC 1948.

The Division bench of the Supreme Court emphatically declared that, the power conferred upon the State by Article 15 (3) is wide enough to cover the entire range of State activity including employment under the state. Thus making Special provisions for women in respect of employment or posts under the States is an integral part of Article 15 (3). This power conferred under Article 15 (3), is not whittled down in any manner by Article 16.

The 73rd and 74th Amendments of the Indian constitution effected in 1992 provide for reservation of seats to the women in Elections to the panchayat and the Municipalities. Perhaps, this is the first attempt by the Parliament to provide reservation for women in legislatures. According to Article 243 D of the constitution of India, not less than one third of the total number of seats to be filled by direct election in every panchayat shall be reserved for woman. Such seats may be allotted by rotation to different constituencies in a panchayat. Not less than one third of total number of offices the chairpersons in the Panchayat at each level shall be reserved for women.

According to Article 243 T of the constitution of India which was added by the constitution (74th Amendment) Act, 1992 makes similar provisions for reservation of seats to women in the direct elections to every Municipality. Therefore there is a successful reservation of 33% seats for woman in local bodies, which acquires poignant importance. It is well documented that the woman of India made a distinguished contribution to the country in all spheres of life Therefore; there is nothing unreasonable or unconstitutional in making reservation for woman in legislatures. It is important to remember that the Article 15 (3) of the constitution of India empowers the states to make special provisions for woman and children.

The parliament introduced the constitution 81st Amendment Bill seeking to reserve one third of seats in Lok Sabha and State Assembly for woman in the month of September, 1996. The bill has been referred to a joint committee of parliament and is yet to be passed. In a way, the move is only an extension of the 73rd and 74th Constitution Amendments, under which a similar quota has been provided for woman in the elected bodies at various levels in the Panchayat Raja and Nagar Palika systems and as such represents a big step forward in empowering the women to play their rightful part in democratic government and in, the political process at the decision making level. This measure is towards correcting the gender injustice.

In the Sarla Mudgal Vs Union of India[24] it was held that Article 23 of the constitution specifically prohibits traffic in human beings. In this context traffic in human beings includes "devadasi system". Trafficking in human beings has been prevalent in India for a long time in the form of prostitution and selling and purchasing human beings for a price just like vegetables. On the strength of Article 23 (1) of the constitution, the legislature has passed the suppression of

[24] AIR 1995 SC 1531

Immoral Traffic Act 1956 (now renamed as The Immoral Traffic (prevention) Act, 1956) which aims at abolishing the practice of prostitution and other forms of trafficking. This is an Act made in pursuance of the International convention signed at New York on the 9th day of May 1950 for the prevention of immoral traffic. Recently the Andhra Pradesh Legislature has enacted the Devadasis (Prohibition of Dedication) Act.1988 to prohibit the practice of dedicating women as Devadasis to Hindu deities, idols and temples etc. which invariably results in evils like prostitution".

The Directive principles of State Policy contained in part IV of the constitution incorporate many directives to the state to improve the status of women and for their protection.

Article 39 (a) directs the state to direct its policy towards securing that the citizen, men and women, equally have the right to an adequate means of livelihood.

Article 39 (d) directs the state to secure equal pay for equal work for both men and women. The state has enacted The equal Remuneration Act, 1976 to this Directive Principle.

Article 39 (e) Specifically directs the State not to abuse the health and strength of workers, men and women.

Article 42 of the constitution incorporates a very important provision for the benefit of women. It directs the state to make provisions for securing just and humane conditions of work and for maternity relief. The state has tried to implement this directive by enacting the maternity Benefit Act, 1961.

Article 44 directs the state to secure for the citizens a uniform civil code through out the territory of India. This particular goal is towards the achievement of gender justice. Even though the state has not yet made any efforts to introduce Uniform civil code in India, the Judiciary has recognised the necessity of the uniformity in application of civil laws like in marriage, succession, adoption and maintenance etc. in the case of Sarala Mudgal vs. Union of India[25] and other cases. Apart from these specific provisions all the other provisions of the constitution are equally applicable to the men and women. This clearly establishes the intention of the framers of the constitution to improve the social, economic, education and political status of the women so that they can be treated with men on equal terms.

In Ramavati Devi Vs State of Bihar[26] the Supreme Court has dealt with the validity of the Chotanagpur Tenancy Act, 1908 of Bihar which denied the right to succession to Scheduled Tribes woman as violative of right to livelihood under Article 21 of the constitution. The Majority Judgment however upheld the validity of the legislation on the ground that such enactment was in accordance with the custom of inheritance / succession of the Scheduled Tribes.

However the dissenting judgment was delivered by Justice K. Rama Swamy who felt that the law made a gender - based

[25] AIR 1995 SC 1531
[26] AIR 1983 SC 154

discrimination and that it violated Articles 15, 16 and 21 of the constitution of India. The Majority Judgment does not appear to be in consonance with the right to equality enshrined in the constitution. During the course of his dissenting opinion Justice K. Rama Swamy had an occasion to refer to various International Declarations and conventions along with the relevant provisions of the Indian constitution as regards the gender discrimination in India. The learned Judge observed:

" Legislative and executive actions must be conformable to and for effectuation of the fundamental rights guaranteed in part III and the directive principles enshrined in Part IV and the preamble of the constitution which constitute the conscience of the constitution. Covenants of the United Nations add impetus and urgency to eliminate gender - based obstacles and discrimination. Legislative action should be devised suitably to constitute economic empowerment of women in socio - economic restructure for establishing egalitarian social order. Law is an instrument of social change as well as the defender of social change. Article 2 (e) of CEDAW (The Vienna convention on the Elimination of all forms of Discrimination Against Women which was ratified by the UNO on 18-12-1979 and which was ratified by the Government of India on 19-6-1993) enjoins this court to breathe life into the dry bones of the constitution, international conventions and the protection of Human Rights Act, to prevent gender - based discrimination and to effectuate right to life including empowerment of economic, social and cultural rights." (at p. 148)

These remarks made by the learned Judge highlighted the plight of the Indian women and also the necessity of the state action that should be taken to rectify the historical inequity that discrimination against the women.

<u>Development of woman law</u> :-

The interpretation of word 'consent' in Mathura's case[27] has in fact became the wind marker to show where the wind blows. In

[27] State of Maharastr V/s. Tukaram AIR 1979 SC 185

changing social scenario there was alarming increase in crime against women. The bride burning, dowry death, rape, crulty, harassment, suicides are evil side of our civilization. The right thinking citizen's social organizations woman activities lawyers & many other leaded the march against such social evil. There was discussion, debate, reporting of this evil which has taken shape in sweeping changes in women's law to cure this menace.

Clause 2nd of S 375of Indian penal code was amended by deleting words "free & voluntary consent" modified the same with only." without her consent " S376 (A) to 376(G) were inserted which relates to custodial rape, gang rape etc. S 498 was inserted in IPC pertaining to combat the ' cruelty' by Husband or relatives of husband mentally or physically. The wider definition of cruelty in S 498 A IPC has brought about a sea change in attitude of Indian womanhood. In fact this legal weapon is in use like anything .It has become the 'shield' of security for married women & hanging

'Sword' to in laws members. The number of cases filed under section 498 A Indian Penal Code no doubt shows the trend of married women's oppression in house & their awareness about their legal rights. I do admit there is misuse of this section but not in all cases.

Apart from it, there are amendments in Indian evidences Act also. The very purpose of the amendments, insertion of some presumption in Indian Evidence act like S 113A,S 113B,S114A is to overcome from the heavily burdened prosecution to cannons of real justice to womenhood, Generally, as per criminal jurisprudence the prosecution has to prove quilt of accused beyond reasonable doubt. In case of atrocities on woman the evidence, which is expected normally, cannot available only because of secondary position of woman in their family & society. Therefore these directory & mandatory presumption are inserted to prove abatement to commit suicide (S 113A) dowry death (S 113 B) about consent in rape S.114 (A) Evidence Act.

As well as Manjushri Sarda's case[28]? is the index to show the development of position of woman in domain of law. S304 (B) is inserted in IPC & Dowry prohibition (amendment) Act 1986 was amended.

<u>In Shaman saheb Vs state of Karnataka</u>[29] held that,

"Composition of offence under section 304B of IPC is vastly different from formation of the offence under section 302 of IPC i.e. Murder under section 302 IPC accused has no burden but under section 304 B if accused failed to rebut the presumption under section 113 B of Evidence Act as a package with section 304 B IPC Dowry death, the court is bound to act on it"

Dowry system

Dowry system is one of the most degrading social practices to offer their daughter to the groom with some agreed money. In old Hindu tenets there was no provision for giving proprietary right to female. Female did not heritate their paternal property. Moreover in society the female can

---

[28] AIR 1984 Sharad Sarada V/s. State of Maharastra

[29] 2001 CrLJ 1075 S.C.

attain her status only on her marriage, which is not in case of male. Consequently, the female gets a secondary position in the family and she became sellable in the pious name of 'kanyadan.' I don't mean to say that the very inception of Dowry system was a evil because it was there with a view to give some proprietary share (though not equal) to female members at the time of marriage.

However, as like other laudable customs in Hindu law, this custom has also taken worst shape in progressive society due to outmost greed of easy money and materialistic approach in marriage bargaining.

The incorporation of section 304 B in IPC and section 113 B in evidence Act and amendment in Dowry prohibition Act is encouraging step towards gender equality. However, still the social atmosphere is not attuning with legal one. It has still one of the instruments of secondary position of woman in society much less in marriage bargaining instead of considering it as 'sacradontal tie'. The rampant thing is that 'marriages are not considered to be made in heaven but settled by hywans'.

In a survey of Shakshi NGO of Delhi of 109 judges[30], the judges attributes pervasiveness of Dowry to number of reasons like unequal economic condition, weak husband, failure of parents to take back the daughter from situation of dowry harassment. The judges laid emphasis on changing woman rather those alerting attitudes, which affect woman adversely. Some judges affirmed that while they would not demand dowry for their son, they would have to provide dowry for daughter where in lies the crux of the problem with gender bias.

Creative role of judiciary in development of women's law

As mention before early 1980's is the most pervasive theme of women's oppression[31], then I have proud to say that early 1990 and 20th century is the righteous recognition and activism of judiciary of woman's emancipation. I have already

30 www.sakshi.org
31

discussed the land mark decisions of our apex court in Sarada's case[32] while understanding social evil of dowry & dowry death the apex court has described the pathetic position of women in family and society which compelled her to bear all the tortures. **The Apex court held**,

"The Indian woman is brought up and trained in a traditional atmosphere and told that it is better to die in the husband's home than return to her parent's home and bring disgrace to them. She finds it very difficult to violate this cardinal principle and prefers to die at her husband's place. This is the social reality of a women's life. The legal agents in power need to understand this and be sensitive to it."

Manjushri Sarda's case moved not only the public opinion but also the apex court. The Apex court in realm protected and guarded the women's right as per letters and sprit of the constitution. Then only there were amendments in Indian penal code, Evidence act and Dowry prohibition (amendment) act 1986 as mentioned supra.

---

[32] AIR 1984 SC 1622

Position of women in early 1990s and onward

In early 80s women faced mainly the domestic violence i.e. cruelty dowry, & gang rape in Mathura's case. However, in 1990s there was a sudden change and addition in crime against woman in a different form. The very 'modesty' of a woman, which is fragrance of her life, was at stake. Such torturer is known as 'sexual harassment'. The cases of molestation came up 24,117 in 1994 i.e.24.37 % of total crime reported against women in 1994.The cases of sexual harassment constituted 10.60% of total crime against women in 1994.[33]

In 1988 Inspector General of Police, Chandigarh molested a senior lady IAS officer. In this case the Supreme Court held the word 'modesty' has not defined in IPC. Ultimate test for ascertaining whether 'modesty' has been outraged or not is the action of offender could be perceived as one, which is capable of shocking the sense of

[33] Roopan Deol Bajaj V/s. KPS Gill AIR 1996 CrLJ 38 SC

decency of a woman. As per oxford dictionary 'modesty' means conduct (in man or woman) reserve or sense of shame proceeding from instinctive aversion to impure or coarse suggestions. Thus appeal filed by IAS officer Rupandeo Bajaj was allowed

Moreover, in the case of state of A.P.Vs. Bodensundra Rao[34] the Apex court came down heavily on A.P.High court for awarding grossly inadequate sentence and held ,

'Crimes against women are on the rise. Imposition of grossly inadequate sentence and particularly against the mandate of legislature not only is an injustice to the victim of the crime in particular and the society as a whole in general but also the rights of the victim of crime and the society at large while considering imposition of the appropriate punishment'.

In another pioneer decision in Bodhi satwa Gautam Vs.Shubra Chakrabarty[35] the apex court held that,

'Rape is not only a crime against a person of a woman (victim) it is a crime against entire

---

[34] AIR 1996 S.C.530

[35] AIR 1996 S.C.922 .

society. Rape is the most hated crime. It is crime against basic human rights and is also violative of the victims most cherished fundamental right namely right to live contained in article 21 of the constitution. The rape laws do not unfortunately take care of the social aspect of the matter and are inept in many respects'.

Relying upon the ruling supreme court in Chairman Railway Board Vs. Chandrima Das[36] where a Bangladeshi national namely Hanoofa Khatoon was gang raped by many including rail way employees in Yatri-nivas at Hawrah station confirming her fundamental right under article 21; the court held that 'state was under constitutional liability to pay compensation to her'.

Despite these decision of our apex court there is no gender sensitivity amongst all strata of society. In fact article 51A (e) of constitution casts a duty on all citizens to renounce practices derogatory of women. Still it is shocking to note that on an average, 41 women are raped in the country every day.

---

[36] 2000 CrLJ 1473 (S.C.)

Actually most of the rape victims preferred not to report this heinous incident as social stigma is attached to it. Thus, incident of rape is not a challenge to a particular woman but it is an indicator to show how the social order is deteriorating. And therefore, there was a social cry that rape accused is hang till death. This offence is serious in nature as it causes experience of death to a victim every day due to shame and spoiling her purity. In such circumstances neither the legal system nor the attitude of society helps the rape victims in any way. Victims suffer in silence and tears.

Vishakha's case on sexual harassment

Vishakh's case reported in Vishakha & others Vs. state of Rajas tan & others[37] is a innovative decision of our apex court has not only shown the stronger contempt to the derogatory practices in society against woman in general but also created a new class of woman working woman and the sexual harassment they suffer at working place.

---

[37] AIR 1997 S C 3011

The plight of social activists Banwaridevi could be seen as an example of a social scenario. Banwaridevi was harassed, ostracised and finally gang-raped when she prevented to child marriages in her village in Rajastan.In male dominated society like Banwari thousands of women have been subjected to various kinds of harassment and exploitation within and out side family circle.

Therefore, some social activists and NGOs moved the supreme court for enforcement of the fundamental rights of working women under article 14,19 & 21 of the constitution in view of prevailing climate in which violation of such rights is not common. With increasing awareness of gender justice there is increase in the effort to guard against violation. The said petition was filed as a class action with an aim of focusing attention towards this societal aberration and assisting in finding suitable methods of the true concept of gender justice and to prevent sexual harassment of working women in all work places through judicial process to fill the vacuum in the existing legislation.

In this case the apex court has elaborately discussed the present constitutional provision and made applicable the international declaration into our Indian law with the aid of article 51&253 of the constitution and defined sexual harassment for this purpose which includes such unwelcome sexually determined behavior (whether directly or by implication) as-

Physical contact and advances

A demand or request for sexual favors

Sexually coloured remarks

Showing pornography

Any other unwelcomes physical, verbal or non-verbal conduct of sexual nature.

The apex court directed all the employer to take preventive steps by forming rules etc.and further held that,

'Sexual harassment of women at work place amounts to violation of right to gender equality and right to life & liberty. And laid down guidelines and norms by taking aid of international convention which is to be treated as law declared under article 141 of the constitution.'

In apparel export Vs.A.K.Chopra[38] the apex court again confirms the above ruling and held

'The sexual harassment of a female at the place of work is incompatible with dignity and honour of a female and needs to be eliminated and there can be no compromise with such a violation admits of no debate'.

Amendment in Maharashtra Civil Service (conduct) Rules & in Bombay High court (conduct rules)

As a result of Vishakh's ruling rule 22 (a) & 22(2) were inserted in Maharashtra civil service (conduct) Rules on 29-9-98 & rule 24 A was inserted in Bombay High Court conduct. Rules on 21-09-2000 about sexual harassment at place of work. & One committee is formed of two Hon able judges out of whom one shall be a lady judge.

Thus we can see the judicial exploration of our apex court from Mathura in 1980s to Vishakha in 20th century.

---

[38] AIR 1999 SC.625

The position of woman in law is not only because of legislative enactments but also due to strong, firm & sensitive role of our apex court who has created the history by adapting the cannons of international conventions & declaration in our laws with aid of article 51 & 253 of our constitution & has become the protecter & guardian of our constitution in realm. Vishakha's case is judicial innovation. The social activists NGOS moved to apex court with outmost belief that the guardian of the constitution would only sail the ship of women's oppression as being saviour.

In progressive society like India like Mains theory of labour to contract & contract to labour just like that the position of women in domain of law is equal from legislation to judicial & judicial to legislation. The public interest litigation has become boon for all the oppressed class of society & mainly for women. The Supreme Court has taken cognizance of all sorts of grievances even on letters sent to it. Thus, the judicial review of all legislative action has made the development of woman in right direction with maintaining pace as per public opinion.

Extension of the Act to the State of J & K.

Role of N.G.O's

For the just a cause the NGO's of our country are playing pivotal role for protection of the victims of sexual abuse & exploitation. Sadhana Mukharjee who forced into prostitution at the age of 15 formed Mahila Samannya Committee comprising 1700 sex workers of Calcutta. She has achieved her mission of dignity & preventing exploitation by a tremendous progress.

The Apex Court & Family Law

The provisions of S.9 of the Hindu Marriage Act 1955 providing for restitution of conjugal rights have been challenged several times on various grounds. The supreme court finally upheld the constitutional validity of S.9.of the Hindu Marriage Act 1955 in Saroj Rani Vs. Sudarshan Kumar[39].

The apex court held,

---

[39] AIR 1984 SC 1562

'The right of the husband or the wife to society of the other spouse is not merely creature of the statute; rather it is inherent in the very institution of marriage. The decree for its restitution serves social purpose as an aid to the prevention of the break up of marriage. Therefore, S.9 is not violative of article 14 of the constitution.

In the matters of Hindu succession, in Pratapsing Vs. Union of India[40] the Supreme Court held

'That section 14(1) of Hindu Succession Act 1956 a providing absolute ownership to a Hindu female over her inherited property was enacted to redress the problems faced by Hindu women who were unable to claim absolute interest in their inherited properties, rather who could only enjoy these properties with the restrictions attached to widow's estate under the Hindu law, as a special provision indented to benefit and protect woman who had been traditionally discriminated against in terms of access to property. And hence, it was not open to Hindu

---

[40] AIR 1985 S.C.1695

males to challenge the provision as hostile discrimination. Such a provision according to the court was protected by article 15(3), which in its view overrides article 15(1) of the constitution.

The apex court in Kalawatibai Vs. Soirabai[41] emphasized on the fact that Hindu Succession Act 1956 was enacted in order to do away with invidious discrimination against women and it was a step towards social amelioration as they had been subjected to gross inequality and discrimination in the matter of inheritance.

The apex court in C.Masilamani Vs. Shri Swaminandaswami reported[42] emphasized that,

"Section 14 of Hindu succession Act should be construed harmoniously consistent with the constitutional goal of removing gender biased discrimination and effectuating economic empowerment of Hindu females. It is imperative for the state to eliminate obstacles and prohibit all kinds of gender-based discrimination as mandated by article 14 and

[41] AIR 1991 SC.1581
[42] AIR 1996 sc.1697

15 of the constitution. It was further held that, 'the state should take all appropriate measures including legislation to modify or abolish all forms of gender based discrimination in the existing laws, regulations, customs and practices which constitute discriminations against women. Legislative action according to court should be devised suitably to constellate economic empowerment of women in socio-economic restructured for establishing and egalitarian social order." Quoting the various provisions of CEDAW the court opined that,

'law is an instrument of social change. Article 2(e) of CEDAW enjoins this court to breathe life into the dry bones of the constitution, international conventions, the protection of human rights act, the act to prevent gender based discrimination and to effectuate right to life including empowerment of economic, social and cultural rights to women.

In a recent landmark decision on gender equality the apex court in Githa Hariharan

Vs.RBI[43] where in RBI has questioned the authority of the mother even when she had acted with the concurrence of the father held, 'That mother was the natural guardian because the father was not taking any interest in his minor daughter's affairs.'

Role of Judiciary in Protection of Human Rights of Women in India

The Indian judiciary has played important role in recognition of enforcement of various human rights of the women & children in India. The Supreme Court in catena of cases held that right to decent life, life with human life & it does not mean animal physical existence. Right to life includes basic necessities of life like right to food, right to health, right to speedy trial, right to education and legal aid, right to compensation to victims and life with human dignity.

In Sunil Batra Vs. Delhi administration[44] the apex court observed,

---

[43] AIR 1999 - 2 Scc 237

[44] AIR 1978 Supreme Court 1675

"That the treatment of a human being which offends the human dignity, imposes avoidable torture and reduces the man to the level of a beast would certainly be arbitrary and can be questioned under article 14 of the constitution.'

It is to be noted that the protection of human rights act 1993 not only covers the fundamental rights but also international covenant. As I have already discussed the Supreme Court has shown great judicial activism while bringing into our law of land all the cannons of the CEDAW Declaration.

Not only the apex court but the various high courts have played vital role in this regard .In Shehnaz sani's case in 1998 the honorable justice Shrikrushna directed employer of Mrs.Sani, a ground hostess in Saudi Arabian Air lines at Bombay to reinstate her with full packages of 13 years during which she was rendered unemployed due to wrongful termination. This is the first even judgment of the high court on sexual harassment at work place has set a new trend in the protection of the human right to dignity of working women in India.

<u>In Sheela Barse Vs. State of Maharastra</u>[45] the apex court entertained the Public Interest litigation on letter of journalist complaining of violence on women prisoners while in police lock up. The court directed a fact finding team to visit the Bombay central jail and interview the women prisoners as together they had been subjected to any torture or ill treatment and to submit report. Then gave direction -

Lock up female only in female lock up guarded by the female constables

Interrogate female prisoners only in the presence of female police officers among other directions.

<u>In All India democratic women's association vs. union of Indian</u>[46] In PIL against 'Sati' allegedly to be committed by Rupkanwar in Rajas than held,

---

[45] AIR 1983 Sc.378

[46] AIR 1989 Sc.1280

'That the restraint imposed on holding chunry ceremony should continue without any variation to prevent glorification of sati.

In Gaurav Jain Vs union of India[47] the apex court issued directions for rescue and rehabilitation of child constitute and the children of fallen women and further directed the establishment of Juvenile Homes for them.

Gender equality principle under constitution in position of woman in different fields :

The preamble of the constitution is the solemn resolve to secure social economic & political justice, liberty, equality & dignity to every person, man & woman. However, this constitutional principles are whittled down by the social evil. They turned their deaf ear to the women's liberation movement & continued to exploit the women in its highest extend. The women were harassed at home & by society at every walk of their life.

---

47. AIR 1997 Sc 3021

Gender Equality :-

The principle of quality is one of the milestones embodied in the preamble of the constitution of India. In order to achieve the goal of gender equality & to provide gender justice to woman. The Government of India has initiated served programmes for empowering women.

Position in Education :-

As per 2001 census report of India three fourth male and a little over half of the literacy has increased from and percent in 1951. 54% in 2001 it shows a positive trend of gender parity in education. But development rate is slow & they are legging far behind in comparison to their male counter parts. Resultantly, there is backwardness in the field of employment.

Position of Women in Employment :-

During 19 th century due to western impact education & advancement & knowledge there had been rise in the awareness of women about their status they became aware to protect their rights. Consequently the doors of empower employment were opened for women. But still they are not freed from their household activities.

The constitution prohibits discrimination & provides that equals should be treated equality because injustice arises when equals are treated unequally. So this principle must be read as equality & injustice. The directive principles lay down guidance & direct state to strive to minimize gender inequality amongst citizens. It directs to all citizens to renounce practices derogatory to the dignity of women. Thus special care has been taken in Indian constitution to provide socio-economic justice to women & to put them on the same footing of equality.

However as per the Decennial censuses from 1991 to 2001, the women workers population is less than half of male workers into men constitute a major chunk of the lebour force in primary sector of Indian industries but it is not productive. The disproportionate representation of female employee also exists in judiciary. Class I services & in other Govt. services.

CHAPTER - IV

POSITION OF WOMEN UNDER PERSONAL LAWS IN INDIA

Position of Women in Family and Society:-

As to provide equal status and position to Hindu women in family & society various LAWS have been enacted. These enactments have removed gender biased inequalities & do not reflect any discrimination against woman. These enactments have been upheld by the courts time & again the enactment in Muslim law received strong reaction & resentment from orthodox Muslims. So no reform would be possible in Muslim law. As for as Christens are concerned, the British enacted special laws though based on egalitarian principles depict discrimination against Christian Woman.

WOMEN AND PERSONAL LAW IN INDIA :-

"All laws which prevent women from occupying such a sanction in society as her conscience shall dictate, or in which place her position inferior to that of man, are certainly to the great precept of nature, and therefore of no force or authority".[48]

[48] Elizabeth Cady Stanton (History of woman Suffrage 1881)

" The institution of marriage is one of the sound social institutions to bring harmony and integration in social fabric.... Therefore due recognition should be accorded for social mobility and integration....."

-The Hon'ble Justice Shri. K. Ramaswamy[49]

(a) Hindu Women And Marriage

(i) Position before 1955

(ii) Position after 1955

(iii) Conditions for a Hindu Marriage

(iv) Abolition of Guardianship of Marriage

(v) Ceremonies

(vi) Registration

(vii) Restitution of conjugal Rights

(viii) Judicial separation

(b) Matrimonial Causes - Rights Of Women

(i) Judicial separation

(ii) Restitution

(iii) Divorce among Hindus

(iv) Grounds of Divorce for a Hindu wife

(a) Common grounds

---

[49] Valsamma Paul v/s. Chochin University (1996) 3 SCC 545

(b) Exclusive grounds

(c) Divorce by mutual consent

India is a known for its rich culture and heritage.It is the abode ofmany religions and philosophies.

Secularism has been one of the features of Indian life from the time immemorial. Perhaps India is the only country in the world which permits persons belonging to different religions to follow their own personal laws in regard to Marriage, divorce, succession, adoption and maintenance. The different personal laws are followed, depending on the religion of the person. This gave rise to different marriage laws, succession laws and divorce laws applicable to different religions like Hindu , Islam and Christian. The different religions confer the different rights on the women as regards these personal matters, in the absence of a Uniform civil code in India.

Thus the Hindus are governed by the Hindu marriage Act, 1955, the Muslims by the tenets of Holy Quran and the Christians are governed by the Christian Marriage act, 1872 and other laws.

The law relating to Hindu women and marriage can be better understood, if the position before the codification of Hindu laws is made clear.

POSITION PRIOR TO 1955 :

Prior to 1955, that is before the enactment of the Hindu marriage Act, 1955, the Hindu Marriage was considered purely to be a sacrament , by all the schools. There were eight forms of marriage among Hindus, out of which four were approved forms and the rest unapproved. The approved forms of marriage were Brahma, Daiva, Arsha and Prajapathya. The unapproved marriages were Asura, Gandharva, Rakshasa and paisacha.

In due course of time only two forms remained in practice viz 'Brahma' , in the approved form and 'Asura'[1] in the unapproved form. In the former type, the women was given as a gift by her father to his son-in -law i.e. the husband of the women. In the latter type, it was considered as a sale by the father to the son-in -law „ "Kanya Sulkam" was the consideration for such sale. Another difference was that in a Branma form of marriage, when the women died, her property devolved upon the legal heirs of the husband, in the absence of the husband and children.

In "Asura" form of marriage, on the death of the wife, in the absence of her husband & children, her property devolved upon her parental side. Polygamy was an accepted practice and there was no limit on the number of women, a Hindu man could marry. Widow remarriage was prohibited till the reformers like Raja Rammohan Rai , Maharshi Karve made some bold attempts to introduce them. Child marriages were rampant, inspite of sustained efforts by certain reforms.

Position of Women After The Hindu Marriage Act of 1955 :-

The Hindu marriage Act, 1955 was the first of the codified Hindu law. It does not specifically provide for any form of marriage. It made the marriage more consensual and secular than religious. It no more considers the marriage as a "Samskara" as considered by Dharms-Sastras. The marriage is solemnized as per the customary ceremonies prevalent in the community to which the bride and bride groom belong.

The Hindu Marriage Act, 1955 (Hereinafter referred to as the Act for Convenience) amended and codified the Hindu law relating to marriage. The Act underwent several amendments by the Hindu marriage Amendment Act (Act 3 of 1956), (Act 44 of 1964). The marriage laws Amendment Act (LXVIII of 1976) and the child marriage Restraint Act of 1978.

The Hindu Marriage Act has made elaborate provisions as to the conditions for Hindu Marriage ceremonies, registration legitimacy of children, nullity of marriage and divorce etc. Even though almost all the provisions are equally applicable to the Hindu husband and wife, a few provisions may be discussed to understand the changed position of the Hindu woman after the Act came into force.

Section 5 of the Act lays down the conditions for a valid Hindu marriage. They are.

Monogamy

Sound mind

A minimum age of 18 years for the girl (bride) and 21years for the boy(bride groom),

The parties are not within prohibited degrees of relationship and The parties are not sapindas to each other.

The last two conditions may be waived if there is a custom each of the parties to the marriage permitting. Thus, it could be seen that the Act of 1955 has introduced radical changes in the marriage laws of Hindus. Section 5 has the effect of abolishing the prohibition on widow's remarriages child marriage and polygamy in one stroke. The woman stands on the same footing as the man in all these matters.

Before 1978, Section 6 of the Act provided that the consent of guardian was necessary for a bride, if she was below the age of 18 years i.e. minor. However the child marriage Restraint (Amendment) Act of 1978 deleted this section in view of the fact that the age of the bride should be at least 18 years at the time of marriage. Therefore when the bride has already completed of 18 years of age question of consent would not arise, as she would be a major.

There is no discrimination between the bride and bride groom with regard to the ceremonies, in view of section 7 of the Act.

The provisions of Section 8 dealing with registration of a Hindu marriage it is equally applicable to the bride and bride groom. There is nothing in the Act to suggest that registration of a Hindu marriage is essential and that failure to do so renders the marriage void.

Sec 9 Restitution of Conjugal Rights :-

This remedy is provided to a Spouse aggrieved by the desertion of the other Spouse, without any reasonable Cause. Section 9 of the Act specifically provides that when either the husband or the wife has withdrawn from the society of the other without reasonable excuse, the aggrieved party may initiate legal proceedings for decree of restitution of conjugal rights. This is a right available to both the Spouses i.e. Wife and Husband equally.

The Supreme Court overruled the decision of the A.P. High Court in the case of Saroj Rani vs. Sudarshan[50] by holding that in the privacy of home and married life, neither Article 21 nor it Article 14 has any place. It may be mentioned in this context that this remedy has been abolished in England by section 20 of the Matrimonial proceedings Act, 1970.

However, in India section 9 affords a remedy to the aggrieved wife against the husband deserting her without any reasonable Cause. If the Court passes a decree in her favour it can be executed as per the procedure contained in Civil procedure code.

Section 10 Judicial Separation

Section 10 of the Act declares the right of either Spouse to a marriage for obtaining judicial separation. This provision is a

[50] AIR 1984 SC 1562

statutory recognition of the right to judicial separation among Hindu Spouses.

In the case of Jat Singh Vs State of U.P. the Supreme Court[51] has explained the consequences of judicial separation. The judicial sanction of separation creates many rights and obligations. A decree or an order for judicial separation permits the parties to live apart. There would no obligation for either party to cohabit with the other. Mutual rights and obligation arising out of a marriage are suspended. The decree however, does not sever or dissolve the marriage. It affords an opportunity for reconciliations and adjustment. Though judicial separation after a certain period may become a ground for divorce, it is necessary and the parties are not bound to have recourse to that remedy and the parties can live separately keeping their status of wife and husband till their lifetime.

Section 13- Grounds for Judicial Separation :-

The grounds for judicial separation for both the husband and wife are the same as the

---

[51] Jat Singh Vs State of U.P

grounds for divorce contained in section 13(1) of the Act. They are Adultery, cruelty, desertion, conversion, unsound mind, venereal diseases, incurable leprosy, renunciation of the world, presumption of death and failure to comply with a decree of restitution of conjugal rights etc. All these grounds are available equally to the husband and wife.

Hindu Wife's Special Grounds for Judicial Separation :-

A from the grounds aforementioned, a Hindu wife may invoke any of the following grounds exclusively available to her. Viz.,

(a) Remarriage by Husband

(b) Husband found guilty of rape, sodomy or bestiality.

(c) Non- resumption of co-habitation inspite of a decree for maintenance of wife and

(d) Option of puberty i.e. at the option of the wife if her marriage was performed before her 15 years of age and she repudiates the marriage after attaining the age of 15 years but before the reaches 18 years of age.

These special grounds have been provided for Hindu wife exclusively by the marriage laws (Amendment) Act, 1976 which amended section 10 and 13 of the Act. The object of this provision is mainly to give time to the Spouses for reapprochement and reconciliation.

Thus, a wife can proceed against the husband on more special grounds than that are available to both the Spouses. This provisions no doubt places the Hindu wife on a better pedestal compared to the Muslim and Christian wives,

Sec 13 Divorce :-

Section 13 of the Act provides several grounds for obtaining divorce by either party to the marriage whether solemnized before or after the commencement of the Act. Unless there is a custom in vogue, no divorce can be obtained by a Hindu couple without approaching a court of law.

The ground common to both the Husband and wife are mentioned in section 13(1). They are :

(a) Other spouse living in adultery

(b) Cruelty of the other spouse

(c) Desertion by the other spouse

(d) Conversion by the other spouse to other religion

(e) Unsound mind of the other spouse

(f) Virulent and incurable form of leprosy to other spouse

(g) Other spouse suffering from venereal diseases

(h) Renunciation of the world by the other spouse and

(i) Presumption of death of the other spouse.

To these grounds, two more grounds common to both the husband and wife were added by an amendment made in 1964[52], in the form of section 13(1-A).

They are - Non-resumption of cohabitation as between the parties to the marriage for a period of one year or upwards after the passing of a decree for judicial separation and

No restitution of conjugal rights as between the parties for a period of one year upwards,

---

[52] Inserted by Act 44 of 1964, Sec. 2.

after passing of decree for restitution of conjugal rights.

These grounds could be invoked by either the Husband or the wife for the purpose of obtaining divorce.

Sec 13(2) Wife's special Grounds For Divorce :-

There are four grounds mentioned in section 13(2) which are available only to a wife, for the purpose of obtaining divorce.

These last two grounds were added by the marriage laws (Amendment) Act, 1976 (68 of 1976). even though these grounds were added in 1976, they can be availed by a wife whether her marriage was solemnized before or after 1976. These grounds are.

Remarriage :-

In the case of any marriage solemnized before the commencement of the Act, if the husband had married again before such commencement or if other wife was alive at the time of marriage of the petitioner, it would be an exclusive ground for the petition of such divorce. Obviously, the right to apply for divorce is available only to the first wife.

Thus, in the case of a petition for divorce by the first wife on the ground that her husband had married with second wife, the fact that the husband divorced his second wife after filing the petition, is on ground to disentitle the first wife for the relief[53].

Husband Guilty Of Rape. Sodomy Or Bestiality :-

This provision enables the wife to obtain divorce where the husband has since the solemnization of the marriage been guilty of rape, sodomy or bestiality as understood under section 375 and 377 of the Indian penal code, 1860.

Non-Resumption Of Cohabitation :-

Where a wife obtains a decree or order for maintenance either under section 18 of the Hindu Adoptions and maintenance Act, 1956 or under Section 125 of Cr.P.C. 1973 and if cohabitation between the parties had not been resumed for one year or upwards after the decree, she can invoke that non- resumption

[53] Naganna vs. Lachmibai AIR 1993 AP 82 :

of cohabitation as a ground for obtaining divorce.

Repudiation of Marriage :-

Where a Hindu girl's marriage was solemnized before she attains the age of 15 years and she repudiates the marriage after 15 years but before attaining 18 years, she can apply for divorce whether the marriage is consummated or not. In this context, the repudiation must be a valid repudiation. However certain authors are doubtful whether any repudiation of marriage done by a wife below the age of 18 years is valid because it amounts to repudiation by minor[54]

It may be seen that similar right is given to a Muslim wife married during her minority in the form of "Khyar-ul-Bulugh" (Option of Puberty).

Sec 13-B Divorce By Mutual Consent:-

Section 13-B of the Act, added by Act 78 of 1976 provided for divorce by mutual consent. Thus when there is total break-down of the of the matrimonial relationship and the

---

[54] Mayne's Hindu Law and Usage (13th ed)

spouses are living out of the matrimonial relationship and the spouses are living separately for a period of one year or more on the mutual agreement between the .parties, divorce can be obtained from a court of law.

This provision is a progressive law as it treats the Hindu wife on equal footing with the Hindu husband.

RELEVANT PROVISIONS OF THE HINDU MARRIAGE ACT, 1955

Conditions for a Hindu Marriage :

A Marriage may be solemnized between any two Hindus, if the following conditions are fulfilled, namely :-

(i) Neither has as spouse living at the time of the marriage: .

(ii)[55]At the time of the marriage, neither party

is incapable of giving a valid consent to it in consequence of unsoundness of mind : or though capable of giving a valid consent, has been suffering from mental disorder of such a

[55] Subs by Act 68 of 1976 section 2 for Cl.(II) Mayne's Hindu Law

kind or to such an extent as to be unfit for marriage and the procreation of children : or has been subject to recurrent attacks of insanity or epilepsy:

(iii) the bridegroom has completed the age of 1 (twenty-one years) at the bride the age of 1 (eighteen years) at the time of marriage: The parties are not within the degrees of prohibited relationship, unless the custom or usage governing each of them permits of a marriage between the two :

The parties are not sapindas of each other, unless the custom or usage governing each of them permits of a marriage between the two :

(Omitted by Act 2 of 1978. section 6 and Schedule)

6. Guardianship in Marriage : - (Omitted by Act. 2 of 1978, section 6 and schedule).

Restitution of Conjugal Rights and Judicial separation

9. (xx) When either the husband or the wife has, without reasonable excuse, withdrawn from the society of the

other, the aggrieved party may apply by petition to

No Bar On Marriage By Divorced Persons:

The Act makes no provision that bars the remarriage by a divorced wife or husband, provided the divorce becomes final (Section 15). It does not attach any stigma to a Hindu woman divorcee and she is not free to contract a fresh marriage.

Relief For Respondent In Divorce And Other Proceedings: -

According to section 23 - A of the Act[56] any proceedings for divorce or judicial separation or restitution of conjugal rights may not only oppose the relief sought by the petitioner but the respondent may also make a counter claim on the grounds of petitioner's adultery, cruelty or desertion. This provision appears to be an effort to avoid filling of two petitions by the two spouses.

Maintenance Pendent Lite and expenses of Proceedings (S.24)

[56] Added by S. 17 of Marriage Laws (Amendment) Act 1976 in Hindu Law

In any proceedings under the Act like the petition for restitution of conjugal rights, Judicial separation or divorce where the respondent spouse has no independent income, sufficient for self-support and also for paying the necessary expenses, the other spouse may be directed by the court to provide maintenance and legal expenses. The quantum of maintenance depends on the petitioner's own income and that of the respondent. This provision helps the spouse in financial distress to face the legal proceedings initiated by the other spouse. This provision is only temporary and lasts till the disposal of the legal proceedings. However the maintenance awarded to a wife under section 24 of the Act is independent and different from the proceedings under section applicable to all the religions.

Permanent Alimony And Maintenance: -

The Indian Divorce Act 1869, The Parsi Marriage and Divorce Act 1936 and the Special Marriage Act – 1954 provide for permanent alimony and maintenance in favour of the spouses. Sections 25 of the Act makes a similar provision. Under this provision the court is empowered to grant permanent maintenance to either spouse, at the time of passing the decree or any time the thereafter at the instance of a spouse who is not able to maintain himself or herself.

However, if the petition of the husband, filed under the provisions of section 9 to 14 of the Hindu Marriage Act, for a decree of restitution of conjugal rights, Judicial separation for divorce is dismissed. No alimony can be granted to the wife under Section 25 of the Hindu Marriage Act. However maintenance can be claimed by her under section 18 (1) of the Hindu Adoptions and maintenance Act or under section 125 cr.p.c.[57]

MUSLIM WOMEN AND MARRIAGE

Islam does not distinguish between the two halves of the spare of humanity. In order to facet a perfect male-female equilibrium in the human society, the Quran speaks in numerous verses of women especially. It even promulgates a special chapter under the title

[57] Chand Dhawan Vs Jawahalala Dhawan (1993) 3 SCC 406

"The woman" "The woman" (surah-al-Nisa) Major parts of surahal-Nisa deal with women and the family. Scattered over many chapters of the Quran also are special exhortations, precepts and commands concerning all stages of female life – childhood, marital life and old age.

Section 20 :- Muslim marriage is regarded as a contract between a muslim man and woman which has for its object procreation and legitimization of children[58]. Once a marriage comes into existence, it is treated with all the essential attributes of a sacred covenant (mithag-i-ghalid). The contractual element attaches to it only at the formative stage: and there it is meant for the mutual benefit of the parties. A man and woman intending to become life partners can, at the very inception mutually, settle down their own terms for the entire duration of the intended partnership and in respect of all its aspects and phases. Perhaps the confusion about the muslim marriage is compounded by the absence of a

[58] D.F. Mulla, Principles of mohammedam law (Bombay, 18th Ed. 1977)

codified law in that regard and the varying practices followed by various schools.

(ix) Divorce

(x) Wife's Special Grounds for Divorce

(xi) Divorce by mutual consent

(xii) No bar on marriage by divorced persons

(xiii) Maintenance pendente lite

(xiv) Permanent alimony

(xv) Custody of children

(xvi) Conslusion.

(b) Muslim women and Marriage

(i) Capacity of a Muslim female to marry
(ii) Marriage guardianship
(iii) Minor's Marriage
(iv) Legal requirements of marriage
(v) Monogomy of Husband-not essential
(vi) Polyandry, not permissible
(vii) Impediments to Muslim marriage
(viii) Mahr
(ix) Muta Marriage
(x) Legal effects of Muta marriage

(c) Christian women and marriage

(a) The Indian Christian marriage Act 1872.

Capacity Of A Muslim Female To Marry: -

Marriage of every muslim, whether male or female, is permissible in law provided the following conditions are satisfied.

Sound mind : and

Puberty (bulugh)

As regards puberty, it is to be understood as a physical phenomenon to be ascertained by evidence and in the absence of evidence to the contrary, it is generally presumed that a person who has completed the fifteenth year of age, has attained puberty[59]. Text book writers maintain that the earliest age of puberty for a boy is, generally twelve years and for a girl it is nine years, Thus even a minor muslim girl also can marry if the consent of a "Marriage-guardian" is obtained for that, purpose.

As regards those persons (both male and female) who are neither minors nor insance, the rules of muslim law are as follows.

Under all schools of muslim law, such a boy can freely marry, personally and without. Under the hanafi and Ithna Ashari laws (not under shafei and Ismaili school), such a girl can freely marry personally and without the consent of any one else.

As regards those persons male and female who are incompetent to contract their own marriage due to insanity or minority, the muslim law lays down as under.

(1) Under none of the schools of muslim law, can an insane person (male or female) or

[59] Mt. Aliqa Begum vs. Ibrahim, AIR 1916 PC 250 as quoted in Tahir Mahmood

a minor contract a marriage without the consent and intervention of his or her "Marriage-guardian".

Under Shafei law: - a girl, though not a minor or insane, cannot contract her first marriage without the consent of her marriage-guardian; but where she is marrying for the first time, this rule does not apply. The same principle applies to Ismaili law.

Thus it could be seen that there is no uniform practice as to the marriage of a muslim male or female even though he or she is a major and of sound mind. It depends on the school to which the person belongs to.

Marriage – Guardianship: -

The authority of a person to contract the marriage of another who is incompetent to contract his or her own marriage is called "marriage – guardianship" (waliyat-e-nikah). The person having such authority is called marriage-guardian (wali-e-nikha) only those persons who can contract their own marriage can act as marriage guardian for another person.

There is no uniformity as to the persons who can act as marriage-guardians. Different schools of muslim law follow different practices in this regard. Eg: In Hanafi law, there are 18 relatives of the bride/bride groom who can act as " Marriage-guardians" they include father, father's father, father's father's father, brother (first full then consanguineous) ect. One after the other. At the shafei, Ithna Ashari, and Ismali laws, the entitlement to marriage-guardianship is extremely restricted. Only the father, or the father's father of a minor can act as the marriage guardian.

However, there is no "Kanyadan" or the "ceremonial giving" of the bride in marriage, as the guardian in marriage acts only as a mediator.

Minor's Marriage And Indian Legislation: -

The Indian majority Act, 1875 does not affect the rules of muslim law relating to minor's marriage[60].

However, the rules of muslim law relating to minor's marriage do confict with

[60] 11 MLA 551.

the provisions of the child marriage Restraint Act, 1929 (popularly known as sarada Act) which is applicable equally to all Indians including muslim. Under the provisions of this Act, every man below the age of 21 years, as also every girl below the age of 18 years is a "Child" every person under the age of 18 years is a "minor" and every marriage either party to which is a child is a " child marriage". As muslims do not enjoy an exemption from any of the aforesaid provisions of the Act of 1929 when a muslim marriage is a "Child marriage" under the Act takes place, various persons responsible for the Act takes place, various persons responsible for it including the bride groom not being a "child", the "marriage-guardian", if any may be prosecuted. However there is violation of its provisions will be invalid.

Legal Requirements Of Marriage: -

As a muslim marriage partakes the character of "Civil contract" there is always a proposal (Ijab) by either party and acceptance (Qubul) by the other party. If the parties to the intending marriage are not competent to contract their own marriage then the proposal and acceptance can be made by their respective marriage guardians. The proposal and acceptance can be made either personally or through a representative. Most of the muslim schools like Hanafi and shafei insist on the presence of witnesses (Gawah) when the contract takes place.

Monogomy of Husband-Not Essential: -

In pre-Islamic Arabia, unlimited polygamy was prevailing. After the advent of Islam, the prophet introduced limited polygamy which fixed the limit of four wives. A Mohammedan male may have four wives at the same time. However it may be remembered that it is only a permission given by the Holy Quran to contract a polygamous marriage and it is not a compulsion. A muslim male can marry more than one woman subject to a maximum of four, only when he can deal with them justly and equitably.

Though limited polygamy has been recognised by Islam, it is tolerated only under certain circumstances. In the case of

Moonshee Byzloor Raheem vs. Shamsonnisa Begum the privy council observed:

"Mohammedan law enforced in India has considered polygamy as an institution to be tolerated but not encouraged and has not enforced upon the husband any fundamental right to compel the first wife to share his consortium with another woman in all circumstances......."

Now after passing of the Dissolution of Muslim Marriage Act, 1939, a mohammedan wife can file a suit for divorce against the husband, on the ground that her husband, having more than one wife, is not treating her equitably[61].

If a muslim male contracts a fifth marriage when his first four marriages are intact, such marriage is void (Batil) as per shia law but is only irregular (fasid) as per the sunni law.

Polyandry In Women, Not Permissible: -

A Muslim woman is not allowed to have at a time more than one husband. If she marries again during the life-time of her husband, she

---

[61] Zubaida Begum vs. Sardar Shah, AIR 1943 Lah 310

will be guilty of committing the offence of Bigamy under section 494 of Indian penal code. The children born to bigamous marriages are illegitimate.

Impediments To Muslim Marriage: -

There are three kinds of prohibitions or impediments to a muslim marriage.

(1) Permanent or Absolute Impediments: -

A Marriage between two muslim is absolutely prohibited.

On the ground of polyandry of the woman.

On the ground of consanguinity (blood relationship)

On the ground of affinity (through earler marriage) and

On the ground of fosterage.

A marriage performed or contracted disregarding these impediments is void (Batil) and it does not give rise to any marital rights or obligations.

(2) Temporary & Relative Impediments: -

On the ground of unlawful conjunction.

On the ground of polygamy

On the ground Iddat period

On the ground Difference of Religion

On the ground absence of witnesses and

On the ground of Divorce (where the divorced female is sought to be remarried by the husband).

All the above mentioned prohibitions are not absolute. Thus in the case of unlawful conjunction i. e. where a Mohammedan male of sunni is prohibited to marry at the same time two wives who are so related each other by blood relationship, affinity or fosterage that if one of them were a male they could have been lawfully married if the husband divorces one, the marriage with the other is valid.

Similarly, a Mohammedan male is prohibited to marry a woman who is undergoing "Iddat" period after the dissolution of her first/ earlier marriage. Here the "Iddat period" varies depending on the cause of dissolution viz. death of husband or divorce etc. A Mohammedan female is prohibited to marry a non – Mohammedan. These impediments are only temporary and can be removed by a subsequent supervening development like divorcing one of the wives, expiry of iddat period and conversion to Islam etc. Any muslim marriage contracted ignoring these impediments is irregular (Fasid) which can be regularized by certain actions or developments.

Mahr (Dower): -

A Muslim wife is also entitled to dower (Mahr) from her husband. Dower or mahr is a sum of money or other property which the wife is entitled to receive from the husband in "consideration of marriage". It is inherent in the concept of marriage under Mohammedan law. It is a sort of deterrented to the husbands absolute power of pronouncing divorce on his wife, so the main object of dower is to offer protection to wife against such arbitrary power[62]. However some of the Mohammedan law commentators do not agree with the idea of identifying mahr as consideration for marriage, but they consider it as an obligation imposed upon a husband as mark of respect for the wife[63].

The Dower may be prompt Dower which is payable at the time of marriage or Deferred

[62] Baillie, I, 18: The Hedaya

[63] Abdur Rahim, "jurisprudence

Dower which may be paid at the time of death of the husband or on the dissolution of marriage. The Quantum of dower depends on the status of the husband and wife.

Muta Marriages: -

In Muslim law the Shia law recognizes 'Muta' marriages but according to sunni law, such marriages are void [2]. Among the shias also the "Ithna ashari School " only permits such marriages.

The literal meaning of the word 'Muta' is enjoyment use. Thus a muta marriage is a contract marriage for a certain period of time as agreed by the parties.

Capacity To Contract A Muta Marriage: -

A Mohammedan male of Ithan Ashari sect of the shias may contract any number of muta marriages, with a female belonging to Islam, Christianity, or Jewish religion. However a female of Ithna Ashari sect of the Shias has capacity to contract a valid muta marriage only with a Mohammedan and nobody else of other religion. A Major shia female of Ithna Ashari School has capacity to contract a valid muta marriage without the consent of her guardian but if she is a minor, she can do so only with the consent of her guardian. The violation of this condition by a minor girl will render the marriage unlawful.

Conditions Of A Valid Muta Marriage: -

In a Muta Marriage, the period of cohabitation and amount of dower must be specified. The condition of proposal and acceptance should be fulfilled along with the use of the word 'Tazwiy' or 'Nikah' or ' Muta'.

Legal Effects Of Muta Marriage: -

The following are the consequences of a valid Muta Marriage.

The parties to a muta marriage will be called the muta husband and the muta wife.

A Muta Marriage does not give rise to mutual rights of inheritance between the rights to inheritance between the muta husband and the muta wife. However this practice can be overridden by an agreement to the contrary.

A Muta wife is not entitled to any maintenance from the husband.

In a muta marriage, the children born out of this union are legitimate and capable of inheriting from both the parents in the same manner as the off springs of a permanent marriage.

If the muta marriage is dissolved by the death of the husband, the muta widow must observe the period of iddat for 4 months and 10 days or till the delivery in the case of pregnancy and Dower or mahr must be specified in a muta marriage.

Thus, the status of a muta wife is very low and insecure, as compared to that of a muslim wife in a permanent marriage.

THE DISSOLUTION OF MUSLIM MARRIAGE ACT, 1939.

(Act VIII of 1939)

(17th March 1939)

WHEREAS it is expedient to consolidate and clarify the provision of Muslim law relating to suits for dissolution of marriage by woman married under Muslim law and to remove doubts as the effect of the renunciation of Islam by a married Muslim woman on her marriage tie: it is hereby enacted as follows:

Short Title And Extent :-

This Act may be called THE DISSOLUTION OF MUSLIM MARRIAGES ACT. 1939.

It extends to the whole of India (except the state of Jummu and Kashmir)[64].

2. Grounds, For Decree For Dissolution Of Marriage :-

A woman married under muslim law shall be entitled to obtain a decree for the dissolution of her marriage on any one or more of the following grounds, namely:-

that the whereabouts of the husband have not been known for a period of four years:

that the husband has neglected or has failed to provide for her maintenance for a period of two years:

that the husband has been sentenced to imprisonment for a period of seven years or upwards :

that the husband has failed to perform, without reasonable cause, his material obligations for a period of three years :

that the husband was impotent at the time of the marriage and continues to be so :

---

[64] Subs. By Act 48 of 1959, Section 3 and sch. I, for certain words (w.e.f.) 1-2-1960

that the husband has been insane for a period of two years or, is suffering from leprosy or a virulent venereal disease :

that she having been given in marriage by her father or other guardian before she attained the age of fifteen years, repudiated the marriage before attaining the age of eighteen years : provided that the marriage has not been consummated that the husband treats her with cruelty, that is to say,

habitually assaults her or makes her life miserable by cruelty of conduct even if such conduct does not amount to physical ill – treatment, or

associates with women of evil repute or leads an infamous life, or

attempts to force her to lead an immoral life, or

disposes of her property or prevents her exercising her legal rights over it, or

obstructs her in the observance of her religious profession or practice, or

if he has more wives than one, does not treat her equitably in accordance with the injunctions of the Quran :

On any other ground which is recognised as valid for the dissolution of marriages under Muslim law :

Provided that :-

no decree shall be passed on ground (iii) until the sentence has become final:

a decree passed on ground (i) shall not take effect for a period of six months from the date of such decree, and if the husband appears either in person or through an authorised agent within that period and satisfies the court that he is prepared to perform his conjugal duties, the court shall set aside the said decree: and before passing a decree on ground (v) the court shall on application by the thousand make an order requiring the husband to satisfy the court within a period of one year from the date of such order that he has ceased to be impotent, and if the husband so satisfies the court within such period, no decree shall be passed on the ground.

3. Notice to be served on heirs of the husband when the husband's whereabouts are not known :- In a suit to which clause (i) of section 2 applies:

the names and addresses of the persons who would have been the heirs of the husband under muslim law if he had died on the date of the filling of the plaint

notice of the suit shall be served on such persons, and

such persons shall have the right to be heard in the suit:

Provided that paternal uncle and brother of the husband, if any, shall be cited as party even if he or they are not heirs :

4. **Effect of Conversion To Other Faith** :-

The renunciation of Islam by a married muslim woman or her conversion to a faith other that Islam shall not by itself operate to dissolve her marriage :

Provided that after such renunciation of conversion the woman shall be entitled to obtain a decree for the dissolution of her marriage on any of the grounds mentioned in section 2 :

Provided further that the provisions of this section shall not apply to a woman converted to Islam from some other faith who re-embraces her former faith.

5. **Rights of Dower Not To Be Affected**:-

Nothing contained in this Act shall affect right which a married woman may have under Muslim law to her dower or any part thereof on the dissolution of her marriage.

6. **Repeal of Section 5 of Act XXVI of 1937**:-

Section 5 of the Muslim Personal Law (Shariat) Application 1937, is hereby repealed.

Conclusion: -

The foregoing discussion amply makes it clear that in a muslim marriage, the female plays an important and almost an equal role as compared to the males. However, female enjoys a very fragile marital life as the muslim husband is vested with an almost absolute right to divorce the wife at any time by resorting to "Triple – Talaq" method. It is not to say that every muslim husband is invoking his right to divorce his wife indiscriminately but only I would like to point out the possibility of its misuse. The law relating to Divorce among muslims and the position of the muslim wife provided in it, has been discussed in detail elsewhere in this work.

CHRISTAIN WOMEN AND MARRIAGE

Every marriage between Indian Christians may be solemnised provided the bride is 18 years of age and the bride groom 21 years. Polygomy is prohibited among the Christians. For the contract of marriage among Christians , the free and intelligent consent of the parties is indispensable . As the Christian do not have a personal law, the law of marriage with special exceptions is codified in the Indian Christian Marriage Act, and Indian Divorce Act.

There are number of enactments in India that deal with the Christian marriages and matrimonial causes. They are the Indian Christian marriage Act, 1872, The marriage's Validation Act, 1892, The Cochin Christian civil marriage Act, 1905, The Indian Matrimonial causes (War marriages) Act, 1948, The convert's marriage Dissolution Act, 1866 and The Indian Divorce Act, 1869 etc.

However many lawyers and jurists are of the opinion that the law relating to Christian marriage is deficient and that it lacks coherency.

(a) The Indian Christian Marriage Act, 1872: -

This the main legislation deals with a Christian marriage in India. This Act lays down various provisions dealing with the marriage registrar, time and place of marriage registration of marriages and the grant of marriage certificates etc. A perusal of various legislations on the topic make it amply clear about a Christian marriage to restitution of conjugal rights, to judicial separation and divorce. Every Christian marriage may be solemnised by complying with certain preliminary procedural formalities like notices of the intended marriage, publication of such notice and declaration by one of the parties.

Registration of such marriage is compulsory. A marriage between the Indian Christians may be solemnised without the preliminary procedural formalities of notice etc., by any person licensed to solemnize such marriages.

The Christian women enjoys equal rights in her marital life along with her husband. There is no ploygomy permitted among the Christians. Similarly, Christians cannot marry each other, if they are within the prohibited degrees of relationships. The child marriage Restraint Act 1929 is applicable to the Christian also. It is clear that a Christian wife enjoys co-equal rights with Hindu and muslim wife even though her status and rights are not governed by a single law.

MATRIMONIAL CAUSES ! - RIGHTS OF WOMEN

The various matrimonial causes that may arise in a marriage are mainly judicial separation, restitution of conjugal rights, divorce and maintenance. The Rights of married women depend on the religion to which she belongs and the personal laws. For the sake of brevity, the topic of marital remedies, can be discussed as under.

SUCCESSION

SYNOPSIS

Hindu Women And Succession

(i) Position before 1956

(ii) Rights in respect of stridhana

(iii) Women's estate

(iv) Position after 1956

(v) Retrospective effect

(vi) Abolition of Limited Estate

(vii) Dilution of Bias against women

(viii) Abolition of reversioners

(ix) Succession to the property of female Hindu

(x) Discrimination in succession to dwelling houses

(xi) Impact of remarriage of widow

(xii) Coparcenary Rights

(xiii) State Amendments - Effect

Muslim Women And Succession:-

(i) Inheritance at Muslim law-position of woman

(ii) Rights of females

(iii) Hanafi law of inheritance

(iv) The sharers

(v) The Reliquaries

(vi) Distant Kindred

(vii) Shia law of Inheritance

Succession Among Christian Women :-

(j) Intestate Succession

INTRODUCTION

The rights of women to succeed to any property vary from religion to religion depending on the personal laws followed by them. The religion played very important role in the devolution of property on the woman in the earlier days. Initially, law of succession was uncodified but with the advent of modern governments and legislatures, most of the succession laws have been codified and consolidated. However there is no uniformity in laws for the women who are following different religions. Even in England, the English women did not enjoy equal rights in the property and succession until the equity courts stared applying the principles of equity.

In India, the women get secondary status in regard to property rights. This unequal status had tried to be removed by certain legislations governing different religions like The Hindu women's Rights to property Act, 1937, The Hindu Disposition of property Act, 1916, The Hindu Inheritance (Removal of Disabilities) Act, 1928, The Indian succession Act, 1925, and The Cochin Christian succession Act, 1902.

The law relating to testamentary succession among Hindu, Christians and Parsis etc. is contained in the Indian succession Act, 1925-. It does not make any distinction between the rights of women and men under a will.

Hindu Women And Succession :-

The Hindu law of intestate succession has been codified in the form of The Hindu succession Act, 1956, which is based on the basic mitakshara principle of propinquity, i.e. preference of heirs on the basis of proximity of relationship, prior to 1956. There are two major schools of Hindu law viz. Mitakshara and Dayabhaga which laid down different principles of succession. There was no uniformity in the rights of the Hindus following different schools to succeed to the property of a Hindu who died intestate i.e. without leaving a will behind him.

Position Of Hindu Woman Before 1956 :-

Before 1956, The property of a Hindu woman was divided into two heads viz (a) Stridhan (b) woman's Estate. "Stridhan" literally means Woman's property. The Hindu law interpreted "Stridhan" as the properties received by a woman by way of gift from relations. It includes movable as well as immovable properties. The texts relating to "Stridhan" except in the matter of succession are fairly adequate and clear. Manu defined "Stridhan" as that what was given. before the nuptial fire, what was given at the bridal procession, what was given in token of love and what was received from a brother, a mother, or a father[65].

The property inherited by a woman from a male or female was not considered as Stridhan and it was not her absolute property for the purpose of inheritance[66]. However Bombay school considered the property

[65] See Mayne's Hindu Law and Usage, 13th Ed. 1995 at p. 875

[66] Mst . Devala vs. Rup. Sir, AIR 1960 MP : 1959 Jab. LJ. 598

inherited by a woman from a male other than a widow, and mother etc. as Stridhan. Under all schools of Hindu law, the property obtained by a woman in lieu of maintenance by adverse possession and property purchased with Stridhan was considered as Stridhan.

Rights In Respect Of Stridhan.:-

1) The Hindu woman had full rights of alienating the "Stridhan " being its absolute owner. She could sell, mortgage, lease or exchange the same in any manner she liked.

2) On her death, all types of Stridhan passed to her own heirs and not to the heirs of her husband. Thus a Hindu woman had unlimited rights of enjoyment, alienation and possession in respect of "Stridhan" as its absolute owner.

Women's Estate:-

The other type of property that could be devolved upon the Hindu woman was called woman's Estate. It was also called widow's estate. A Hindu woman could be the owner of woman's Estate in the same way as any individual subject to two basic limitations.

(a) She could not alienate the property (Corpus) and

(b) On her death, it devolved upon the next heir of the last full owner.

In other words, she had only 'limited estate' in respect of this kind of property. She had full powers of possession, management and enjoyment of such property but she had virtually no power of alienation or transfer. However, she could alienate the property in certain exceptional cases like (a) legal necessity i.e. for her own needs and for the need of the dependants of the last full owner, (b) for the benefit of estate and (c) for the discharge of indispensable religious duties such as marriage of daughters, funeral rites of husband, his "Stridhan" and alms to poor for the salvation of his soul. In other words, she could alienate the property for the spiritual benefit of the last full owner but not for her own spiritual benefit. So the rule in

Hanooman prasad vs. Babooee Mumraj[67] applied to alienation of woman's estate also. The woman's estate was normally taken by the woman either by way of property obtained by inheritance or as share obtained on partition.

The foregoing brief discussion makes it amply clear that the position of Hindu woman in relation to property and succession was not satisfactory and uniform. The rights varied depending on the school to which she belonged and the nature of property that devolved upon her. The Hindu women's Right to property Act, 1937 made some changes in succession in respect of separate property of a mitakshara Hindu and in respect of all properties of a Dayabhaga Hindu. It provided for right or survivorship and right of partition to a Hindu widow of Mitakshara School in coparcenary property. However she was not accorded the status of a coparcener. This uncertainly was put to rest by codifying the entire Hindu law of succession in 1956.

---

[67] (1856) 6 MIA, 393. Also see Harisatya vs. Mahadev, AIR 1983 Cal 76.

Position After 1956 :- Sec 14 of Hindu succession Act

The parliament has enacted the Hindu succession Act, 1956 to amend and codify the law relating to intestate succession among Hindus. This Act is applicable to all the Hindus, Buddhists, Jainas and Sikhs by religion, Section 14 of the Act made radical changes in the rights of a Hindu women to succeed to a property, "Property" in this context includes both movable and immovable property acquired by a female Hindu by inheritance or device or at a partition or in lieu of maintenance or by gift from any person, before or after her marriage[68]. It is a comprehensive definition which covers all kinds of property and also covers the erstwhile women's estate.

Retrospective Effect :

Section 14 has been specifically made applicable to the prior Act women's estate also and it has been given retrospective effect. Thus the rule of full ownership is

[68] Mayne's Hindu Law See Explanation to S. 14 of the Act.

applicable to all kinds of properties vested in and held by a woman when the Act came into force.

Abolition Of Limited Estate And Ownership :-

The Act abolished the limited ownership of a Hindu woman in respect of the property held by her as woman's estate, by converting it into full ownership. Limited owner commonly means a person with restricted rights as opposed to full owner with absolute rights. In relation to property absolute, Complete or full ownership comprises various constituents such as the right to possess, actual or constructive, power to enjoy i.e. to determine the manner of use extending even to destroying, right to alienate, transfer or dispose off, etc. Any restriction or limitation on exercise of these rights may result in limited or qualified ownership[69]. Now after 1956, no distinction could be made between the Stridhan and women's estate, as the erstwhile women's estate is converted into 'Stridhan' by section 14 of the Act.

[69] Kalavati V/s BaiSoiryaBai, (1991) 3 SCC 410 at 424.

Where any property is given to a female Hindu in lieu of her Maintenance before the commencement of the Hindu Succession Act, such property becomes the "absolute property" of such female Hindu on the commencement of the Act provided the said property was possessed by her, by virtue of section14 (1) of the Act. This is not withstanding the limitations, or restrictions contained in the instrument, grant or award where under the property is given to her[70].

Dilution Of Bias Against Women :-

The mitakshara school's bias of preference of males over females and of agnates over cognates has been considerably whittled down by the Act. An analysis of the various provisions of the Act makes it clear that the position of women has improved considerably, as compared to the pre-Act position in the matter of succession. In the matter of succession to the property of a Hindu Male dying intestate. Section 8 lays

[70] Nazar Singh and other vs. Jagjit kaur and others, (1996)1 SCC 35 See

down that, it shall also kalavati Bai vs. Sourya Bai (1991) 3 SCC 410.

Devolve firstly upon the heirs specified in class-l of the schedule to the Act, Secondly, in the absence of any class - I heirs on the class-II heirs: Thirdly in the absence of class-l and II heirs upon the agnates of the deceased. And lastly If there are no agnates, thereupon the cognates[71] of the deceased. It is worthwhile to note that there are as many as 8 females in Class-l heirs. They are (1) Daughter (2) Mother (3) Widow, (4) Daughter of a predeceased son (5) daughter of a pre-deceased daughter, (6) Widow of the pre-deceased son (7) Daughter of a pre-deceased £on of a predeceased son and (8) the widow of a pre-deceased son of a pre-deceased son. All these female class-l heirs take their shares on par with their male counter parts as per the scheme of distribution contained in section 10 of the Act. Similarly, there are number of females among the class-II heirs. With regard to the remote heirs, the rule of agnatic preference over coganatic heirs reasserts

[71] Defined by section 3 (a) of the Hindu Succession Act, 1956

itself, which is an indication that there is still some degree of discrimination against females.

Succession To The Property Of Hindu Female :-

Section 15 deals with succession to a property of a female Hindu. This is the first statutory provision dealing with succession to the property of female Hindu. The previous enactments like the Hindu law of inheritance Act, 1929 and the Hindu woman's rights to property Act, 1937, dealt with succession to the property of a male. For the purpose of succession, a female Hindu's property is divided into three categories: (1) Property inherited by a female from her father or mother (2) property inherited from her husband or father-in-law and (3) Property which she herself required any other manner from any other source as her absolute property.

The property mentioned in the first two categories devolves upon her death intestate upon the heirs of her father in the absence of any son or daughter of the deceased and upon the heirs of the husband respectively. Her absolute property mentioned in the third category above devolves upon any of the five classes of the heirs described in Section 15 (1) subject to the rules set out in section 16 : her sons, daughters who include children of pre-deceased son or daughter and husband take precedence over the heirs of the husband.

Discrimination In Succession To Dwelling Houses :-

Section 23 makes special provision respecting dwelling houses. The object of the section seems to be to prevent fragmentation or disintegration of a family dwelling house at the instance of a female heir to the prejudice of the male heirs[72] if a female Hindu inherits a dwelling house along with male heirs she has no right to claim partition of such house until the male heirs divide their respective shares. However, a female heir, not being an unmarried daughter is entitled to reside in the dwelling house. A deserted wife or a female separated from her husband or a widow are

---

[72] Janabai Amma vs. Palani Mudaliar, (TAS) 1981 Mad. 62.

entitled to a right of residence in the dwelling house. A share in a dwelling house cannot be claimed by married daughters[73].

The expression 'dwelling house though not defined by the Act, is referable to the dwelling house in which the intestate Hindu was living at the time of his/her death: he/she intended his/her children who continued to normally occupy and enjoy it. He/She regarded it as his/her permanent abode[74]. Under section 23 a female heir's to claim partition of the dwelling house of Hindu dying intestate is to be deferred or kept in abeyance during the life time of even of a sole surviving male heir of the deceased until he chooses to separate his share or ceases to occupy it or lets it out.

Impact Of Remarriage Of Widow On Her Right To Succession:-

Section 24 lays down a disqualification for succession against (i) the widow of a pre-deceased son (ii) the widow of a pre-deceased

---

[73] Dharma Singh vs. Aso and another, 1990 (Supp). SCC 684

[74] Narsimham Murthy vs. Sheetala Bai, (1996) 3 SCC 644

son of a pre-deceased son (iii) the widow of a brother of Hindu intestate if such widow has remarried on the date when the succession opens. The remarriage, if takes place after the opening of the succession does not divest such females of the property[75]. The disqualification is confined to only three classes of widows mentioned supra and not to the other widows. In other words, once the succession is opened a widow can not be executed from succession even if she marries again.

Coparcenary Rights:-

Coparcenary means that part of a Joint Hindu family which consists of persons who by virtue of relationship, have the right to enjoy and hold the joint property, to restrain the acts of each other in respect of it, to burden it with their debts, and at their pleasure to enforce its partition[76]. A female Hindu was not considered as a coparcener[77]. Thus, she should not enjoy the right of survivorship.

---

[75] Chanda vs. Khubala AIR 1983 Pat. 33

[76] State of Maharashtra vs. Narayana Rao, AIR SC 716 (Para 279).

[77]. CED -VS. Harish Chandra, (1987) 167 ITR 230 (All)

She had only certain interior rights such as that of maintenance since she was not a coparcener, she was not entitled to act as the manager or karta of a joint Hindu family. The Hindu women's rights to property Act 1937, makes a serious in-road upon the rule of survivorship, by making the wives of a coparceners entitled to the interests of male coparcener in a Mitakshara family on their death. However, under the provisions of this Act, *the male* issue of the deceased coparcener remained coparcener along with the other surviving coparcener. The Hindu succession Act, 1956 did not disturb this principle and still retained the same concept of Mitakshara coparcenery.

Effect Of The State Amendments :

Certain State in India like Andhara Pradesh, Tamil Nadu and Maharashtra have realised the difficulty that arise by excluding the daughter's right to claim partition in coparcenry under the Hindu mitakshara law, these state legislatures have amended the Hindu Succession Act, 1956 to achieve the constitutional mandate of equality.

On the time of the Andhra Pradesh Amendment inserted by Andhra Pradesh Amendment Act 13 of 1986 & Tamil Nadu Amendment Act 1990 i.e. 25.3.89, in Maharastra also Hindu Succession (Maharastra Amendment) Act 1994 (46 of 1994) W.C. F. 22.6.94 was amendment as follows :-

(i) The daughter of a coparcener shall become a coparcener by birth in her own right and her status is equal to that of a son. She enjoys the same rights in the coparcenary property as a son. She is entitled to all the rights of survivorship. She will be subject to the same habitats and disabilities in respect of coparcenary property as the son (s.29-A).

(II) She becomes the absolute owner of the property inherited by her as a coparcener (S.29-A).

(iii) when a female Hindu dies after coming into force of this amendment (i.e) after 22.6.94), having at. That time interest in mitakshara coparcenry , her, interest will be devolved by survivorship upon the other coparceners. But if the deceased dies leaving behind any children or children of pre-deceased child at the time of death, the devolution will be in accordance with the provisions of the Hindu succession Act and not by survivorship. (S-29-B). This legislation is beneficial to the women who form part of valnerable sections of the society and it is necessary to give a liberal effect to them[78].

Muslim Women And Succession :-

The Muslim law of succession is basically different from the other indigenous systems of India. The distinction between the self acquired and ancestral properties, Survivorship and partition etc. are not known to islamic law of succession which is based on the tenets of the holy Quaran. no women is excluded from inheritance only on the basis of sex. Women have like mean, right to inherit property in lieu of maintenances Every women who inherits some property is its absolute owner like a man. There is no concept of either 'Shridhan' or 'women's limited estate.' Consequently, there is no scope of any reversion upon the death of a

[78] Sai Reddy vs. Narayan Reddy, (1991) 3 SCC 647.

Muslim woman because it devolves upon her own shares and not on those of her husband. The Muslim law of succession which is unmodified, makes no distinction between a property of deceased male or female. Some authors on Muslim law feel that the Muslim law of property and succession in India has been considerably influenced by the local concepts and institutions

(i) **Inheritance at Muslim Law**: - Position of this topic may be discussed under two heads.

(a) **Principles on pre- Islamic Law** :- The principles of the pre-Islamic customary law may be summarized as under.

(1) The nearest male agnate (s) succeeded

(2) Females and cognates were excluded

(3) Descendants were preferred to ascendants and ascendants to collaterals.

(4) Where the agnates were equally distant, the estate was divided per capita.

It is clear that the females were discriminated against. As they were virtually excluded from the inheritance.

(b) **Principles of Islamic Law** :-

The main reforms introduced by Islam may be stated briefly as under[79].

(1) The husband /wife was made an heir

(2) Female and coinages were made competent to inherit.

(3) Parents and ascendants were given the right to inherit even when there were male descendants.

(4) As a general rule, a female was given one half the share of a male.

The newly created heirs were mostly females, but where a female was equal to the customary heir in proximity to the deceased, the Islamic law gave her half the share of the male. For example, if a daughter coexisted with the son, or a sister with a brother, the female obtained one share and the male two shares.

(Hi) **Rights of Females** :-

At present, males and females have no equal rights over property. This is manifest when there are two heirs of opposite sex in the same degree. Then the male heir takes two

[79] A.A.A. Fyzee : Outlines of Mohammedan Law (4th ed), at 390.

shares and the female heir takes only one share. Thus, a daughter does not, however, by reason of her sex, suffer from any disability to deal with her share of the property. She is the absolute owner/ master of her inheritance. The same rule applies to a widow or a mother.

There is no such thing as a widow's estate, as in Hindu law, or the disabilities, of a wife, as under the older English common law.

Hanafi law of Inheritance :-

Under the hanafi law, the heirs of a deceased, male or female, fall under the following classes.

(i) The sharers (ii) The Reliquaries,

(iii) The Distant Kindred and

(iv) The state by escheat. The Sharers :-

There are twelve shares in number who are given specific shares. However their shares are not permanently fixed as each heir may be affected by the presence of other sharers. Sometimes, a sharer may be totally excluded from inheritance. The sharers include father, True Grandfather, Husband. Wife, mother, True Grandmother, Daughter

Son's Daughter how so ever, uterine Brother, Idetltrine Sister, Full sister, son sanguine sister. There are as many as 8 female sharers who could inherit the property of a deceased muslim.

The Residuaries:-

They are certain shares who are excluded from taking their specified sharer, if a residuary of equal rank co -exists. In such a case they become residuaries. They are entitled to inherit, if there are no shares, but there is a residue left satisfying their claims. In the presence of such circumstances either the whole inheritance or the residue as the case may be devolves upon Residuaries in the order prescribed by the Koranic Text[80].

These Residuraries include.

(i) Descendants viz (1) son (2) Son's how so ever.

(ii) Ascends viz (3) father (4) True Grandfather How High so ever

(iii) Descendants of father viz (5) Full brother (6) Full Sister (7) Consanguine Brothers (8)

---

[80] Mulla : Principles of Mohemmadan Law Ed. By M. Hidayatullah, 19th ed, 1990. 54,55.

Consanguine sisters (9) Full brothers Son (10) Consanguine Brothers' Son (11) Full Brother's (12) Consanguine Brother's Son.

(iv) Descendents of True Grandfather how high so ever.

Viz. (13) Full paternal uncle.

(14) Consanguine paternal uncle's Son.

(15) Full paternal uncle's Son

(16) Consanguine paternal uncle's Son

(17) Full paternal uncle's Son.

(18) Consanguine paternal uncle's Son's son.

(19) Male descendants of more Remote True Grand father.

It may be noted that, in all, only four females are included among the Residuaries in the form of full sister, consanguine sister, the daughter and the son's daughter how low so ever, No other female can inherit as residuaries with corresponding males of a parallel grade. Of the five heirs that are always entitled to some share of the inheritance and who are not liable to exclusion in any case viz (1) the child i.e. Son or daughter (2)father (3) mother (4) husband

(5) wife, there could be three females in the form of mother, daughter and wife.

Distant Kindred :-

In the absence of sharers and Residuaries, the inheritance is divided among "distant Kindred" which consists of four classes viz the Descendants of the deceased, ascendant of parents and descendants of immediate grand parents. There are number of females in all these four classes, who are remotely related to the deceased. The first of the class exclude the second and the second excludes the third, so on.

Shia law of Inheritance :-

The shias divide heirs into two groups. (1) heirs by consanguinity i.e. blood relations and (ii) heirs by marriage i.e. husband and wife. Among the blood relations mother, daughter, Sister, Grandfather, Paternal aunt and maternal aunt are the females who are entitled to inherit the property of the deceased. They are called sharers. They take different shares depending on certain conditions like existence of other sharers and relatives. However it may be noted that wife takes normally 1/8th share in the property of the husband , and husband takes 1/4th share in the property of the wife i.e double the share of the wife in similar circumstances. Among the Shias, there is no separate class of heirs corresponding to the distant kindred on Sunni law.

Discrimination :-

Even though the protagonists of the Muslim law claim that there is absolute equality among the women and men in the matter of succession, there are certain provisions which are loaded in favour of the male inheritors as they take more shares, compared to their female counter parts. For example, among the shias, a childless widow takes no share in her husband's land but she is entitled to her one fourth share in the value of trees and building standing thereon, as well as in his movable property[81].

[81] Mulla : Principles of Mohammedan Law, 1990 at para 113, p. 98.

SUCCESSION AMONG CHRISTIAN WOMEN :-

The entire Christian law of succession is codified and governed by the Indian succession Act 1925. The Act regulates the in-testate as well as testamentary succession among the Christians and also others.

Intestate succession :-

Part V of the Act, and Section 29-56 deal with the intestate succession. This part is not applicable to the property of any Hindu, Muhammandan, Buddhist, Sikh or Jaina. In other words this part is applicable to the property of the Christians and Parsis only. Chapter-II of part V of the Act dealt with the Rules in cases of Intestate other than Parsis. According to section 32, the property of an intestate devolve upon the wife or husband on upon those who are kindred of the deceased.

According to section 33, where the intestate has left a widow and also any lineal descendants, one third of his property shall belong to his widow and the remaining two thirds shall go to his lineal descendants. But if there are only distant kindred left along with the widow but no lineal descendants, one half of his property shall belong to his widow. If he has not left behind any lineal descendants or distant kindred but only the widow, She takes the entire property. Therefore the share of the wife is not fixed and is variable depending on certain circumstances.

Thus, the widow is made to share the property along with the other relatives of the husband in certain cases. On the whole the position of the Christian women is not so unhappy as was the case of the Hindu women prior to the Act of 1956. the lineal descendants and the kindred also consist of many female heirs who take their shares in the property of the intestate as per the Rules of distribution contained Sections 36 to 49 of the Indian succession Act, 1925.

MAINTENANCE

SYNOPSIS

(a) **Hindu Women And Maintenance** :

(i) Maintenance under the Hindu Adoptions and Maintenance Act, 1956.

(ii) Definition of maintenance.

(iii) Maintenance of wife.

(iv) Maintenance under the Hindu Marriage Act.

(v) Maintenance of widowed daughter-in-law.

(b) **Maintenance Of Muslim Women** :

(i) Wife.

(ii) Maintenance on divorce

a. Under Muslim personal law.

b. Under Cr.p.c.

c. Under the Act of 1986.

RELEVANT PROVISIONS OF THE HINDU ADOPTIONS AND MAINTENANCE ACT, 1956

==================================

(No. 78 of 1956)

An Act to amend and codify the law relating to adoptions and maintenance among Hindus

Definitions :- In this Act. unless the context otherwise requires :-

(b) " Maintenance" includes :-

1) In all cases, provisions for food, clothing, residence, education and medical attendance and treatment :

in the case of an unmarried daughter, also the reasonable expenses of and incident to her marriage:

(c) "Minor" means a person who has not completed his or her age of eighteen years.

Maintenance

18. **Maintenance of wife** :-

(1) Subject to the provisions of this section, a Hindu wife, whether married before or after the commencement of this Act. shall be entitled to be maintained by her husband during her life time.

(2) A Hindu wife shall be entitled to live separately from her husband without forfeiting her claim to maintenance if is guilty of desertion, that is to say of abandoning her without reasonable cause and without her consent or against her wish, or of willfully neglecting her: if he has treated her with such cruelty as to cause a reasonable apprehension in her mind that it will be harmful or injurious to live with her husband:

if he is suffering from a virulent form a of leprosy :

if he has any other wife living :

if he keeps a concubine in the same house in which his wife is living or habitually resides with a concubine elsewhere :

if he has ceased to be a Hindu by conversion to another religion :

if there is any other cause justifying her living separately.

(3) A Hindu wife shall not be entitled to separate residence and maintenance from her husband if she is unchaste or ceases to be a Hindu by conversion to another religion.

19. Maintenance Of Widowed Daughter-In-Law :-

(1) A Hindu wife, whether married before or after the commencement of this Act. shall be entitled to be maintained after the death of her husband by her father-in-law :

Provided and to the extent that she is unable to maintain herself out of her own earnings or other property or, where she has on property of her own, is unable to obtain maintenance –

From the estate of her husband or father or mother, or

from her son or daughter, if any, or his or her estate.

(2) Any obligation under sub- section (1) shall not be enforceable if the father-in-law has not the means to do so from any coparcenary property in his possession out of which the daughter-in-law has not obtained any share, and any such obligation shall cease on the remarriage of the daughter-in-law.

20. Maintenance Of Children And Aged Parents :-

(1) Subject to the provisions of this section a Hindu is bound, during his or her lifetime, to maintain his or her legitimate or illegitimate children and his or her aged or infirm parents.

(2) A legitimate or illegitimate child may claim maintenance from his or her father or mother so long as the child is a minor.

(3) The obligation of a person to maintain his or her aged or infirm parent or a daughter, who is unmarried extends in so far as the parent or the unmarried daughter, as the case may be, is unable to maintain himself or –

herself – out of his or her own earnings or other property.

Explanation :- In this section "parent" including a childless stepmother.

21. Dependants Defined :- for the purposes of this chapter "dependants" mean the following relatives of the deceased:

his or her father:

(ii) his or her mother:

his widow, so long as she does not remarry:

his or her son or the son of his predeceased son or the son of a pre-deceased son of his pre-deceased son, so long as he is a minor: provided and to the extent that he is unable to obtain maintenance, in the case of a grandson from his father's or mother's estate, and in the case of a great grandson, from the estate of his father or mother or father's or father or father's mother:

his or her unmarried daughter, or the unmarried daughter of his pre-deceased son or the unmarried daughter of a pre-deceased son of his pre-deceased son, so long as she remains unmarried:

provided and to the extent that she is unable to obtain maintenance, in the case of a grant-daughter from her father's or mother's estate and in the case of a great-father's father or father's mother:

his widowed daughter: provided and to the extent that she is unable to obtain maintenance-

From the estate of her husband or

From her son or daughter if any, or his or her estate:

From her father-in-law or his father or the estate of either of them:

Any widow of his son or of a son of his pre-deceased son, so long as she does not re-marry:

provided and to the extent that she is unable to obtain maintenance from her son or daughter, if any, or his or her estate: or in the case of a granson's widow, also from her father-in-law's estate:

His or her minor illegitimate son, so long as he remains a minor:

His or her minor illegitimate daughter, so long as she remains unmarried.

22. Maintenance of dependants :-

(1) Subject to the provisions of sub-section (2) the heirs of a deceased Hindu are bound to maintain the dependants of the deceased out of the estate inherited by them from the deceased.

(2) Where a dependant has not obtained, by testamentary or intestate succession, any share in the estate of a Hindu dying after the commencement of this Act, the dependant shall be entitled, subject to the provisions of this Act. to maintenance from those who take the estate.

(3) The liability of each of the persons who takes the estates shall be in proportion to the value of the share or part of the estate taken by him or her.

(4) Notwithstanding anything contained in sub- section (2) or sub- section (3) non person who is himself or herself a dependant shall be liable to contribute to the maintenance of others, if he or she has obtained a share or part the value of which is, or would, if the liability to contribute were enforced, become

less than what would be awarded to him or her by way of maintenance under this Act.

23. Amount of Maintenance:-

(1) It shall be in the discretion of the court to determine whether any and if so what, maintenance shall be awarded under the provisions of this Act, and in doing so the court shall have due regard to the considerations set out in sub- section (2) or sub-section (3) as the case may be, so far as they are applicable.

(2) In determining the amount of maintenance if any, to be awarded to a wife, children or aged or infirm parents under this Act, regard shall be had to-

The position and status of the parties:

The reasonable wants of the claimants:

If the claimant is living separately, whether the claimant is justified in doing so:

The value of the claimant's property and any income derived from such property, or from the claimant's own earnings or from any other source:

The number of persons entitled to maintenance, under this Act.

(3) In determining the amount of Maintenance, if any, to be awarded to a dependant under this Act. regard shall be had to—

The net value of the estate of the deceased after providing for the payment of his debts:

The provision, if any made under a will of the deceased in respect or the dependant:

the degree of relationship between the two:

The reasonable wants of the dependant:

The past relations between the dependant and the deceased:

The value of the property of the dependant and any income derived from such property: or from his or her earnings or from any other source:

The number of dependants entitled to maintenance under this Act.

24. Claimant to Maintenance should be a Hindu :-

No person shall be entitled to claim maintenance under this chapter if he or she has ceased to be a Hindu by conversion to another- religion.

25. Amount of maintenance may be altered on change of circumstances:-

The amount of maintenance, whether fixed by a decree of court or by agreement, either before or after the commencement of this Act. may be altered subsequently if there is a material change in the circumstances justifying such alteration.

26. Debts To Have Priority :-

Subject to the provision contained in section 27 debts of every description contracted or payable by the deceased shall have priority over the claims of his dependants for maintenance under this act.

27. Maintenance When To Be A Charge :-

A dependant's claim for maintenance under this Act shall not be a charge on the estate of the deceased or any portion thereof, unless on has been created by the will of the deceased, by a decree of court, by agreement between the dependant and the owner of the estate or portion, or otherwise.

28. Effect Of Transfer Of Property On Right To Maintenance :-

Where a dependant has a right to receive maintenance out of an estate, and such estate or any part thereof is transferred, the right to receive maintenance may be enforced against the transferee if the transferee has notice of the right, or if the transfer is gratuitous: but not against the transferee for consideration and without notice of the right.

Hindu Guardians and Wards Act :-

On pondering over the provisions under personal laws; it seems that –

The old Hindu law was primarily based on Shastric concepts. Marriage under old and present law also is not contract unlike Muslim law and even Christen law . It has a sanctify of its own old Hindu law was codified, as Hindu marriage Act, Hindu Adoption and Maintance Act, Hindu Succession Act and Child Marriage Restraint Act also. Marriage is not indissoluble. It is still considered a sacrament. **Saptpati** still remain as a necessary sacrament. That itself shows that Hindu Marriage Act does not violate the basic tenets of old shastric Hindu Law.

However, due to change circumstances into entire atmosphere provisions of divorce have also been made under Hindu Marriage Act. But at the same time baseless allegations can not entitled a party of braking the marital tie. The provisions for divorce are that way very strict though it does not permit divorce by mutual consent under certain circumstances.

Thus provisions for women under old Hindu law has been liberated to a considerable extent. The same thing is about Hindu Succession Act formerly women has no right to succession under the very exceptional circumstances it was virtually denied for them. Now however they are not only entitled to succeed to the estate of their parents like but the state like Maharastra and others states have been given status by the birth right in family, Sec. 14 of the Hindu Succession Act has made a vary important provisions to the effect that property held by women even though originally was limited owner shall be deemed to be her absolute property if she is in possession of the concern property on the date of enactment.

Maintenance is a very touchy subject concerning all women apart from Sec. 125 of Cr.P.C. now a women is entitled to get maintenance even during pendency of matrimonial litigation . Not only that the legislature has made further stringent provision that a party failing to give maintenance to his wife forfeits his right of Defence. Their are important provisions so far as women is concerned under the Hindu Adoption and Maintance Act. Under the new act a female can be adopted under certain specified condition and this is no doubt a very important provision, having for recharge consequences of the very concept of hatred of daughters is failed to be put to an end by this Act.

Thus, the new Hindu Law no doubt has made .... changes with a view to improve the position of women in general unfortunately, even after all these enactment's the position of women particularly in villages is for from satisfactory these needs to be revolutionary changes in the attitude of men towards women. It is strange that, violence against women is not only limited to villages now but virus has spread to cities and big cities also. There are hundreds of pictures books and serials on the T.V. harping on this topic. The constant educative alone can improve the situation.

Hindu law (Hindu succession Act 1956) :

The legislators by enacting the provisions of S.14 & 15 of the Hindu succession Act 1956 has no doubt brought a revolutionary & see change benefit to the rights & interest of Hindu woman over the property possessed by her, even from Vedic age, the Indian law never touched the women's right to such a high scale. This Act turned their limited right over the property to full & absolute ownership. Adhering to the preamble of constitution legislature enacted these provisions to equalize the right to property amongst the Hindu male & female. It has given unfettered right to heritage & absolute ownership with right to dispose of it.

CHAPTER - V

POSITION OF WOMEN UNDER VARIOUS LAWS ABOUT MOTHERHOOD AND CHILDHOOD.

PROVISION OF INDUSTRIAL LAW AND WOMEN: -

"Motherhood and childhood are entitled to special care and assistance. All children whether born in or out of wedlock shall enjoy the same social protection".

-Art 25(2) of The Universal Declaration of Human Rights.

"Women are one-half of the world but until a century ago-..... it was a man's world. The laws were man's laws the Government a man's Government. The country a man's country... The man's world must become a man's and woman's world....

--Martha Thomas, American Educator (1908)

Introduction: -

In the sphere of Industrial Law, the women have been assigned a special position in view of their unique characteristics, physically and mentally. The Constitution of India which is the fundamental law of the land contains number of provisions to protect the interest of woman and also to prohibit gender discrimination. The preamble specifically declares that one of the main purposes of the constitution is to secure social, economic and political justice along with equality of status and of opportunity to all the citizens. This is irrespective of the sex. This specific mandate given to the state has resulted in number of protective, beneficial and health provisions made in various enactments for the benefit of woman.

Article 42[82] to the Constitution of India directs the State to make provisions for securing just and humane conditions of work and for maternity relief. In pursuance of this objective, the Parliament has passed the Maternity Benefit Act, 1961 to regulate the employment of women in certain establishment for certain periods before and after child birth and to provide for maternity and other benefits. This enactment consists of 30 sections and has been amended in 1970,72,73,76,88, and recently in 1995 to make it more effective and beneficial for women.

Prohibition of employment or work.

After The Delivery Or Miscarriage etc: -

[82] Dr. J.N. Pandey – The Constitutional Law of India

According to Section 4, of the Act no woman who delivers a child or who undergoes Medical Termination of pregnancy or miscarriage shall be employed during the six weeks immediately following the date such a movement.

Before The Delivery Or Miscarriage Etc: -

No pregnant woman is required to do any work which is of an arduous nature or which involves long hours of standing or which in any way interferes with her pregnancy or the Normal development of the foetus or likely to pass her miscarriage or adversely affect her health, during the period of one month immediately preceding the period of six weeks, before the date of or expected delivery and during any period of six weeks for which the pregnant woman does not avail of leave of absence. Thus a pregnant woman in her last stages of pregnancy should not be assigned any difficult or hard work that may affect her pregnancy.

Maternity Benefit Covers Miscarriage And Medical Termination Of Pregnancy Also [83]: -

[83] The Medical Termination Of Pregnancy Act 1971

In view of the amendment made in 1995 the benefits conferred on a woman in case of her delivery or miscarriage also cover the Medical Termination of pregnancy under the provisions of Medical Termination of pregnancy Act, 1971. Therefore, in the case of abortion also a woman can claim the said benefit.

Other Benefits: -

Section 8 :- Payment of Medical Bonus :-

Every woman who is entitled to maternity benefit is also entitled to receive medical bonus of Rs. 250/- from her employer, if the employer does not provide pre-natal and post-natal care free of cost.

Section 9 :- Leave For Miscarriage Or Medical Termination Of Pregnancy

In case of miscarriage or medical termination of pregnancy, the woman is entitled to leave with wages at the rate of maternity benefit, for a period of six weeks immediately after such an event.

Section 9A :- Leave With Wages For Tubectomy Operation : -

In case of family planning operation that is tubectomy performed on a woman employee, she is entitled to leavc with wage at the rate of maternity benefit for a period of two weeks immediately after such operation.

Section 10 :- Leave For Illness Due To Pregnancy, Delivery Ect. : -

Any woman employee suffering from illness arising out of pregnancy, delivery, pre-mature birth of child, miscarriage, medical termination of pregnancy or tubectomy operation is entitled to leave with wages at the rate of maternity benefit for maximum period of one month. This leave period is in addition to the period of absence allowed to her for any individual event aforementioned as applicable under the Act.

Section 11 :- Nursing Breaks: -

Every woman who returns to duty after delivering a child is entitled to two breaks in the course of her daily work until the child attains the age of 15 months. These breaks and provided for the purpose of nursing the child and are in addition to the regular intervals of rest allowed to her. According to

Rule 6 of the maternity Benefit (Mines and Circus) Rules, 1963 each of the two breaks shall be of fifteen minutes duration where a distance is to be covered for the purposes of journey to and from the place where the child is kept, an extra period of live to fifteen minutes duration can be given to the woman.

Section 2 :- No Dismissal During Absence Of Pregnancy : -

When a woman absents herself from work in accordance with the provisions of this Act, her employer cannot discharge or dismiss her during or due to such absence. The employer also shall not give notice of such discharge or dismissal. If the woman employee is discharged or dismissed as mentioned above, it shall not have effect of depriving her of the maternity benefit or medical bonus. In other word the dismissal or discharge during absence of pregnancy is unlawful for the purpose of claiming maternity and other benefits conferred by the Act.

However if the woman employee is dismissed for any gross misconduct, she will forfeit the maternity benefit or medical bonus or both. Under Rule 8 of The maternity Benefits (Mines and Circus) Rules, 1963, the following acts constitute gross misconduct for the purpose of dismissal under section 12 of the Act.

(a) Wilful destruction of employer's goods or property.

(b) Assaulting any superior or co-employee at the place of work.

(c) Criminal offence involving moral turpitude resulting resulting in conviction in a court of law.

(d) Theft, fraud or dischonesty in connection with the employer's business or property: and.

(e) Wilful non- observance of safety measures or rules on the subject or wilful interference with safety devices or with fire fighting equipment.

<u>Section 21, 22 :- Penalties</u> : -

If any employer fails to pay any amount of maternity benefit to a woman under this Act or violates any of the provisions of this Act, he is liable to be punished with a minimum imprisonment of three months but which may extend to one year also with fine. Similarly if an employer obstructs the Inspector or any other authority appointed by the government under this Act from implementing the provision of this Act, the same is an offence and is punishable. Thus this Act creates special offences in so far as non-implementation of the provision of this Act is concerned.

Other Benefits: -

Apart from the above provisions with regard to the working hours, permitted intervals and prohibition of employment of woman, number of enactments provide various other benefits to the woman employees. They include maternity Benefit, Insurance, crèches for the infants of woman employees and Nursing breaks. Some of this benefits have already been discussed in the preceding chapters. The following paras explain the provision with regard to crèches etc.

****

SEX DETERMINATION TESTS AND FEMALE FOETICIDE

I. Sex Determination Tests: -

(i) Introduction.

(ii) Sex-Determination and misuse of Techniques.

(iii) Regulations of pre-natal diagnostic techniques.

(iv) Scheme of legislation.

(v) Regulations of Techniques and permitted use.

(vi) Prohibition of Sex-Determination.

(vii) Safeguards before use of Techniques.

(viii) Constitution of central Supervisory Authority.

(ix) Registration of Genetic centers etc.

(x) Prohibition of Advertisement.

(xi) Penal provision.

II. Termination of Pregnancy : -

(i) Introduction.

(ii) The medical Termination of pregnancy Act.

(iii) Circumstances permitting Termination of pregnancy.

(iv) Grave injury to mental health.

(v) Age of the pregnant woman.

(vi) Consent of pregnant woman.

(vii) Place of Termination of pregnancy.

Pre-Natal Diagnostic Techniques (Regulation and Prevention of Misuse) Act 1994[84] : -

Introduction :- Like in any other countries in India also the female foeticide and infanticide are on the rise. In the old days when the scientific techniques were not advanced, it was impossible to determine the sex of the child being carried in the womb of mother until it was delivered.

However with the advent of modern techniques developed in the recent times, it became quite possible to ascertain the sex of the child in the womb even in the early stages of pregnancy. The technique used to diagnose the condition, and sex of the fetus is medically called 'amniocentesis' which is one of the many pre-natal diagnostic techniques. These techniques are actually intended to test or analyze the amniotic fluids, blood or any tissue of a pregnant

[84] Pre-Natal Diagnostic Techniques Act, 1994

woman for the purpose of detecting any genetic or metabolic disorders or chromosomal abnormalities or congenital anomalies or sex linked diseases. The procedures used for conducting any pre-natal diagnostic tests include all gynecological or obstetrical or medical procedures such as ultra sonography, taking or removing samples of blood or any tissue of a pregnant woman etc.

Scheme of Legislation :-

The Pre-Natal Diagnostic Techniques (Regulation and prevention of misuse) Act, 1994 consists of 34 Sections spread over in 8 chapters. The Act regulates the use of such techniques and prevents their misuse for sex-determination, not only by individuals such as Gynecologist, Medical geneticists, and Pediatricians but also by any Genetic counseling centre, Genetic Laboratory or Genetic clinic.

Regulation of Techniques & Permitted Use:-

According to section 4 of the Act, the pre-diagnostic techniques may be conducted only for the purpose of detecting any abnormality like chromosomal abnormality, genetic metabolic disease, sex-linked genetic disease. Or congenital anomaly etc. Thus, if a womán is pregnant and is tested HIV positive, pre-diagnostic technique may be legally applied to determine whether her child in the womb also is HIP positive. Similarly, if the pregnant mother is suffering form venereal Disease, the technique may be applied to test whether the child in the womb also is affected with such disease.

These technique may be used or conducted only when any of the following conditions is satisfied.

(i) When the pregnant woman is above 35 years, of age:

(ii) When the pregnant woman has already undergone 2 or more abortions or fetal loss:

(iii) Where the pregnant woman has been exposed to potentially dangerous agents like drugs, radiation, infection or chemicals.

(iv) Where the pregnant woman has a family history of mental retardation or physical deformities such as spasticity or any other genetic disease etc.

Therefore, no relative or husband of the pregnant woman can seek or encourage the conduct of any pre-natal diagnostic techniques except when any one of the above conditions is fulfilled.

Section 6 : - Prohibition of Determination of Sex:-

The Act absolutely prohibits the determination of the sex of a fetus and communication there of by any Genetic Centre, laboratory or clinic. Therefore techniques like ultra-sonography can be used only for detecting the genetic disorders or abnormalities and not for determination of sex of the fetus.

Section 5 :- Safeguards Before Use of Techniques:-

Before using or conducting a per-natal diagnostic technique, on a pregnant woman the concerned Genetic counseling centre, Laboratory or clinic must fulfill the following conditions.

(i) It must explain the possible side effects and consequences of using the techniques to the pregnant woman.

(ii) Obtain her written consent to undergo such procedure in the prescribed form, in the language she understands.

(iii) Give her a copy of her written consent.

Under no circumstances, the sex of the fetus should be communicated to the woman concerned or her relatives.

Section 7 and 16 :- Constitution of Central Supervisory Authority:-

The Act empowers and directs the central Government to constitute an authority called the central Supervisory Board consisting of the minister for family welfare, the secretary of such ministry / Department and 21 other members including eminent geneticists, gynecologist, Social scientists and woman parliament members etc. for a period of 3 years. The functions of the board include advising the Government on policy matters related to the use of pre-natal diagnostic techniques, creating public awareness and properly implementing the Act.,

Section 18–21 :- Registration of Genetic Centers :-

Under section a8 of the Act, every Genetic counseling centre, Genetic Laboratory or Genetic clinic must be registered under the Act, after the commencement of the Act. No person shall open any such centre unless such registration is made separately or jointly.

The Government is vested with the power to cancel or suspend the registration, if it is found that such centers have misused the techniques.

<u>Section 22 :- Prohibition of Advertisement Regarding Sex Determination</u> :-

The Act provides that, no person, organization or Genetic centre should advertise in any form regarding the facility of the pre-natal determination of sex available at such centre or laboratory. Therefore no publicity can be given as to the existence or availability of the facility.

If advertisement is given, in contravention of the above provision, the same is punishable with imprisonment up to 3 years or with fine up to 10,000 Rs.

<u>Section 22-28 :- Penal Provisions</u> :-

Any contravention of the provisions of this Act. is made an offence. The guilty individual is liable to be punished with various punishments depending on the nature of the contravention.

If a company commits such an offence, any person who is the incharge of such company at the time of offence shall be deemed to be guilty of the offence. Thus vicarious liability is imposed on the individuals heading the companies or organizations violating.

The Law views the offences committed under this Act as very serious. This could be seen from section 27 of the Act which makes every offence under the Act, a cognizable, non-bailable and non-compoundable.

The above discussion makes it amply clear that the state wants to protect the dignity and status of women and punishes those who attempt to commit or help commit female infanticide either directly or indirectly. The offence of causing miscarriage are discussed in greater detail elsewhere in this book.

Termination of Pregnancy

Introduction :-

In India, Termination of pregnancy by unregistered medical practitioners and quacks is common place. The reasons for such abortions are many which include superstitions and carrying illegitimate children etc. prior to 1971 a termination of pregnancy was not regulated by any law. However the Indian Penal Code provides for many provisions to punish the persons responsible for miscarriage,. Sections 312 to 316 of the Indian Penal Code punish the persons causing miscarriage, preventing a child being born life or causing the death of quick unborn child. Inspite of these penal provisions the practice of causing miscarriage continued in India for various social and medical reasons.

Therefore the parliament has decided to provide for the termination of certain pregnancy by registered medical practitioners.

The termination of pregnancy by quacks, and unregistered and unqualified medical practitioners caused irreparable damage to the woman concerned and also caused death in many cases. The practice has been found to be hazardous to the health of the woman who are pregnant. In most of the cases the abortion was forcefully carried out to prevent the birth of a female child and in the process most of the women also lost their lives besides certain other medical damages. These were the main reasons that prompted the Parliament to make a law to regulate termination of pregnancy only in certain cases and only by registered medical practitioners. The main purpose of the Legislation called The Medical Termination of Pregnancy Act, 1971 is to provide for the termination of pregnancy by registered medical practitioners where it continuance would involve a risk to the life of the pregnant woman or grave injury to her physical or mental health or where there is a substantial risk that if child were born.

The Medical Termination of Pregnancy Act, 1971[85] :-

The Parliament has passed this enactment to provide for the termination of certain pregnancies by registered medical practitioners and other matters connected with such termination. The Act consist of 8 Sections dealing with various aspects like the time, place and circumstances in which a pregnancy may be terminated by medical practitioners legally. Here the 'Medical Practitioners' means the persons who posses any recognized medical qualifications as defined in The Indian Medical Council Act, 1956 and whose name has been entered in State Medical

[85] The Medical Termination of Pregnancy Act, 1971

Register. Such person must have experience or training in gynecology and obstetrics.

Section 3 :- Circumstances In Which Pregnancy May be Terminated :-

A pregnancy may be terminated by a medical practitioner only when any of the following conditions is fulfilled :-

(a) Where the length of pregnancy does not exceed 12 weeks that is three months, it may be terminated by a single registered medical practitioner.

-Or-

(b) Where the length of pregnancy exceed 12 weeks but does not exceed 20 weeks, it may be terminated by not less than two registered medical practitioners.

Such termination can take place only when such medical practitioners (s) forms (s) an opinion in good faith that,

(i) The continuance of pregnancy would involve a risk to the life of the pregnant women or of grave injury to her physical or mental health : or

(ii) There is substantial risk that if the child were born, it would suffer from such physical or mental abnormalities as to be serious handicapped.

Therefore it is clear that termination of pregnancy can take place only on medical grounds that too when the registered medical practitioner has formed above opinion in good faith.

Grave Injury To Mental Health :-

If the pregnancy is alleged to be caused by rape, the anguish caused by such pregnancy is presume to constitute grave injury to mental health. The result of failure of any family planning device used by any married woman or husband, the anguish caused by such unwanted pregnancy is presumed to constitute grave injury to the mental health of the pregnant woman. Therefore a pregnancy caused by rape or which is unwanted may be medically terminated under section 3 of the Act.

Section 3 :- Age of The Pregnant Woman :-

Section 3 (4) of the Act specifically provides that the pregnancy of woman, who has not attained the age of 18 years cannot be terminated except with the written consent of her guardian. Similarly if the pregnant woman is above 18 years of age and is a lunatic, then also the written consent of her guardian is essential.

Section 4 :- Place of Termination of Pregnancy :-

A medical termination of pregnancy can be made only at a hospital established or maintained by the Government or at other places approved for that purpose by the Government. Therefore the termination of pregnancy may be carried out only at a hospital which is fully equipped with all the medical facilities.

Overriding Effect of The Act :-

The Medical Termination of pregnancy Act, 1971 has been given overriding effect over The Indian Penal code, 1860, which deals with the

Relevant Provisions of

FACTRORES ACT, 1948[86]

(Relevant Portions)

19. Latrines and Urinals :-

(1) In very factory-

(a) Sufficient latrine and urinal accommodation of prescribed types shall be provided conveniently situated and accessible to workers at all times while they are at the factory :

(b) Separate enclosed accommodation shall be provided for male and female workers:

(c) Such accommodation shall be adequately lighted and ventilated, and no latrine or urinal shall unless specially exempted in writing by the chief Inspector, communicate with any work-room except through an intervening open space or ventilated passage:

[86] Factories Act, 1948

(d) All such accommodation shall be maintained in a clean and sanitary condition at all times:

(e) Sweepers shall be employed whose primary duty it would, be to keep clean latrines, urinals and washing place.

22. Work On Or Near Machinery In Motion :-

(2)[87] No woman or young person shall be allowed to clean, lubricate or adjust any part of a prime mover or of any transmission machinery while the prime mover or transmission machinery is in motion, or to clean, lubricate or adjust any part of any machine if the cleaning, lubrication or adjustment thereof would expose the woman or young person to risk of injury from any moving part either of that machine or of any adjacent machinery).

27. Prohibition of Employment of Women And Children Near Cotton –Openers :-

No woman or child shall be employed in any part of a factory for pressing cotton in which a cotton – opener is at work:

[87] Subs by Section 6 of Act 25 of 1954 for the original sub – section (2).

Provided that if the feed – end of a cotton – opener is in a room separated from the delivery end by a partition extending to the roof or to such height as the Inspector may in any particular case specify in writing, women and children may be employed on the side of the partition where the feed – end is situated.

48. <u>Creches:-</u>

(1) In every factory wherein more than (thirty women workers)[88] are ordinarily employed there shall be provided and maintained a suitable room or rooms for the use of children, under the age of six years, of such women.

(3) <u>The State Government May Make Rules</u>:-

(a) Prescribing the location and the standards in respect of construction, accommodation, furniture and other equipment of rooms to be provided, under this section:

(b) Requiring the provision in factories to which this section applies of additional facilities for the care of children belonging to women workers, including suitable provision of

[88] Subs by Section 23 Act. No. 94 of 1976 for fifty women worker's (w.e.f. 26-10-1976)

facilities for washing and changing their clothing:

(c) Reacquiring the provision in any factory of free milk or refreshment or both for such children:

(d) Requiring that facilities shall be given in any factory for the mothers of such children to feed them at the necessary intervals.

66. Further Restrictions On Employment Of Women :-

(1) The provisions of this chapter shall, in their application to women in factories, be supplemented by the following further restrictions, namely.

(a)No exemption from the provisions of section 54 may be granted in respect of any woman:

(b) No woman shall be (required or allowed to work in any factory)[89] except between the hours of 6 a.m. and 7 p.m.

Provided that the state Government may, by notification in the official Gazette, in respect of (any factory or group or class or description of

---

[89] Subs by Section 29, ibid, for employed in any factory' (w.e.f.26-10-1976)

factories)[90], very the limits laid down in clause (b) but so

(a)In sub- section (1) the latter and brackets "a" before the words "in the case of sickness," the word "and" after the words "sickness allowances" and clause (b) shall be omitted:

(b) In sub- section (2) the words "or maternity" shall be omitted.

30. Repeal :-

i) To mines, the mines maternity Benefit Act 1941 (19 of 1941) : and

ii) To factories situate in the Union territory of Delhi, the Bombay maternity Benefit Act, 1929 as in force in that territory, shall stand repealed.

[90] Subs. By section 29, ibid, for any class or description of factories; (w.e.f.26-10-1976)

RELEVANT PROVISIONS OF THE EMPLOYEE'S STATE INSUTANCE ACT, 1948[91].

MATERNITY BENEFIT

In exercise of powers conferee by section 97 of the Act, the central Government has framed the above Regulations. The Regulations 87 to 95 deal with the maternity benefit available to an insured woman.

87. Notice of pregnancy :-

An insured woman, who decides to give notice of pregnancy before confinement, shall give such notice in form 19 to the appropriate local office by post or otherwise and shall submit, together with such notice, a certificate of pregnancy in form given in accordance with these regulations on a date not earlier than seven days before the date on which such notice is given.

---

[91] THE EMPLOYEE'S STATE INSUTANCE ACT, 1948

88. Claim For Maternity Benefit Commencing Before Confinement:-

Every insured woman claiming maternity benefit before confinement shall submit to the appropriate local office by post or otherwise

(i) A certificate of expected confinement in form 21 given in accordance with these regulation, not earlier than fifteen days before the expect date of confinement :

(ii) A claim for maternity benefit in form 22 stating therein the date on which she ceased or will cease to work for

(iii) Within thirty days of the date on which her confinement takes place, a certificate of confinement in form 23 given in accordance with these regulations.

89. Claim For Maternity Benefit Only After Confinement Or For Miscarriage :-

Every insured woman claiming maternity benefit for miscarriage shall within 30 days of the date of the miscarriage, and every insured woman claiming maternity benefit after confinement, shall submit to the appropriate office by post or otherwise a claim for maternity benefit in form 22 together with a certificate of confinement or miscarriage in form 23 given in accordance with these regulations.

89-A. Claim For Maternity Benefit After The Death Of An Insured Woman Leaving Behind The Child :-

For the purposes of the proviso to sub- section (2) of section 50 of the Act, the person nominated by the deceased insured woman on form 1 or on such other form as may be specified by the Director-General in this behalf and if there is no such submit to the appropriate office by post or otherwise a claim for maternity benefit, as may be due, in form 24-A within 30days of the death of the insured woman together with a death certificate in form 24-B given in accordance with these Regulations.

89-B. Claim For Maternity Benefit In Case Of Sickness Arising Out Of Pregnancy, Confinement, Premature Birth Of Child Or Miscarriage :-

(1) Every insured woman claiming maternity benefit in case of sickness arising out or pregnancy,

confinement, premature birth of child or miscarriage, shall submit to the appropriate office by post or otherwise a claim for benefit in one of the forms (12-A, 13, and 13-A)[92] appropriate to the circumstances of the case together with the appropriate medical certificate in form 8,9,10, or 11 as the case may be, given in accordance with these Regulations.

(2) The provisions of Regulations 55 to 61 and 64 shall, so far as may be, apply in relation to a claim submitted and a certificate given in accordance with this Regulation as they apply to certification and claims under those Regulations.

90. Other Evidence In Lieu Of A Certificate :-

The corporation may accept any other evidence in lieu of a certificate of pregnancy, expected confinement, confinement death during maternity, miscarriage or sickness arising out of pregnancy, if in its opinion, the circumstances of any particular case so justify.

[92] Substituted by Notification No. 12/13/1/90-P&D, dated 17-5-1991 (w.e.f. 15-6-1991).

91. Notice Of Work For Remuneration :-

Except as provided in Regulation 89-B every insured woman who has claimed maternity benefit shall give notice in form 24 if she does work for remuneration on any day during the period for which maternity benefit would be payable to her but for her working for remuneration.

92. Date Of Payment Of Maternity Benefit :-

No certificate required under any of the Regulations 87 to 89-B shall be issued except by the insurance medical officer to whom the insured woman has or had been allotted or by an Insurance medical officer attached to a dispensary, hospital clinic or other institution to which the insured woman is or was allotted and such Insurance medical officer shall examine and if in his opinion the condition of the woman so justifies or in case of death of the insured woman or the death of the child, if satisfied about such death issue to such insured woman or in case of her death to her nominee or legal representative as the case may be, free of charge any such certificate when reasonably required by such insured woman or her nominee or legal representative, as the case may be, under or for the purposes of the Act or any other enactment of these Regulations.

Provided that such officer may issue a certificate, as aforesaid, under these Regulations, to or in respect of an insured woman who is or was not allotted to him or to the dispensary, hospital, clinic or other institution to which such officer is attached, if such officer is attending the woman for prenatal care, for confinement, for miscarriage or for sickness arising out of pregnancy, confinement, pre-mature birth of child or miscarriage or in case of death, was attending the deceased insured woman or the child at the time of the death of the insured woman or the child:

Provided further that a certificate of pregnancy, of expected confinement, of confinement or miscarriage required under these Regulation may be issued by a registered midwife which shall be accepted by the corporation on counter – signatures by the Insurance Medical Officer:

Provided that such officer may issue a certificate of pregnancy, expected confinement or confinement under these regulations to an insured woman who is not allotted to him or to the dispensary, hospital, clinic or other institution to which such officer is attached, if such officer is attending the woman for pre-natal care or for confinement :

Provided further that a certificate of pregnancy, of expected confinement or of confinement required under these regulations may be issued by a registered midwife which shall be accepted by the corporation on counter signature by the insurance Medical Officer.

THE MATERNITY BENEFIT ACT, 1961

(Act 53 of 1961 as amended by Acts 51 of 1970, 21 of 1972, 52 of 1973[93], 53 of 1976[94], 61 of 1988[95] and 29 of 1995[96])

(12th December, 1961)

An Act to regulate the employment of women in certain establishments for certain periods before and after child – birth and to provide for maternity benefit and certain other benefits.

Be it enacted by parliament in the Twelfth year of the Republic of India as follows :-

1. **Short Title, Extent And Commencement** :-

(1) This Act may called the maternity benefit Act, 1961.

(2) It extends to the whole of India[97](***).

---

[93] Act 52 of 1973, enforced w.e.f. 1-3-1975 vide noti. Nos. o. 113-A (E) dt. 27-2-1975.

[94] Act 53 of 1976, enforced w.e.f. 1-5-1976 vide not. No. S.O. 337 (E) dt. 30-4-1976.

[95] Act 61 of 1988, enforced w.e.f. 10-1-1989 vide Noti No. S.Q. 47 (E) dt. 6-1-1989.

[96] Act 29 of 1995 menforced w.e.f. 1-2-1996

(3) It shall come into force on such date[98] as may be notified in this behalf in the official gazette,

(a)[99] in relation to mines and to any other established wherein persons are employed for the exhibition of questrian, acrobatic and other performances, by the central Government, and)

(b) In relation to other establishment in state by the state Government.

2. **Application of Act** :-

("(1) It applies , in the first instance -

(a) to every establishment being a factory. Mine or plantation including any such establishment belonging to Government and to every establishment wherein persons are employed for the exhibition of equestrian, acrobatic and other performances.

---

[97] Omitted by Act 51 of 1970

[98] The Act came into force w.e.f. 1-11-1963 in relation to mines in the territories to which it extends vide Not, no S.O. 2920, dt. 5-10-1963

[99] Sub by Act 52 of 1973.

(b) to every shop or establishment within the meaning of any law for the time being in force in relation to shops and establishments in a state in which ten or more person are employed or were employed, on any day of the preceding twelve months".)

Provided that the state Government may, with the approval of the central Government, after giving not less than two months' notice of its intention declare that all or any other establishment or class of establishments, industrial commercial, agricultural or otherwise.

(2) [100](Save as otherwise provided in [101](Section 5-a and 5-b) nothing contained in this Act) shall apply to any factory or other establishment to which the provisions of the Employees state Insurance Act 1948 (48 of 1948) apply for the time being.

(3) <u>Definitions</u> :-

In this Act, unless the context otherwise requires,-

---

[100] Subs, by Act 61 of 1988 (w.e.f. 10-1-1989).

[101] Subs, by Act 21 of 1972.

(a) "Appropriate Government" means in relation to an establishment being a mine [3](or an establishment where persons are employed for the exhibition of equestration, acrobatic and other performances), the central Government and in relation to Government:

(b) "Child " includes a stillborn child:

(c) "delivery " means the birth of a child:

(d) "employer" means –

(i) in relation to an establishment which is under the control of the Government , a person or authority appointed by the Government for the supervision and control of employees or where no person or authority is so appointed the head of the department :

(ii) in relation to an establishment under any local authority , the person appointed by such authority for the supervision and control of employees or where no persons is so appointed, the chief executive officer of the local authority :

(iii) In any other case, the person who or the authority which, has the ultimate control over the affairs of the establishment and where the said affairs are entrusted to any other person whether called a manager, managing director, managing agent, or by any other name, such person :

(e)[102] "establishment " means –

(i) a factory :

(ii) a mine :

(iii) a plantation :

(iv) an establishment wherein persons are employed for the exhibition of equestrian, acrobatics and other performances : (.....)[103]

"(iva)[104] a shop or establishment : or"

(v) an establishment to which the provisions of this Act have been declared under sub–section (4) of section 2 to be applicable :)

---

[102] Subs, by Act 52 of 1973

[103] Omitted by Act 61 of 1988 (w.e.f. 10-1-1989)

[104] Ins. by Act 61 of 1988 (w.e.f. 10-1-1989)

(f) "Factory" means a factory as defined in clause (m) of section 2 of the factories Act, 1948 (63 of 1948) :

(g) "Inspector" means and inspector appointed under Section 14:

(h) "Maternity benefit" means he payment referred to in sub-section (1) of section : 5

((ha)[105] "Medical termination of pregnancy" means the termination of pregnancy permissible under the provisions of the medical Termination of pregnancy Act, 1971 (34 of 1971)

(i) "Mine" means a mine as defined in clause (j) of section 2 of the Mines Act, 1952 (35 of 1952)

(j) "Miscarriage" means expulsion of the contents of pregnant uterus at any period to or during the twenty sixth week or pregnancy but does not include any miscarriage the causing of which is punishable under the Indian Penal Code (45 of 1860) :

[105] Ins by Act 29 of 1995 Section 2 (w.e.f. 1-2-1996).

(k) "Plantation" means a plantation as defined in clauses (f) of section 2 of the plantation Labour Act, 1951 (69 of 1951) :

(i) (1) "Prescribed" means prescribed by rules made under this Act

(m) "State Government" in relation to a Union territory means the Administrator thereof:

(n) "Wages" means all remuneration paid or payable in cash to a woman, if the terms of the contract of employment, express or implied were fulfilled and includes.

(1) Such cash, allowances (including dearness allowance and house rent allowance) as a woman is for the time being entitled to :

(2) incentive bonus : and

(3) the money value of the concessional supply of foof grains and other articles but does not include -

 (i) any bonus other than incentive bonus :

 (ii) overtime earnings and any deduction or payment made on account of fines ;

(iii) any Contribution paid or payable by the employer to any pension fund or provident fund or for the benefit of the woman under any law for the time being in force : and

(iv) any gratuity payable on the termination of service :

(v) "woman" means a woman employed, whether directly or through any agency, for wages in any establishment.

4. Employment Of Or Work By, Women Prohibited During Certain Period -

(1) No employer shall knowingly employ women in any establishment during the six weeks. Immediately following the day of her delivery or [106](miscarriage or medical termination of pregnancy)

(2) No woman shall work in any establishment during the six weeks immediately following the day of her delivery or miscarriage or medical termination of pregnancy.

(3) Without prejudice to the provisions of section 6, no pregnant woman shall on a request being made

---

[106] Subs by section 3 of the maternity Benefit (Amendment) Act no 29 of 1995) for "--------------------" w.e.f. 1-2-1996.

by her in this behalf, be required by her employer to do during the period specified in subsection (4) any work which is of an arduous nature or which involves long hours of standing or which in any way is likely to interfere with her pregnancy or the Normal development of the fetus or is likely to cause her miscarriage or otherwise to adversely affect her health.

(4) The period referred to in sub-section (3) shall be---

(a) the period of one month immediately preceding the period of six weeks, before the date of her expected delivery :

(b) any period during the said period of six weeks for which the pregnant woman does not avail of leave of absence under section 6.

(5) Right To Payment Of Maternity Benefit :-

(1) Subjects to the provisions of this Act, every woman shall be entitled to and her employer shall be liable for the payment of maternity benefit at the rate of the average daily wages for the period of her actual absence, that is to say, the period immediately

preceding the day of her delivery, the actual day of her delivery and any period immediately following the day)

Explanation :-

For the purpose of this sub-section the average daily wages mean the average of the woman's wages payable to her for the days on which she has worked during the period of three calendar months immediately preceding the date from which she absent herself on account of maternity ("the minimum rate of wage fixed or revised under the minimum wages Act 1948 (11 of 1948), or ten rupees, whichever is the highest".

(2) No woman shall be entitled to maternity benefit unless she has actually worked in an establishment of the employer from whom she claims maternity benefit for a period of not less than (Eighty days in the twelve months immediately preceding the date of her expected delivery:

Provided that the qualifying period of (Eighty days aforesaid shall not apply to a woman who has immigrated into the state of Assam and was pregnant at the time of the immigration.

Explanation: -

For the purpose of calculating under this sub-section the days on which a woman has actually worked in the establishment, (the days for which she has been laid –off or was on holidays declared under any law for the time being in forces to be holidays with wages), during the period of twelve months immediately preceding the date of her expected delivery shall be taken into account.

(3) "The maximum period for which any woman shall be entitled to maternity benefit shall be twelve weeks of which not more than six weeks shall precede the date of her expected delivery".

Provided that where a woman dies during this period, the maternity benefit shall be payable only for the days up to and including the day of her deaths.

(Provided further that where a woman, having been delivered of a child, dies during her delivery or during the period immediately following the date of her delivery for which she is entitled for the maternity benefit, leaving behind in either case the child, the employer shall be liable for the maternity benefit for that entire period but if the child also dies during the said period, then, for the days up to and including the date of the death of the child".

(5-A. Continuance Of Payment Of Maternity Benefit In Certain Cases[107]:-

Every woman entitled to the payment of maternity benefit under this Act shall, notwithstanding the application of the Employee's State Insurance Ac, 1948 (31 of 1948), to the factory or other establishment in which she is employed, continue to be so entitled until she becomes qualified to claim maternity benefit under section 50 of that Act).

(5-B. Payment Of Maternity Benefit In Certain Cases [108]:-

Every woman-

(a) Whose is employed in a factory or other establishment to which the provisions of the employees' State Insurance Act, 1948 (34 of 1948) apply,

---

[107] Ins by Act 21 of 1972.
[108] Ins. by Act 53 of 1976 (w.e.f. 1-5-1976)

(b) Whose wages (excluding remuneration for overtime work) for a month exceed the amount specified in sub- clause (b) of clause (a) of section 2 of that Act, and

(c) Who fulfils the conditions specified in sub- section (2) of section 5, Shall be entitled to the payment of maternity benefit under this Act).

5. Notice Of Claim For Maternity Benefit And Payment There Of

(1) Any woman employed in an establishment and entitled to maternity benefit under the provisions of this Act may give notice in writing in such form as may be prescribed to her employer, stating that her maternity benefit and any other amount to which she may be entitled under this Act may be paid to her or to such person as she may nominate in the notice and that she will not work in any establishment during the period for which she receives maternity benefit.

(2) In the case of a woman who is pregnant, such notice shall state the date from which she will be absent from work, not being a date earlier than six weeks from the date of her expected delivery.

(3) Any woman who has not given the notice when she was pregnant may give such notice as soon as possible after the delivery".

[109]("(4) On receipt of the notice, the employer shall permit such woman to absent herself from the establishment during the period for which she receives the maternity benefit."

(5) The amount of maternity benefit for the period preceding the date of her expected delivery shall be paid in advance by the employer to the woman on production of such proof as may be prescribed that the woman is pregnant, and the amount due for the subsequent period shall be paid by the employer to the woman within fort-eight hours of production of such proof as may be prescribed that the woman has been delivered of a child.

(6) The failure to give notice under this section shall not disentitle a woman to maternity benefit or any other amount under this Act if she is spector may either of his own motion or on an application made to him by the woman, order the payment of such

---

[109] Subs by Act 61 of 1988 (w.e.f. 10-1-1989).

benefit or amount within such period as may be specified in the order.

(7) **Payment Of Maternity Benefit In Case Of A Woman:-**

If a woman entitled to maternity benefit or any other amount under this Act, dies before receiving such maternity benefit or amount, or where the employer is liable for maternity benefit under the second proviso to sub-employer is liable for maternity benefit under the second proviso to sub-section (3) of section 5, the employer shall pay such benefit or amount to the person nominated by the woman in the notice given under section 6 and in case there is no such nominee, to her legal representative.

8. **Payment Of Medical Bonus:-**

Every woman entitled to maternity benefit under this Act shall also be entitled to, receive from her employer a medical bonus of [110](two hundred and fifty rupees), if no prenatal confinement and

[110] Subs by Act 61 of 1988 (w.e.f. 10-1-1989)

postnatal care is provided for the employer free of charge.

[111](9). **Leave For Miscarriage Ect.:-**

In case of miscarriage or medical termination of pregnancy, a women shall, on production of such proof as may be prescribed, be entitled to leave with wages at the rate of maternity benefit, for a period of six weeks immediately following the day of her miscarriage or, as the case may be, her medical termination of pregnancy.

[112](9-A. **Leave With Wages For Tubectomy Operation :-**

In case of tubectomy operation, a woman shall, on production of such proof as may be prescribed, be entitled to leave with wages at the are of maternity

[111] Subs by Section 4 of the maternity benefit (Amendment)Act, 1995 (Act no – 29 of 1995) for " in case of miscarriage, a woman shall, on production of suh proof as may be prescribed, be entitled to leave with wages at the rate or maternity benefit for a period of six weeks immediately following the day of her miscarriage") w.e.f. 1-2-1996.

[112] Inserted by section 5 of the maternity Benefit (Amendment) Act. 1995 Act No. 29 of 1995).

benefit for a period of two weeks immediately following the day of her tubectomy operation."

10. <u>Leave For Illness Arising Out Of Pregnancy, Delivery, Premature Birth Of Child Or Miscarriage, Medical Termination Of Pregnancy Or Tubectomy Operation</u>:-

A woman suffering from illness arising out of pregnancy, delivery, permuted birth of child.

[113](miscarriage, medical termination of pregnancy or tubectomy operation) shall, on production of such proof as may be prescribed, be entitled, in addition to the period of absence allowed to her under section 6, or, as the case may be, under section 9, to leave with wages at the rate of maternity benefit for a maximum period of one month.

11. <u>Nursing Breaks</u>:-

Every woman delivered of a child who returns to duty after such delivery shall, in addition to the interval for rest allowed to her, be allowed in the course of her daily work two breaks of the prescribed

---

[113] Subs. by section 6 of the maternity Benefit (Amendment) Act 1995, (Act no–29 of 1995) for the words" or Miscarriage") w.e.f.1-2-1996

duration for nursing the child until the child attains the age of fifteen months.

12. <u>Dismissal During Absence Or Pregnancy</u>:-

(1) Where a woman absent herself from work in accordance with the provisions of this Act, it shall be unlawful for her employer to discharge or dismiss her during or on account of such absence or to give notice' of discharge or dismissal on such a day that the notice will expire during such absence, or to vary to her disadvantage any of the conditions of her service.

(2) (a) This discharge or dismissal of a woman at any time during her pregnancy, if the woman but for such discharge or dismissal would have entitled to maternity benefit or medical bonus refereed to in section 8, shall not have the effect of depriving her of the maternity benefit or medical bonus.

Provided that where the dismissal is for any prescribed gross misconduct the employer may, by order in writing communicated to the woman, deprive her of the maternity benefit or medical bonus or both.

[114]((b) Any woman deprived of maternity benefit or medical bonus or both, or discharged or dismissed during or on account of her absence form work in accordance with the provisions of this Act, may, within sixty days from the date on which order of such deprivation or discharge or dismissal is communicated to her appeal to such authority as may be prescribed, and the decision of that authority on such appeal, whether the woman should or should not be deprived of maternity benefit or medical bonus, or both, or discharged or dismissed shall be final".

---

[114] Subs by Act 61 of 1988 w.e.f. 10-1-1989.

(c) Nothing contained in this sub-section shall affect the provisions contained in sub-section (1).

13. No Deduction Of Wages In Certain Cases:-

No deduction from the normal and usual daily wages of a woman entitled to maternity benefit under the provisions of this Act shall be made by reason only of ---

(a) the nature of work assigned to her by virtue of the provisions contained in sub – section (3) of section 4;

or

(b) breaks for nursing the child allowed to her under the provisions of section 11.

14. Appointment Of Inspector :-

The appropriate Government may, notification in the official Gazette, appoint such officers as it thinks fit to be Inspectors for the purpose of this Act and may define the local limits of the jurisdiction within which they shall exercise their functions under this Act.

15. Powers And Duties of Inspectors:-

An Inspector may, subject to such restrictions or conditions as may be prescribed, exercise all or any of the following powers, namely:-

(a) enter at all reasonable times with such assistants, if any, being persons in the service of the Government or any local or other public authority as he thinks fit, any premises or place where women are employed or work is given to them in an establishment, for the purposes of examining any registers, records and notices required to be kept or exhibited by or under this Act and require their production for inspection:

(b) examine any person whom he finds in any premises or place and whom he has reasonable cause to believe, is employed in the establishment:

Provided that no person shall be compelled under this section to answer any question or give any evidence tending to incriminate himself.

(c) require the employer to give information regarding the names and addresses of women employed, payments made to them, and applications or notices received from them under this Act: and

(d) take copies of any registers and records or notices or any portions thereof.

16. Inspectors Toe Be Public Servants:-

Every Inspector appointed under this Act shall be deemed to be a public servant within the meaning of section 21 of the Indian Penal Code (45 of 1860).

17. Power Of Inspector To Direct Payments To Be Made :-

[115]("(1) Any woman claiming that-

(a) Maternity benefit or any other amount to which she is entitled under this Act and any person claiming that payment due under section 7 has been improperly withheld:

Her employer has discharged or dismissed her during or on account of her absence from work in

---

[115] Subs. by Act No. 61 of 1988 w.e.f. 10-1-1989.

accordance with the provisions of this Act, may make a complaint to the Inspector.

(2) The Inspector may, of his own motion or on receipt of a complaint referred to in sub- section (1) make an inquiry or cause an enquiry to be made and if satisfied that.-

(a) Payment has been wrongfully withheld, may direct the payment to be made in accordance with his orders:

(b) She has been discharged or dismissed during or on account other absence from work in accordance with the provisions of this Act, may pass such orders as are just and proper according to the circumstances of the case".

(3) Any person aggrieved by the decision of the inspector under sub- section (2) may within thirty days from the date on which such decision is communicated to such person, person, appeal to the prescribed authority.

(4) The decision of the prescribed authority where an appeal has been referred to it under sub- section (3) or of the Inspector where no such appeal has been preferred, shall be final.

((5) Any amount payable under this section shall be recoverable by the Collector on a certificate issued for that amount by the Inspector as an arrear of land revenue").

18. Forfeiture Of Maternity Benefit :-

If a woman works in any establishment are she has been permitted by her employer to absent herself under the provisions of section 6 for any period during such authorized absence she shall for – feit her claim to the maternity benefit for such period.

19. Abstract Act And Rules Thereunder To Be Exhibited:-

An abstract of the provisions of this Act and the rules made thereundre in the languages of the locality shall be exhibited in a conspicuous place by the employer in every part of the establishment in which women employed.

20. Registers, Ect. :-

Every employer shall prepare and maintain such registers, records and muster-rolls and in such manner as may be prescribed.

("21. **Penalty For Contravention Of Act. By Employer**:-

(1) If any employer fails to pay any amount maternity benefit to a woman entitled under this Act or discharges or dismisses such woman during or on account of her absence from work in accordance with the provisions of this Act, he shall be punishable with imprisonment which shall not be less than three months but which may extend to one year and with fine which shall not be less than two thousand rupees but which may extend to five thousand rupees:

Provided that the court may, for sufficient reasons to be recorded in writing, impose a sentence of imprisonment for a lessor term of fine only in lieu of imprisonment.

(2) If any employer contravenes the provisions of this Act or the rules made there under, he shall, if, no other penalty is elsewhere provided by or under this Act for such contravention, be punishable with imprisonment which may extend to one year, or with fine which may extend to five thousand rupees, or with both:

Provided that where the contravention is of any provision regarding maternity benefit or regarding payment of any other amount and such maternity benefit or amount has not already been recovered, the court shall, in addition, recover such maternity benefit or amount as if it were a fine and pay the same to the person entitled thereto")

22. Penalty For Obstructing Inspector :-

Whoever fails to produce on demand by the Inspector any register or document in his custody kept in pursuance of this Act or the rules made there under or conceals or prevents any person from appearing before or being examined by an Inspector, shall be punishable with imprisonment [1](which) may extend to one year, or with fine which may extend to five thousand rupees), or with both.

[116](**23. Cognizance Of Offences:-**

(1) Any aggrieved woman, an office- bearer of a Trade Union registered under the Trade Unions Act,1926 (16 of 1926) of which such woman is a member or a voluntary organization registered under

[116] Subs. by Act 61 1988 (w.e.f. 10-1-1989).

the societies Registration Act, 1860(21 of 1860) or an Inspector, may file a complaint regarding the commission of an offence under this Act in any court or competent jurisdiction and no such complaint shall be filed after the expiry of one year from the date on which the offence is alleged to have been committed.

(2) No court inferior to that of a Metropolitan magistrate or a Magistrate of the first class shall try any offence under this act".

24. <u>Protection Of Action Taken In Good Faith</u> :-

No suit, prosecution or other legal proceeding shall lie against any person for anything which is in good faith done or intended to be done in pursuance of this Act or of any rule or order made thereunder.

25. <u>Power Of Central Government To Give Directions</u> :-

The central Government may give such directions as it may deem necessary to a state Government regarding the carrying into execution the provisions of this Act and the state Government shall comply with such directions.

26. Power to exempt establishments:-

If the appropriate Government is satisfied that having regard to an establishment or a class of establishments providing for the grant of benefit which are not less favorable than hose provided in this Act, it is necessary so to do, it may, by notification in the official Gazette, exempt subject to such conditions and restrictions, if any, as may be specified in the notification, the establishment or class of establishments from the operation of all or any of the provisions of this Act or of any rule made thereunder.

27. Effect Of Laws And Agreements Inconsistent With This Act :-

(1) The provisions of this Act shall have effect notwithstanding anything anything inconsistent therewith contained in and other law or in the terms of any award., agreement or contract of service whether made before or after the coming into force of this Act:

Provided that where under any such award, agreement, contract of service or otherwise, a woman is entitled to benefits in respect of any matter which are more favorable to her than those to which she would be entitled under this Act, the woman shall continue to be entitled to receive benefit in respect of other matters under this Act.

28. <u>Power To Make Rules</u> :-

(1) The appropriate Government may, subject to the condition of previous publication and by notification in the official Gazette, make rules for carrying out the purposes of this Act.

(2) In particular, and without prejudice to the generality of the foregoing power, such rules may provide for –

(a) The preparation and maintenance of registers, records and muster rolls:

(b) The exercise o powers (Including the inspection of establishments) and the performance of duties by Inspector for the purposes of this Act:

(c) The method of payment of maternity benefit and other benefits under this

Act in so far as provisions has not been made therefore in this act:

(d) The form of notices under section6 :

(e) The nature of proof required under the provisions o f this Act:

(f) The duration of nursing breaks referred to in section 11:

(g) Acts which may constitute gross misconduct for purposes of section 12:

(h) The authority to which an appeal under clause (b) of sub- section (2) of section 12 shall lie, the form and manner in which such appeal may be made and the procedure to be followed in disposal thereof :

(i) The authority to which an appeal shall lie against the decision of the Inspector under section 17: the form and manner in which such appeal may be made and the procedure to be followed in disposal thereof:

(j) The form and manner in which complaints may be made to Inspector under sub- section (1) of section 17 and the procedure to be followed by them when making inquiries or causing inquiries to be made under sub- section (2) of that section:

(k) Any other matter which is to be, or may by prescribed.

(3) Every rule made by the central Government under this section shall be laid as soon as may be after it is made, before each house of parliament while it is in session for a total period of thirty days which may be comprised in one session[117] (for in two or more successive sessions, and if, before the expiry of the session immediately following the session or the successive sessions, aforesaid), both Houses agree that the rule should not be made, the rule shall thereafter have effect only in such modified form or be of no effect, as the case may be: so however, that any such modification or annulment shall be without prejudice to the validity of anything previously done under that rule.

29. <u>Amendment OF Act 69 Of 1981</u> :-

In section 32 of the plantations Labour Act, 1951-

---

[117] Subs. by Act No. 52 of 1973.

Chapter VI

POSITION OF WOMEN UNDER CRIMINAL LAWS & CRIME AGAINST WOMEN & VARIOUS REPORT ON GENDER JUSTICE

CRIME AGAINST WOMEN

Every declaration has its root or cause in suppression. Like declaration of bill of right., declaration of independence in freedom fighters movement just like that the broken - hearted position of women in the society aroused the women hood which includes her strongness (Shakti) at international level. Their strongness and determination can be realized from the Veinna Declaration and Programe of Action in U.S. which declared

Be ready when the hour comes to show that women are human and have the pride and dignity of human beings. Through such resistance our cause will triumph we fight that our pride, our self respect, our dignity may not be sacrificed in future as they have been in the past.

"Women must stand ereet now and forever more. Then, even if they should not win it at least they will deserve success and that is what matters more than all beside"

In CEDAW the preamble explicitly acknowledges extensive discrimination against women continues to exist and emphasizes that such discrimination violates the principles of equality of rights and respects for human dignity."

The agenda for equality is specified in the 14 Articles on three dimensions civil right, legal status of women and human rights.

In 18th December, 1979. United Nations general assembly adopted the CEDAW declaration and policy. It entered into force as an international treaty on 3rd Sep., 1981 the twentieth country has rectified it. By the Tenth anniversary of the convention in 1989. almost one hundred nations have agreed to be bound by its provisions.

INTRODUCTION :-

In Indian mythology woman is known as "Shakti" "Devi" or "Grihlaxmi". On festive occasions Indians do worship this "Shakti" with "Bhakti". They praise shakti that is goddess Adishakti or Parwati but they never treated this Shakti-female with humanity. In fact woman by her nature itself is closely associated with he/family. She feels secure in family, expects protection from them, not because she is weak but only because of her weaker sex. Women are exploited and spoiled since years together only because of her weaker sex. In male dominated society violence against women is a bleak reality and dark side of our civilization.

India has witnessed glorified culture in golden days and vedic days. However due to sudden shift in the rule over India mainly by Muslim rulers the very culture and respect for women turned into bondage of bundle of rigid customs and restrictions on woman in the name of chastity. The lifestyle of women is nothing but poverty, ignorance^ fear of violence and insecurity.

The word 'Domestic' has reference to an idealized family unit functioning in a protected and Secluded manner appropriately shielded from public. Family has been considered as place of intimacy love and devoid of conflicts of interests. It is considered as purely private matter. So the safest place for men to commit violence is the home. In fact has it has become least safe place for women.

In orthodox societies marriage is the main source of violence against married women. Each year more than 10 million married women experience violent episodes.-Pain or serious injuries on them.

Married women are burned with matches, cigarettes and hot iron stamped or strangled by their intoxicated husbands. The threat of married violence is more pervasive now, only because of the increased frequency off dowry deaths more than ever. Each years 5000 dowry death cases are reported which is a clear evidence of horrifying situations and a major setback to women liberation movement. A women's traditional position of being her husband's property, alcoholic intoxication of husband and economic inequality are the main factors that can be attributed to such violence.

In our society, the majority of women being economically inactive are dependent upon their husband for financial support in whatsoever manner they are treated. In our economic system, man control the whole economic institutions, own most property, direct economic activity, both within and outside family and also determine the nature of different productive activities. In contrast, most household works are done by women is neither recognized nor paid for. If their productive activities are hired by private employer they poorly paid. The position of women who work on daily wages basis is too worse as they are more susceptible to violence and sexual exploitation by the person who engage them on contract or daily wage basic.

FUNDAMENTAL DUTIES :-

Article 51 (e)- To renounce practices derogatory to the dignity of women.

Article 21 of our constitution provides that, "No person shall be deprived of his life or personal liberty except according to the procedure establishment by law.

In special leave petition before the apex court[118] the state relies on Cl 3rd S 375 I PC which runs as follows thirdly, with her consent when her consent has been obtained by putting her in fear of death or of hurt.

[118]Tukaram V/s. State of Maharastra Apr. 1979 SC 185.

It was held High Court did not give finding that such fear was shown to be that of death or hurt, in absence of such finding and the girl was taken away from amongst her near and dear etc. the alleged fear would not vitiate the 'consent'. Thus reversed the conviction and acquitted appellants / accused.

CRIMINAL LAW (SECOND AMENDMENTS) ACT 1983 - f Anti Rape Amendment Act)

Mathura's decision was widely criticized that it was extraordinary decision sacrificing right to privacy of women under law and constitution. The Maharasthra Government filled review petition. It was dismissed. The judicial approach on the factum of 'consent' moved the public opinion and ultimately the criminal law (Second Amendment) Act 1983 was passed.

RAPE - VIOLATION OF FUNDAMENTAL RIGHT OF LIFE AND LIBERTY:-

Rape is worst side of violence against women. Women of all ages even girls of 2 - 3 years are victims of lust-loaded violence i.e. Rape. The boundaries of her physical body are violated. Her purity is taken away at the hands of individuals, groups or gangs. Rape destroys the entire psychology of a woman and pushes her into deep emotional crisis -sometimes to the extent of committing even suicide. It is only by her shyer will power. She rehabilitates herself in society which on coming to know of the rape looks down upon her with contempt.

The social organizations, women activists and many others took up the cause to cure this evil and for reaching reforms and sweeping changes in law came to be made to cure this malady by inserting new section S. 376 a to q 2nd of S. 375 was amended by deleting words "free and voluntary consent" and modify the same with only "without her consent" As well as S 376 (A) to 376 (g) were inserted which relate to custodial rape and gang rape. Amendments S174, 198A, 176 and 327 Cr. P. C and made this proceeding as in camera. Apart from this S113 A and 114 A were inserted in evidence Act. These sections enable courts to raise presumption in favour of women.

<u>Sexual Offences Against Women-Rape SYNOPSIS</u>

(i) Introduction

(ii) Sexual Intercourse with wife

(iii) Punishment of rape

(iv) Exploration Criminal Law (Second Amendment) Act

(v) Marital rape

(vi) Corresponding changes in law

(vii) Punishment for disclosure of rape Victim's name.

(viii) Presumption of rape

(ix) Compensation to rape victims

(x) Rape of unchaste woman

(xi) Delay in lodging complaint.

The Indian penal code deals with the various sexual offences against women in sections 375 to 376 D, section 354 and 509. Of these offences, rape is the most brutal, which violates not only the body of woman but also mind psyche of women more than one way.

(i) Rape (i) Introduction :-

Section 375 defines the statutory offence of rape. It denotes the sexual intercourse with a woman first, against her will, secondly without her consent. Thirdly, with her consent obtained by putting her in fear of death or hurt fourthly with her consent when man knows that he is not her husband and if consent is given under her misconception of his identity as her husband fifthly with her consent when at the time of giving such consent she is under the influence of unsoundness of mind or administration of some substance to make her give consent sixthly, with or without consent when she is under of sixteen years age. Thus, it could be seen that it is a comprehensive definition by any standards.

The Explanation to section 375 provides that mere penetration is sufficient to constitute the sexual intercourse necessary to the offence of rape. Therefore it is not necessary that there must be

Sexual Intercourse With wife :-

According to the Exception to section 375, sexual intercourse by a man with his own wife if she is not under the age of fifteen years does not amount to rape. However in certain countries like U.K. and Sweden, marital rape has been made an offence.

Punishment For Rape :-

Section 375 provides for punishment to the offender who commits rape. It is important to know that this section imposes a minimum and mandatory punishment with imprisonment of not less than 7 years which may extent to either ten or even life imprisonment depending on certain circumstances. Sections 375 and 376 have been substantially changed by the criminal law (Amendment) Act, 1983 the same Act has also introduced several new sections viz, sections 376 A, 376B, and 376C, and 376D. Indian penal code. Of these, Section 376 A Punishes Sexual intercourse with wife without her consent by a judicially separated husband, section 376 B Punishes sexual intercourse by a public servant with woman in his custody, Section 376C Punishes sexual intercourse by superintendent of Jail, remand home etc., with inmates in such institution and section 376D Punishes sexual intercourse by any member of the management or staff of a hospital with any woman in that hospital.

Marital Rape :-

However it is felt that section 376 A dealing with rape by judicially separated husband should be treated as an ordinary rape. Lessor punishment of two years imprisonment is prescribed on the ridiculous reason " to facilitate reconciliation." It is noteworthy that marital rape is an offence in United State of America, Sweden, Denmark, and Australia.

These new section have been introduced with a view to stop sexual abuses of women in custody, care and control by various categories of persons which though not amounting to rape were nevertheless considered highly reprehensible. The amended section 376 now prescribes minimum punishment as mentioned earlier. For combating the vice of custodial rape, rape on pregnant woman, rape on girls under 12 and gang rape, a minimum punishment of ten years imprisonment has been made compulsory. However, for special reasons to be recorded in the judgment the court in either case can impose* a sentence lesser than seven or ten years, as case may be.

Corresponding changes in Law :-

A further improvement in the law relating to sexual offences has been made in the provisions of section 228A, Indian penal code, section 327 (2) of Cr.P.C. and section 114 A of the Indian Evidence Act, which too were introduced by the same amendment Act, 1983. The first provision aforementioned punishes a person who discloses the names or identity of the rape victim. The second provisions provides a similar protection to the rape victim to the effect that the inquiry and the trial of rape should be conducted in camera.

The third provision incorporates a presumption in the Indian evidence Act, that where sexual intercourse by the accused with the prosecutor is proved, the court shall presume that she did not consent. All these provisions are intended for the protection and benefit of the rape victims.

Punishment For Disclosure Of Name Of Rape Victim etc.:-

Section 228A of the I PC punishes a person who prints or publishes the name or any matter which may identify any person against whom rape was committed or alleged to be committed under sections 376, 376A, 376B, 376C, and 376D. This protection is introduced to proted the rape victims from the public ridicule and the stigma they carry if their identity is disclosed, the Supreme Court has held that in Gurumitsingh case[119] trial of rape cases must invariably be held in camera "The Supreme Court further held that the

[119] State of Pubjab vs. Gurmit Singh, 1996 (1) Supreme 485.

courts should, as far as possible, avoid disclosing the names of the prosecutrix in their orders to save further embarrassment to the victim of. The anonymity of the victim of the crime mist be maintained throughout. Section 327 (2) of the code of criminal procedure, 1973 also makes a similar provision to the effect that the inquiry into and trial of rape or an offence under section 376 shall be conducted ' in camera.'

Presumption Of Rape:-

Under Section 114 A of the Indian Evidence Act, 1872, in a prosecution of rape under section 376 of Indian penal code where sexual intercourse by the accused is proved and the question is whether there was consent of the woman alleged to have been raped, the court shall presume that she did not consent[120].

Thus, the courts shall always presume that she did not consent. The reason for such a presumption appears to be that a rapist not only violates the victims personal integrity but also degrades the very sole of the helpless female.[1"] In the case of Doctor Sudhanshuy Shekhar Sahoo in . State of Orissa the Accused was a DMO alleged to have committed rape of a lady supervision. The prosecutrix was an educated lady of status. Her statement

---

[120] Dharma vs. Nirmal Singh 1996 (1) Supreme 780.

Maddan Gopal Kakkad vs. Naval Dubey, (1992) 3 SCC 204.

was believable, credible and consistent and same was made basis for conviction of the accused. In the case of rape, conviction can be based on the sole testimony of the prosecutrix without any corroboration if her testimony is otherwise worthy of credence. However, corroboration by medical evidence can be insisted upon where such evidence is forth coming .

Compensation To Rape Victims :-

The Supreme court, in Delhi Domestic working women's forum vs. Union of India[121] Suggested the formulation of a scheme for awarding compensation to rape victim at the time of convicting a person found guilty of rape. The Supreme Court Suggested that the Criminal Injuries Compensation Board or the court should award compensation to the victims by taking into account pain, suffering, and shock as well as loss of earnings due to pregnancy and the expenses of child birth if this occurs as a result of the rape.

The Supreme Court suggested the setting up of a criminal Injuries compensation Board under the Directive principals contained under Article 38(1) of the constitution of India. However it is unfortunate that the Government has not implemented the said directive of the court till today.

[121] 1995(1) SCC 14.

The Apex Court in recent case of state of Punjab vs. Gurmit Singh[122] took cognizance of the above fact.

The Supreme Court lamented about the crimes against woman and specially the rape in the following words: -

Of late , crime against women in general and rape in particular has the increase. It is an irony that while we are celebrating women's rights in all spheres, we show little or no concern for her honour. It is a sad refection on the attitude of indifference of the society towards the violation of human dignity of the victims of sex crimes. We must remember that a rapist not only violates the victim's privacy and personal integrity, but inevitably causes serious psychological as well as physical harm in the process. Rape is not merely a physical assault. It is often destructive of the whole personality of the victim. A murderer destroys the physical body of his victim, a rapist degrades the very soul of the helpless female. The Courts therefore shoulder a great responsibility while trying an accused on charges of rape. They must deal with such cases with utmost sensitivity. The courts should examine the Border probabilities of a case and not get swayed by minor contradictions or insignificant discrepancies in the statement of the prosecutrix, which are not a fatal nature, to throw out an otherwise reliable prosecution case. If

[122] 1996 (1) Supreme 485

evidence of the prosecutrix inspires confidence, it must be relied upon without seeking corroboration of her statement in material particulars. If for some reason the Court finds it difficult to place implicit reliance on her testimony, it may look for evidence which may lend assurance to her testimony, short of corroboration required in the case of an accomplice. The testimony of the prosecutrix must be appreciated in the background of the entire case and the trial court must be alive to its responsibility and be sensitive while dealing with cases involving sexual molestations".

In the same case the Supreme Court categorically held that trial of rape case in camera should be the rule and an open trial in such cases an exception.

In the case of Kuntimon vs. State it was desired that the victim has to be compensated and that the courts compensate her for her deprivation, as nearly as possible.

Interim Compensation: -

In the case of Bodhisattwa Goutham vs. Subhra chakraborty[123] a person developed sexual relationship with the prosecutrix on false assurance of marriage.

Rape of Unchaste Woman :-

Rape victim need not be woman of chaste character. The Supreme court has laid down that the unchastity of a woman does not make her "open to any and every person to

[123] (1996) 1 SCO 490.

violate her person as and when he wishes. She is entitled to protect her person if there is an attempt to rape her. She is equally entitled under protection of law. Therefore, merely because she is a woman of easy virtue, her evidence cannot be thrown overboard. Thus in the case of state of Maharashtra vs. Madhukar N. Mardikar[124] the Supreme Court held even a prostitute has a right to privacy and no person can rape her just because she is a woman of easy virtue.

The foregoing discussion makes It clear that rape is considered as a serious offence that not only affects the body of a woman but also her basic human dignity which includes her privacy also.

"By the end of the decade, it was obvious that the amendments had failed to evoke the desired response. Simultaneously, newer issues, which had remained unaddressed, began to surface. Central among these was the patriarchal presumption that vaginal penetration by the penis amounts to ultimate violation 'a state worse that death'. A paradoxical situation prevailed in criminal law where all assaults are rendered grievous if a weapon is used as the risk of bodily injury is aggravated. Only in rape cases it is the reverse. A range of sexual violence meted out

---

[124] (1991)1 SCC 57.

to little girls by inserting objects like bottles, sticks and iron rods into their tender and as yet not fully formed vaginas, causing multiple injuries and risk to life, got swept away under the nomenclature of 'violating modesty' punishable with a maximum of two years of punishment. The legal explanation was that the male sexual organ was not involved, however gruesome the sexual assaults may have been and hence the offence could not be brought within the favour corners of the offence of rape.

As far as women's situation is concerned, throughout the two decades of struggle, not a single case of a reversal of gender roles, in the realm of sexual offence, had ever surfaced in the Indian context nor at any time formed part of the discourse. In this entire history, no one has ever advanced the plea of sexual violation by women. On the contrary, the core concern has been sexual violations by men not only of women, but children – both male and female and other men. The social sanction awarded to aggressive male sexuality, expressed through violent, penetrative sex, both within and outside marriage, in the closeted secrecy of bedrooms and the public domains of civilian spaces; and the violations by the state in custodial situations – these has been the central focus of the debate. And yet, paradoxically, while addressing this concern, women have now been posed as offenders and have been made culpable for an offence, which is far removed from the ground reality of their social existence.

The premise of gender neutrality has been supported by the three women's rights groups who had been consulted, perhaps by adopting a Western model where laws have been rendered gender neutral through active intervention of feminists. But subsequently, this model has been criticized by feminist legal scholars who have felt that the equality model has had detrimental impact on women and children. For instance, Martha Fineman has commented that reformers can and often do create new and even more complex difficulties through the ill considered strategies which they seem inevitably to employ when using the law to attempt to construct a more ideal society. The rhetoric of equality defines and confines the reforms. She suggests that in order to do equity one must move away from 'equality' as the grand principle of reform.

In conclusion, though the move to reform rape laws is in the right direction and is long overdue, unless it is fine tuned to the specific needs of the concerned segments, its aspirations will remain at the level of rhetoric at best or result in misery and humiliation at worst".[125]

Delay in Lodging Complaint :-

In rape cases, merely because the complaint was lodged less than promptly, it does not raise the inference that the complaint is false. The reluctance to go to the police is because of society's attitude towards such woman. It casts doubt and shame upon her rather than comfort and sympathies with her.

Offences Relating to Marriage :-

Chapter XX of Indian Penal Code in sections 493 to 498 deals with the offence relating to marriage. They are.

(1) Cohabitation by a man with a woman who is not his wife by deceit (section 493).

(2) Bigamy during the life time of a spouse (section 494 and 495).

(3) Mock marriage with fraudulent intention (section 496).

(4) Adultery (section 497) and.

(5) Enticing or taking away or detaining a married woman with criminal intention.

---

125 Feminist Jurisprudence – Flavia Agnes

Non - Applicability to (Muhammadan) Males :-

Under the Muhammadan law, a male can marry four wives at a time. It is important to remember that it is only a permission but not a compulsion to have four wives at a time. Therefore section 494 which punishes bigamy is not applicable to a Muslim male contracting a bigamous marriage. However the exception is only in respect of Muslim males and section 494 applies to Muhammadan females, and to Hindus, Christians, and Parsis of either sex. A person found guilty under section 494 is punishable with a maximum imprisonment of seven years and also fine.

The offence of bigamy has the following ingredients.

(1) Existence of the first wife or husband when the second marriage is performed.

(2) The second marriage being void due to the subsistence of the first marriage.

Exceptions :-

A person can marry for the second time during the subsistence of the first marriage in the following cases.

(a) When the other spouse is continuously missing for a minimum period of seven years.

(b) The absent spouse not having been heard of by the other party as being alive within that time : and.

(c) The party marrying must inform the person with whom he or she marries of the above fact.

These exceptions are based on the presumption of death of a person if he is unheard of for seven years by those who normally have heard of him under section 108 of The Indian Evidence Act 1872.

Section 495 of I PC punishes the aggravated form of bigamy. It provides that whoever contracts a subsequent marriage by concealing the former marriage is punishable with maximum imprisonment of ten years.

Adultery :-

It is an offence against marriage. In England it is not a offence but only a tort. Section 497 of the Indian Penal Code punishes a man having sexual intercourse with a woman knowing that she is the wife of another man and without the consent or connivance of such other man.

The following remarks made by the Supreme Court in the instant case refect the thinking of the framers of the Indian Penal code who did not confer any right on the wife to prosecute the husband who has committed adultery with another woman.

" The philosophy underlying the scheme of these provisions appears to be that as between the husband and the wife social good will be promoted by permitting them to 'make up' or 'break up' the matrimonial tie rather than to drag each other to the criminal court. They can either condone the offence in a spirit of 'forgive and forget' and live together or separate by approaching a matrimonial court and snapping the matrimonial tie by securing divorce. They are not unable to send each other to jail. Perhaps it is as well that the children (if any) are saved from the trauma of one of their parents being jailed at the instance of the other parent. Whether one does or ctees ©f does not subscribe to the wisdom or philosophy of these provisions is of little consequence. For the court is the arbiter merely of the constitutionality of the law".

The Supreme Court Division Bench speaking through Justice s. Rathnavel Pandian has suggested the following measures for the purpose of eradicating the evil of prostitution.

(1) All the state Governments and the Governments of Union territories should direct their concerned law enforcing authorities to take appropriate and speedy action under the existing laws in eradicating child prostitution without giving room for any complaint of remissness or culpable indifference.

(2) The State Government and the Governments of Union territories should set up a separate Advisory Committee within their respective zones consisting of the secretary of the Social welfare Department sociologists, members of the women's organisations, members of Indian Council of child welfare and Indian Council of Social welfare as well the

members of various voluntary social organizations and associations etc., the main objects of the Advisory committee being to make suggestions of:

(a) The measures to be taken in eradicating the child prostitution, and

(b) The social welfare programs to be implemented for the care, protection, treatment, development and rehabilitation of the young fallen victims namely the children and girl rescued either from the brothel houses or from the vices of prostitution,.

(3) All the State Governments and the Governments of Union territories should take steps in providing adequate and rehabilitative homes manned by well-qualified trained social workers, psychiatrists and doctors.

(4) The Union Governments should set up a committee of its own in the line, we have suggested under direction No. (2) the main object of which is to evolve welfare programs to be implemented on the national level for the care, protection, rehabilitation etc. of the young fallen victims namely the children and girls and to make suggestions of amendments to the existing laws or for enactment of any new law, if so warranted for the prevention of sexual exploitation of children.

(5) The central Government and the Governments of States and Union territories should devise a machinery of its

own for ensuring the proper implementation of the suggestions that would be made by the respective committees: and.

(6) The Advisory committee can also go deep into Devadasi system and Jogin tradition and give their.

S. 498-A[126] Husband or Relative of Husband of A Woman Subjecting Her to Cruelty:-

Whoever, being the husband or the relative of the husband of a woman, subjects such woman to cruelty shall be punished with imprisonment for a term which may extend to three years and shall be liable to fine.

Explanation :-

For the purposes of this section " Cruelty" means -

(a) any willful conduct which is of such a nature as is likely to drive the woman to commit suicide or to cause grave injury or danger to life, limb or health (whether mental or physical) of the woman : or.

(b) Harassment of the woman where such harassment is with a view to coercing her or any person related to her to meet any unlawful demand for any property or valuable security or is on account of failure by her or any person related to her to meet such demand.

In a case under section 498A IPC, the Bombay High Court held that it is not every harassment or

[126] Ins by Act. 46 of 1983, Section 2 (w.e.f.25.11.1983)

every type of cruelty that could attract S. 498A. It must be established that beating and harassment was with a view to force the wife to commit suicide or to fulfill illegal demands of husband or in-laws. The court held that beating and harassment was with a view to force the wife to commits suicide or to fulfill the illegal demands of the husband was not established.

It the famous Manjusree Sarda case[127] the husband who was involved with another women killed the wife by poisoning her. The Sessions Court convicted the husband. The Bombay High Court confirmed the order. But the husband was acquitted by the Supreme Court. The Court held that the guilt of the husband was not proved beyond reasonable doubt and the wife might have committed suicide out of depression.

In the case of Vibha Shukla,[128] Vibha was found burnt while the husband was present in the house. Huge amount of dowry was paid at the time of the wedding and there were several subsequent demands for dowry. Vibha's father-in-law was an Assistant Commissioner of Police in Bombay. When

---

[127] sharad sarda vs. state of Maharashtra Cr.L.J 1986

[128] State of maharashtra vs. Ashok shukla Bombay high court Judgement dt. 14th October 1986

Vibha had delivered a daughter the family did not accept the child and she was left behind in Vibha's parents house. In-spite of this, the Bombay High Court set aside the order of conviction of the Sessions Court and acquit the husband of the offence of harassment u/s. 498A. The Court held that the offence of murder could not be proved beyond reasonable doubt and further that occasional cruelty and harassment cannot be construed as cruelty u/s 498A IPC.

RELEVENT PROVISIONS OF THE INDIAN EVIDENCE ACT, 1872,

Section 113 A – Indian Evidence Act

Presumption as to abetment of suicide by a married woman had been abetted by her husband or any relative of committed suicide within a period of seven years for the date of her marriage & that her husband & such relative of the court may presume having required to all the other circumstances of the case that such suicide had been abetted by her husband or by such relative of her husband.

Explanation – In the purpose of this Act section cruelty shall have the same meaning as in S. 498 A of IPC.

By virtue of this amendment the mental to order to wife also brought within encompass of criminal law in view of the rebuttal presumption under S. 113 A if the change u/s. 498 A is proved & it is proved that the woman died within seven years from her marriage the Court can evince the presumption for abetment to commit suicide u/s. 306 of IPC &before that it was impossible to convict erring husband for want of direct evidence. As offence generally occurred in house or in secrecy it was impossible to do justice to a victim of such cruelty.

In Jeevan Babu Desai V/s. Sate of Mah.[129]. the apex court has given wider interpretation to and cruelty which encompasses changes against a wife of infidelity. In **Madhavi V/s. Mukund Chitnis**[130] it was held filing false & defaming proceedings for unlawful demand is also cruelty.

In Balkrishna Moghe V/s. State of Maharastra[131], it was held S. 498 A is valid piece of legislation. Having regard to social evil that was sought to be remedied, classification of the husband & his relatives as a separate class is no

---

129 1992 CrHJ 2996
130 1989 MHJ 58
131 1998 MHJ 331

discrimination or violation of the guarantee Act 14 of constitution. About definition of 'cruelty' it was further held that, there is no vagueness or obscurity in the definition – There is a valid nexus between S. 498 A & the object sought to be achieved.

Section 113-B[132]. Presumption As to Dowry Death :-

When the question is whether a person has committed the dowry death of a woman and it is shown that soon before her death such woman had been subjected by such person to cruelty or harassment for, or in connection with, any demand for dowry, the court shall presume that such person had caused the dowry death.

Explanation :-

For the purpose of this section "dowry death" shall have the same meaning as in section 304-B of the Indian Penal code (45 of 1860).

the additional functions to be performed by the Dowry prohibition officers under sub – section (2) of Section 8 – B.

[132] Ins by Act. 43 of 1986, Section 12 (w.e.f.8.9.1986)

limitation and conditions subject to which a Dowry prohibition officer may exercise his functions under sub – section (3) of Section 8 – B.

(3) Every rule made by the State, Government under this section shall be laid as soon as may be after it is made before the state Legislature.

THE DOWRY PROHIBITION ACT 1961[133]

"The Standards of the law are standards of general application. The law takes no account of the infinite varieties of temperament, intellect and education, which make the internal character of a given act so different in different men. It does not attempt so see men as God sees them"[134]........

...- Oliver Windell Holmes (The Common Law,1881)

"Bride burning is a shame of our society. Poor never resort to it. Rich do not need it. Obviously because it is basically an economic problem of a class which suffers both from Ego & complex......... Social Ostracisation is needed to curtail increasing malady of bride burning"

Justice R. M. Sahai in Ashok Kumar Vs State of Rajasthan[135]

****

Introduction :-

The evil of dowry system has been a matter of serious concern to every one in view of its ever increasing and disturbing proportions. In order to prohibit the evil practice of giving and taking of dowry the parliament has passed the Dowry prohibition Act, 1961. The Act has been substantially

[133] The Dowry Prohibition Act 1961
[134] Oliver Windell Holmes (The Common Law,1881)
[135] (1991) I SCC 166

amended by the amending Acts in 1984 and 1986. However this is not the first legislative effort to eradicate the pernicious dowry system. Number of steps have been taken by the Legislature even before the Act came into force, to tackle this issue. As the problem is essentially a social one, it was sought to be tackled by the conferment of improved property rights on women by legislations like the Hindu Succession Act, 1956. The statement of objects and Reasons to the Bill and to the amendment Acts of 1984 and 1986 clearly explain the intention of the legislature.

For the sake of Convenience the problem of dowry has been discussed under three heads namely, The dowry prohibition Act, Dowry Death and suicide, and cruelty by Husband for Dowry.

I The Dowry Prohibition Act, 1961

SYNOPSIS

Statement of objects and Reasons

Judicial cognizance of the evil

Act not a complete code

Non-applicability to certain gifts

Definition of Dowry

Dower, Not Dowry

Penalty for taking Dowry

Presents tiven without demand

Penalty for demanding Dowry

Demand for dowry and cruelty

Time for demanding dowry

Ban on advertisements

Mere Advertisements, Punishable

Dowry agreements, void

Civil consequences of taking dowry

Failure to transfer

Death of wife before transfer

Burden of proof

Procedural aspects of the Act

Sanction for prosecution

Application of code of criminal procedure

Non- bailable and non- compoundable

****

II Dowry Death And Dowry Suicide

SYNOPSIS

Introduction

Dowry related offences and Indian penal code

Dowry Death

Unnatural Death, Whether suicide or homicide

Abetment to commit suicide

Dying Declaration

Burden of proof of innocence

Indirect harassment

Abnormal circumstances of Death

Causing dowry death, not “rarest of rare “

******

III Cruelty By Husband Or Relatives For Dowry

SYNOPSIS

Introduction

Cruelty by vexatious litigation

Mere demand of dowry on offence

Every kind of harassment, not covered

Jurisdiction

Suicide by mistress

New provisions

Compounding of complaint

******

I The Dowry Prohibition Act, 1961

Statement Of Objects And Reasons :-

The object of this Bill is to prohibit the evil practice of giving and taking of dowry. This question has been engaging the attention of the Government for some time past, and one of the methods by which this problem, which is essentially a social one, was sought to be tackled was by the conferment of improved property rights on women by the Hindu Succession Act, 1956. It is however felt that a law which makes the practice punishable and at the same time ensures that any dowry, if given. Does ensure for the benefit of the wife will go a long way to educating public opinion and to the eradication public opinion and to the eradication of this evil.

There has also been a persistent demand for such a law both in and outside parliament. Hence the present Bill. It, However, takes care to exclude presents in the form of clothes, ornaments. etc., which are customary at marriages. Provided the value thereof does not exceed Rs. 2000. Such a provision appears to be necessary to make the law workable.[136]

[136] Gazette of India 1959,Extra., Pt. II 2, p.397. See Joint committee Report, pp.1191.93.

Application Of Cr. P. C. (S.8) To The Offences Under The Act :-

The code of Criminal procedure, a 973 is applicable to the offences under this Act, as if they are cognizable offences. Thus demand and taking of dowry are cognizable offences by virtue of section 8 of the Act. The offences are cognizable for the purposes of investigation of such offences.

Non-Bailable And Non-Compoundable Offences.:-

Every offence under the Dowry prohibition Act is a non-bailable and non-compoundable offence.

The Criminal procedure code defines "cognizance offence" as an offence for which a police officer may, arrest the accused without any warrant. (S.2 (c)

Dowry Death And Dowry Suicide

Introduction :-

The parliament has taken a serious view of the increasing number of dowry deaths. The law commission of India also suggested number of measures in its 91 st amend to eradicate the evil of dowry deaths. Consequently the Indian Penal code 1860, has been amended and also the Indian Evidence Act, 1961 to create the special offences of dowry death. The criminal law (2nd Amendment) Act, 1983 which effected the relevant amendments has explained reasons for the same in its statement of objects and Reasons which is as under :

"Statement Of Objects And Reasons :-

(1) The increasing number of dowry deaths is a matter of serious concern. The extent of the evil has been commented upon by the Joint committee of the Houses to examine the working of the Dowry Prohibition Act, 1961. Cases of cruelty by the husband and relatives of the husband which culminate in suicide by, or murder of, the hapless woman concerned, constitute only a small fraction of the cases involving such cruelty. It is, therefore, proposed to amend the Indian Penal Code, the Code of Criminal procedure, and the Indian Evidence Act suitable to deal effectively not only with cases of dowry deaths but also cases of cruelty to married women by there in – laws.

The bill seeks to achieve the above objects."

Thus it is clear from the above statement of objects and reasons that the amendment of the Indian penal code and the Indian Evidence Act has been made to curb the inhuman practice of dowry deaths and to bring the culprits of such offences to the book effectively.

Dowry Related Offences And Indian Penal Code:-

The Indian Penal Code, 1860, contains two specific provisions in the form of section 304 B and section 498A to deal with two distinct offences namely causing dowry death and subjecting a woman to cruelty for dowry respectively.

Dowry Death:-

According to Section 304 B inserted by Act No. 43 of 1986, Section 10) where the death of woman is caused by any burns or bodily injury under obnormal circumstances within seven years of a marriage such death is called dowry death and the husband or relative of such deceased wife shall be deemed to have caused her death. The offence has the following ingredients.

The death of a woman should be caused by burns or bodily injury or otherwise that under normal circumstances.

Such death should have occurred within seven years of her marriage.

She must have been subjected to cruelty or harassment by her husband or any relative of her husband.

Such cruelty or harassment should be for or in connection with demand for dowry.

Un-natural Death, Whether Suicide or Homicide:-

Where the death occurred under unnatural circumstances, it is immaterial whether it was the result of a suicide or homicide. Even assuming that it is a case of suicide even then it would be death amounting to dowry death under Section 304 B[137].

In a case the deceased pregnant woman died due to 100% burns and the occurance took place at mid night in the house of the accused husband. There was a total absence of any cries or her shouts of the deceases. The Supreme Court held in the case of Prabhudayal vs State of Maharashtra[138] that it was a case of Homicide and not suicide.

Manjushree Sarada's Case :-

Earlier I have discussed that Mathura's case became a stepping stone for anti rape amendment Act 1983. In the same way Manjushree case went ahead in regard to major changes in Dowry law & thus this case is the root cause of Dawry prohibition (Amendment) Act 1986 (Bride-borning Act).

In the case of Sharad Sarda V/s. State of Maharastra[139] (Manjushree Case) the prosecution

[137] Shanti vs. State of Harayana, AIR SC 1226
[138] (1993) 3 SSC 573
[139] AIR 1984 Sc 1622

came with a case of murder as accussed/appellant administered strong dose of poison to his wife Manju on account of his illicit relatives with one lady & he wanted to perform marriage with her. For this purpose Manju was treated that Manju committed suicide by poison. The trial court convicted accused u/s. 302 of IPC & sentenced to death. The Bom. High Court confirmed the same. The supreme court held that when two views are possible, the benefit must go to the accused. It was further held this coordinal principle has a special relevance in cases wherein the quilt of the accused is sought to be established by circumstantial evidence.

On account of alarming increase in bride burning & suicide cases the question before Supreme Court was where death in question was horricidal as per prosecution or was accidental or suicide as per defence offence of murder, the process of elimination is a useful & legitimate exercise also in possibility of accident is ruled out to arrive at a definite finding of suicide of the offence of Dowry death could not come within the ambit of murder.

Dowry Prohibition (Amendment) Act 1986 –

Therefore, legislature rightly thought to fill up the deficiency by new Act in cases of dowry related deaths. Hence the legislature for the first time created a new offence known as "Dowry Death" by inserting S. 304 B in IPC. I also inserted a legal presumption as to the cause of death in cases of dowry related deaths.

Section 304 B IPC – Dowry Death

For moving offence u/s. 304 B the following are the essentials –

1) Death of women by burn or bodily injury or otherwise than normal circumstances.

2) Death within 7 yrs of marriage.

3) Subjected to cruelty by husband or his relative.

4) Such cruelty should be for or in connection with any demand for dowry.

5) Such cruelty or harassment must be "soon before her death."

S. 113 B of Evidence Act

The legislature has made this presumption as mandatory as word "shall presume" is used. It is presumption of law, of course rebuttable.

Justice Khalid, Chief Justice of J & K H C said valedictory function in VGC that, Hard remedy is necessary when crimes are hard such a departure from the normal rule alone can infuse bear in the minds of erring endividuals."

In Kundalabala V/s. State of A.P[140]**.** a student of enter medical class, 18 yrs Act was married with a young man with a handsome dowry, Rs. 50,000/- cash 50 sovereigns of and six acres of land. The father gave Rs. 50,000/- 15 gold soverrings & possession of land but insisted registry in the name of daughter. This became cause of ill-treatment brighten kitchen, she was kept like a prisoner & her mother in law & husband ignited her by pouring kerosene & setting her on fire. She gave oral O-Os to neighbours accordingly.

The trial court acquitted the accused. The High convicted u/s. 302 of IPC & the Supreme Court upheld the conviction & dismissed appeal. It was observed that, "Awakening of collective consciousness is the need of the day, change of heart & attitude is what needed. Laws are not enough to combat the evil. A wider social movement of educating women their rights, to conquer the menace is needed. The courts would deal with such matter with a realistic manner & not insignificant procedural technicalities or lacunae in evidence. The courts are expected to be sensitive in cases involving crime against women.

---

[140] 1993(2) SCC 684

The Supreme Court in recent judgment repeated in Shamnsaheb V.s, State of Karnataka[141] held that,

Composition of the offence under S. 304 B of IPC is vastly difference from formation of the offence murder u/s. 302 of IPC. Hence, former cannot be regarded as minor offence u/s. a u/s. the latter. Held that, S. 304 B has been brought on statute on 9-11-86 as a package with S. 113 B Evidence Act. In S. 302 accused has no burden. But u/s. 304 B without notice to him would deprive him opportunity to disprove the burden cast on him by law. If he fails to rebut the presumption the court is bound to act on it.

Abetment To Commit Suicide By Dowry Harassment:-

Where it was proved that the mother-in-law and sister-in-law of the diseased were taunting the bride for bringing less dowry and having given birth to a female child thereby driving her to commit suicide, it would amount to causing dowry death[142].

Dying Declaration:-

---

[141] 2001 CrLJ 1075 SC

[142] State of Punjab vs. Kirpal Sing, 1992 (2)

Where a woman who was not in a position to speak at the time of giving dying declaration and as such her dying declaration was recorded by a magistrate on the basis of some nods and gestures made by her, making it clear that she was burnt, not accidentally but by her husband, such a dying declaration was held to be admissible and relied upon for conviction of the accused[143].

Similarly the Supreme Court has held in number of cases that the conviction of the accused can be based on dying declarations of the deceased if they are voluntary and trust worthy[144].

Burden Of Proof Of Innocence On The Family:-

Every member of the family of the deceased, with whom she had been living before her death has the burden to prove his or her innocence. This burden of proof is imposed by section 113 B of the Indian Evidence Act, 1872[145].

Indirect Harassment For Dowry And Suicide :-

In the case of State of Punjab vs. Iqbal Singh[146] a woman set herself and her three children ablaze. She was working as a teacher. Soon after the

[143] Meesala Ramkrishna vs. State of A.P. 1994 (2) Crimes 114 (SC)
[144] See Mangath Ram vs. State 1994 (3) Crimes 685, hannu Raja vs. State of M.P. 1976 (2) SCR 761, Ramavathi Devi vs. State of Bihar, AIR 1983 SC – 154 – etc.
[145] Added by the criminal Law Amendment) Act, 1983.
[146] AIR 1991 SC 1532.

marriage there were disputes between the husband and wife on the question of dowry. The demand for extra dowry strained the relation between them and as a result the husband began to ill – treat the deceased wife.

She also lodged a police complaint but could not pursue the same due to some understanding. Inspite of the same, the situation did not improve and she was compelled to take the extreme step of putting an end to the life of herself and her three children. The Supreme Court convicted the accused husband under section 304 B and 306 of the Indian Penal Code.

Abnormal Circumstances Of Death :-

The Courts in India have held that death by drowning, by poisoning, due to burns, by hanging, by strangulation etc. are the instances of abnormal circumstances of death of a woman if it takes place within seven years of marriage. Where the death is unnatural it is immaterial whether it was caused due to suicide or homicide and section 304 B will be attracted in either case[147].

[147] Shanti vs. State of Harayana, AIR 1991 SC 1226.

Causing Dowry Death, Not "Rarest Of The Rare" :-

The Supreme Court[148] has held that dowry death has ceased to belong to the species of "the rarest of the rare". In the instant case a wife was brutally murdered by her husband and her head was severed and her body was cut into nine piece for causing disappearance of the evidence relating to her murder. The murder was caused in relation to dowry. However. Unless a dowry death is considered as the ' rarest of rare' case, death penalty cannot be imposed.

Cruelty By Vexatious Litigation :-

Where out of a sense of vindictiveness, the husband instituted vexatious litigation against his wife and she was feeling humiliated and tortured by reason of execution of search warrants and seizures of personal property, it was held that the section was wide enough to encompass a cruelty committed through an abuse of the litigative process. The trial Court had imposed a sentence of six months RI, the appellate court, going by the age, occupation and family condition of the husband, substituted the jail term with a fine of Rs. 6,000. The Bomaby High

[148] Ravindra Trimbak Chouthmal vs. State of Mah (1996) 4 SCC 148

Court held that though the substitution of the Jail sentence was justified, a modest fine of Rs. 6,000 was not justified. The amount was accordingly increased to Rs. 30,000[149].

Mere Demand of Dowry An Offence :-

The Calcutta High Court has expressed the opinion that by virtue of clause (b) of the Explanation to Section 498A, mere demand of dowry would be an offence. But, for the purposes of Section, 4 2(1) of the Dowry prohibition Act,1961, it is necessary that dowry should have been given or agreed to be given[150]. In a subsequent case under the section, it was on record that the husband accompanied his deceased wife to his in – laws to ask not only for additional dowry. This was held to be sufficient to constitute an offence under this section[151].

Jurisdiction :-

A wife, Maltreated for dowry, was sent back to her father where she became ill because of shock and after effects of cruelty. The Court having jurisdiction at the place was held competent to entertain a complaint both under section 498A in respect of

---

149 Madhuri M. Chitnis vs. M.M. Chitnis, 1992, Cri. LJ. 273
150 Shankar Prasad vs. State, 1991 Cri. LJ. 639 Cal.
151 Vadde Rama Rao vs. State of A.P. 1990 Cri. LJ. 1666 (A.P.)

cruelty and also under section 181 (4) of Cr.Pc, 1973 in respect of misappropriation of stridhan[152].

The Commission of Sati (Prevention) Act, 1987[153].

On 4th Sep. 18 yrs old Roop Kanwar burnt herself on the pure of her husband in Deorala Dist Sikar Rajsthan. His incident & its glorifications started country wide denouncement of practice of Sati & Ultimately led to passing of the special enactment. The preamble States Sati or burning or burying alive of widows is revolting to feeling of human nature.

[152] Vijay Rathan Sharma vs. State of U.P. 1988 Cri LJ. 1581 All.
[153] The Commission of Sati (Prevention) Act, 1987

THE INDECENT REPRESENTATION OF WOMEN (PROHIBITION) ACT, 1986[154]

(60 of 1986)

23rd December, 1986

An Act to prohibit indecent representation of women through advertisements of in publication, writings, painting, figures or in any other manner and for matters connected therewith or incidental thereto.

Be it enacted parliament in the Thirty-seven year of the Republic of India as follows :-

1. **Short Title, Extent And Commencement** ;-

This Act may be called the indecent Representation of women (prohibition) Act, 1986.

It extends to the whole of India except the state of Jammu and Kashmir.

It shall come into force on such date[155] as the central Government may, by notification in the official Gazette, appoint.

---

[154] Published in the Gazette of India Extra pt. II section I, dated 23rd December, 1986.

[155] 2-10-1987 vide Noti. No. G S.R.821(e) dated 25th September, 1987, see Gazette of India, Extra, 1987, pt., II, Section 3 (1).

2. <u>**Definitions**</u> **:-**

In this Act, unless the context otherwise requires –

"**Advertisement**" includes any notice, circular, label, wrapper or other document and also includes any visible representation made by means of any light, sound, smoke or gas:

"**Distribution**" includes distribution by way of samples whether free or otherwise:

"**Indecent representation of women**" means the depiction in any manner of the figure of a women, her form or body or any part thereof in such a way as to have the effect of being indecent, or derogatory to, or denigrating, women, or is likely to deprave, corrupt to injure the public morality or morals:

"**Label**" means any written, marked, stamped, printed or graphic matter, affixed to, or appearing upon, any package:

"**Package**" includes a box, carton, tin or other container :

"**Prescribed**" means prescribed by rules made under this Act.

3. Prohibition Of Advertisements Containing Indecent Representation Of Women :-

No person shall publish, or cause to be published, or arrange or take part in the publication of exhibition of any advertisement which contains indecent representation of women in any form.

4. Prohibition Of Publication Or Sending By Post Of Book, Pamphlets, Etc, Containing Indecent Representation Of Women :-

No person shall produce or cause to be produced, sell let to hire, distribute, circulate or send by post any book, pamphlet, paper, slide, film, writing, drawing, painting, photograph representation or figure which contains indecent representation of women in any form :

Provided that nothing in this section shall apply to –

Any book, pamphlet, paper, slide, film, writing, drawing, painting, photograph, representation or figure-

The publication of which is proved to be justified as being for the public good on the ground that such book, pamphlet, paper, slide, film, writing, drawing, painting, photograph, representation or figure is in the interest of science, literature, art, or learning or other objects of general concur: or

Which is kept or used bona fide for religious purposes:

Any representation sculptured, engraved, painted or otherwise represented on or in –

Any ancient monument with in the meaning of the Ancient Monument and Archaeological sites and remains Act, 1958 (24 of 1958) : or.

Any temple, or on any car used for the conveyance of idols, or kept or used for any religious purposes

Any film in respect of which the provisions of part II of the cinematography Act 1952 (37 of 1952,). Will be applicable.

5. Powers To Enter And Search :-

(1) Subject to such rules as may be prescribed, any Gazetted officer authorized by the state Government may, within the local limits of the area for which he is so authorized,

Enter and search at all reasonable times, with such assistance, if any, as he considers necessary, any place in which he has reason to believe that an offence under. This Act has been or is being committed :

Seize any advertisement or any book, pamphlet, paper, slide, film, writing, drawing, photograph, representation or figure which he has reason to believe contravenes any of the provisions of this Act :

Examine any record, register, document any or other material object found in any place mentioned in clause (a) and seize the same if has reason to believe that it may furnish evidence of the commission of and offence punishable under this Act :

Provided that no entry under this sub- section shall be made into a private dwelling house without a warrant:

Provided further that the power of seizure under this sub- section may exercised in respect of any document, article or things which contains any such advertisement, including the contents, if any, of such documents, article or thing if the advertisements cannot be separated by reason of its being embossed or otherwise from such document, article or thing without affecting the integrity, utility or saleable value thereof.

(2) The provisions of the code of criminal procedure, 1973 (2 of 1974), shall, so far as may be, apply to any search or seizure under this Act as they

apply to any search made under the authority of a warrant issued under section 94 of the said code.

(3) Where any person seizes anything under clause (b) or clause (c) of sub- section (1) he shall,. As soon may b, inform the nearest Magistrate and take his orders as to the custody there of.

6. Penalty :-

Any person who contravenes the provisions of section 3 or section 4 shall be punishable on first conviction with imprisonment of either decription for a term which may extend to two years, and with fine which may extend to two thousand rupees, and in the event of a second or subsequent conviction with imprisonment for a term of not less than six months but which may extend to five years and also with a fine not less than ten thousand.

7. Offences By Companies :-

(1) Where an offence under this Act has been committed by a company, every person, who, at the time the offence was committed, was in charge of , and was responsible to the company for the conduct, of the company, as well as the company, shall be deemed to be guilty of the offence and shall be liable to be proceeded against and punished accordingly :

Provided that nothing contained in this sub- section shall render any such person liable to any punishment, if he proves that the offence was committed without his knowledge or that he had exercised all due diligence to prevent the commission of such offence.

(2) Notwithstanding anything contained in sub-section (1) where any offence under this Act has been committed by a company and it is proved that the offence has been committed with the consent or connivance of, any director, manager, secretary or other officer of the company, such director, manager, secretary or other officer shall be proceeded against and punished accordingly.

Explanation :-

For the purposes of this section…

"Company" means any body corporate and includes a firm or other association of individuals : and

"Director", in relation to a firm, means a partner in the firm,.

8. Offences To Be Cognizable And Bailable :-

(1) Notwithstanding anything contained in the code of criminal procedure, 1973 (2 of 1974), an offence punishable under this Act shall be bailable.

(2) An offence punishable under this Act shall be recognizable.

9. Protection Of Action Taken In Good Faith :-

No suit, prosecution or other legal proceeding shall lie against the central Government or any state Government or any officer of the central Government or any state Government for anything which is in good faith done or intended to be done under this act.

10. Power To Make Rules :-

(1) The central Government any, by notification in the official Gazette, make rules to carry out the provisions of this Act.

In particular and without prejudice to the generality of the foregoing power, such rules may provide for all or any of the following matters, namely :-

The manner in which the seizure of advertisements or other articles shall be made and the manner in which the seizure list shall be prepared and delivered to the person from whose custody any advertisement or other article has been seized :

Any other matter which is required to be, or may be, prescribed.

(3) Every rule made under this Act, shall be laid as soon as may be after it is made, before each House of

Parliament, while it is in session for a total period of thirty days, which may be comprised in one session or in two or more successive sessions, and if, before the expiry of the session immediately following the session or the successive sessions aforesaid, both houses agree in making any modification in the rule shall thereafter have effect only in such modified form or be of no effect, as the case may be: so however, that any such modification or annulment shall be without prejudice to the validity of anything previously done under that rule.

THE IMMORAL TRAFFIC PREVNTION ACT 1956[156]

" Prostitution always remains as a running sore in the body of civilization and destroys all moral values. The causes and evil effects of prostitution maligning the Society are so notorious and frightful that none can gainsay it. This malignity is daily and hourly threatening the community at large slowly but steadily making its way onwards leaving a track marked with broken hopes. Therefore, the necessity for appropriate and drastic action to eradicate this evil has become apparent……."

-- Supreme Court in Vishal Jeet Vs. Union of India[157]

*****

[156] THE IMMORAL TRAFFIC PREVNTION ACT 1956
[157] (1990) 3 S C C 3181

Introduction

Indian Legislation on Immoral Traffic

Scheme of Legislation

Purpose of Legislation

Important Definitions

Salient features

Rehabilitative and Remedial Provisions

Suggested measures.

Introduction :-

The prostitution is said to be the oldest among the professions in the world of human need for gratification of sexual urge impelled men and women, of all ages and in all countries of the world to exploit either sex. This profession or trade has existed in all civilized countries from the time immemorial though was regulated in some countries by law or regulations.

Indian Legislation On Immoral Traffic :-

Article 23 of the constitution of India, Trafficking in human beings is prohibited. The Right against exploration is a fundamental right which aims at putting an end to all forms of trafficking in human beings including prostitution and 'Begar' India has also signed the 1950 which required a legislation to implement the same. There had been number of local acts in force in Indian in some states but they were neither uniform nor effective.

In the light of all these circumstances, the Indian parliament has thought it fit and desirable to pass a central law that will not only secure uniformity through out the country, but also would implement the fundamentals rights in Article 23 of the constitution and also conventional obligation of 1950.

Accordingly the parliament has passed the Suppression of Immoral Traffic in women and Girls Bill of 1954 which became the Immoral Traffic in women and girls Act, 1956 and it was shortly known as SITA. This Act was covering only the females and children.

Subsequently it has been realized that prostitution is not confined only to the females and children but also covers the males. In order to cover even the males, the Act was renamed as the Immoral Traffic (Prevention) Act, 1956 by an Amendment in females, as it uses the expression 'Persons'. Power to make Rules has been vested in the State Governments and accordingly many states have framed Rules for carrying out the purposes of the Act effectively.

Scheme of Legisltaion :-

The immoral Traffic (Prevention) Act, 1956 contains 25 sections. Those provisions are supplemented by the Rules framed by various state Governments. The Act underwent two major Amendments in 1978 and 1986, which introduced radical changes in the scope of the legislation. The persons covered there under and the definition of 'prostitution' etc., The Act also contains number of penal provisions which aim to punish those who keep or manage a brothel, who procure, induce or take a person for prostitution and who carry on prostitution in the vicinity of a public place etc.

Purpose of Legislation:-

The purpose of the enactment was to inhibit or to abolish commercial vice namely traffic in women men and children for the purpose of prostitution as an organized means of living. The aim was not to render prostitution 'per se' a criminal offence or punish a woman merely because the prostitutes herself. A careful scrutiny of the act clearly reveals that it was aimed at the suppression of commercialized vice (Ratnamala)[158]. What is

[158] AIR 1962 Madras 31 (33)

punishable under the act is sexual exploitation for commercial purpose, or to make a living thereon.

Salient Features of The Act:-

The Act contains the following salient features :-

Punishment For Keeping A Brothel etc.:-

Section 3 of the Act punishes any person who keeps or manages or assists such keeping or manages a brothel. Under this section any landlord owner, lessor, tenant occupier or lessee is 'punishable' if he knowingly uses the premises for prostitution or allows it for such use. The knowledge of the person is very important.

Punishment For Living On The Earnings of Prostitution :-

Section 4 provides that any person who is over 15 years of age, who lives wholly or in part of the earnings of prostitution of a person is liable to be punished.

A Person Is Liable To Be Punished Under This Section If:-

He is above 15 years of age.

He lives with or is habitually in the company of prostitute.

He exercises control, action or influence over the movements of a prostitute and.

He acts as a pimp or tout on behalf of prostitute.

Therefore the pimps or touts can be punished under this provided the above ingredients are satisfied.

Punishments for procuring a person for prostitution: Section 5 of the Act punishes a person who procures a person, for the propose of prostitution. Similarly a person who induces a person or takes a person from one place to another with a view to his / her carrying on prostitution also is liable to be punished under this section.

This provision is similar to the one under section 366, 372, and 373 of Indian penal code.

Punishment for a person for immoral purpose:

According to section 6 of the act, detention of a person by another whether with or without the consent of the detenue, in a brothel or any other promises for immoral purposes, is punishable with imprisonment and fine. It is punishable with a minimum imprisonment of 7 years but the punishment may extend to life imprisonment or 10 years.

Subsection 2-A of section 6 raises a presumption when a child or a minor is found in a brothel and is medically found to be sexually abused that the child/minor is detained for the purpose of prostitution.

Punishment for prostitution in the vicinity of public place:

According to section 7 of the Act, carrying on of prostitution in any premises within a distance of two hundred meters from any place of public religious worship, educational institution hostel, hospital, nursing home of public place notified as such by the commissioner of police or the district magistrate, an offence. In such case not only the woman who carries on the offence but also the man with whom she indulges in prostitution are punishable with an imprisonment which may extend to three months. But if the offence is committed in respect of child or a minor, the punishment is higher.

Punishment for seducing or soliciting for prostitution: section 8 of the Act makes it a penal offence for any person to seduce or solicit for the purpose of prostitution in any public place or within sight of it. Here the soliciting may be by any communicable from like words, gestures, willful exposure of her person or otherwise tempting any person for prostitution. Seducing normally means drawing aside from the path of rectitude and duty in any manner: to entice to evil or to induce to surrender chastity.

Punishment for custodial seduction:

Section 9 of the Act punishes custodial seduction i. e. seduction by any person having the custody, charge or care of or in a position of authority over any person. It is a grave offence which attracts a minimum imprisonment of 7 years and also fine. This provision is similar to the provisions of Indian penal code contained in section 376-B.C.D.

Rehabilitative And Remedial Provisions :-

The Immoral Traffic (prevention) Act, 1956 is not a pure penal legislation. It is also a social welfare legislation and aims at the rehabilitation and correction of female and child offenders found guilty of indulging in prostitution. According to S.10.A of the Act, a female offender found guilty of an offence of carrying on prostitution at a public place etc., may be ordered to be detained in a corrective institution for a term not less than 2 years and not more than 5 years.

Suggested Measures :-

In view of the explosion of sex related deceases and more particularly the dreaded AIDS disease which is fast spreading in developing countries like

India, the immoral Traffic (prevention) Act should be adequately amended further.

First and foremost the definition of "Prostitution" should be amended so as to bring even the promiscuous intercourse carried by a single person within it purview. At present prostitution 'per se' is not an offence under the Act and is punishable only under certain circumstances. It is desirable that prostitution is made punishable irrespective of the circumstances under which it is committed, so that this social evil can be combated effectively.

In the case of Vishal Jeet vs. Union of India[159]. The Supreme Court has taken note of the fact that many poverty stricken children and girls in the prime of youth are taken to "Flesh Market" and forcibly pushed into the flesh trade which is being carried on in utter violation of all canons of morality, decency and dignity of human kind.

------

159 (1990) 3 SSC 318

The crimes against women in 1998 reported, an increase of 8.3 per cent and 4.8 per cent over previous year 1997 and 1996 respectively. In absolute numbers an increases of 10,073 cases was reported at All India level in 1998 over 1997. The crime head wise incident of reported crimes during 1996 to 1998 along with percentage variation is presented below.[160]

Sr. No.	Crime Head	1996	Year 1997	1998	percentag veriation 1998
1	2	3	4	5	6
1.	Rape	14846	15330	15031	2.0
2.	Kidnapping and Abduction.	14877	15617	16381	4.9
3.	Dowry death	5513	6006	6917	15.9
4.	Torture	35246	36592	41318	1.2.9
5.	Molestation	28939	30764	31 046	0.9
6.	Sexual Harassment	5671	5796	8123	40.1
7.	Importation of Girls.	182	78	146	87.2
8.	Sati prevation Act	000	01	000	100.00
9.	Immoral Traffic(P) Act	7706	8323	8695	4.5
10.	Indecent Rep. of women (P) Act	96	73	192	163.0
11.	Dowry prohibition Act	2647	2685	3489	29.9
	Total	115723	121265	131338	8.3

160 Judicial Colloquia on Gender and Law - 2001

Status of Women in India – Select Indicators				
1991			1951	
Female	Male		Female	Male
927	1000	Sex Ratio.. Females per 1000 Males	946	1000
58.1	57.7	Life Expectancy at Birth	31.7	32.5
18.3 19.5 (Combined)	23.3 (1981)	Mean Age at Marriage	15.6	19.9
27.2	25.9	Death Rates (0-4 years)	55.1	51.7
74	73	Infant Mortality Rate (1992)	131	123
324		Maternal Mortality Rate per Lakh live births	468	
1991			1951	
39.19% 54.16 (2001)	64.13% 78.85 (2001)	Literacy	8.86%	27.16%
46.4 mn	61.8 mn (1993-94)	School Enrolment	504 mm	13.8 mn
10.2 to total		No of Women in polytechnics	7.4 to total	
22.27	51.61	Work participation Rate	(1971) 14.22	52.75
40.27 lakhs (1993)	14.8%	Women in Orgnised Sector	(1971) 19.3 lakhs	(11% to total)
7.5% in 1990	Women in Central Government		1971 in 2.5%	
8% (1999)	Women in Parliament		(1952) 5.47%	

Extract from Chapter 5, Crime in India 1998, published by National Crime Records Bureau

5.1.1 The global campaign of elimination of violence against women, in the recent years indicates the enormity as well as the seriousness of the atrocities committed against women that are being witnessed the world over. Development along with its progressive changes in personal life style, living standards varied economic growth caused by urbanization and changes in social ethos contributes to a violent attitude and tendencies towards women which has resulted in an increase in crimes against women. Such incidents are a matter of serious concern and its containment is a necessity so that the Women of India attain their rightful share and live in dignity, freedom, peace and free from crimes and aspersions. The battles against crime against women, has to be waged by the various sections of society through campaigns and various programmes with social support along with legal protection, safeguards and reforms in the Criminal Justice System.

5.1.2 Despite all these safeguards, the women in our country continue to suffer, due to lack of awareness of their rights, illiteracy and oppressive practices & customs. The resultant consequences are many viz. a constant fall in the sex ratio, high infant morally rate, low literacy rate, high drop out rate of girls from education, low wages rates etc.

Legal Rights

5.2.1 To uphold the Constitutional mandate, the State has enacted various legislative measures intended to ensure rights, to counter social discrimination and various forms of violence and atrocities and to provide support services especially to working women.

5.2.2 Although Women may be victims of any of the crimes such as "Murder", "Cheating" etc., the crimes which are directed specifically against Women are characterized as ":Crime Against Women". These are broadly classified under two categories.

(1) The Crimes Identified Under the Indian Penal Code

(IPC)

(i) Rape (Sec. 376 IPC)

(ii) Kidnapping & Abduction for different purposes (Sec. 363-373 IPC)

(iii) Homicide for Dowry, Dowry Deaths or their attempts (Sec. 302/304-B IPC)

(iv) Torture, both mental and physical (Sec. 498-A IPC)

(v) Molestation (Sec. 354 IPC)

(vi) Sexual Harassment * (Sec. 509 IPC)

(vii) Importation of girls (upto 21 years of age) (Sec. 366-B IPC)

(* referred in the past as Eve-Teasing")

(2) The Crimes identified under the Special Laws (SLL)

5.2.3 Although all laws are not gender specific, the provisions of law affecting women significantly have been reviewed periodically and amendments carried out to keep pace with the emerging requirements. Some acts which have special provisions to safeguard women and their interests are :

(i) The Employees State Insurance Act, 1948

(ii) The Plantation Labour Act, 1951

(iii) The Family Courts Act, 1954

(iv) The Special Marriage Act, 1954

(v) The Hindu Marriage Act, 1955

(vi) The Hindu Succession Act, 1956

(vii) Immoral Traffic (Prevention), Act, 1956

(viii) The Maternity Benefit Act, 1961 (Amended in 1995)

(ix) Dowry Prohibition Act, 1961

(x) The Medical Termination of Pregnancy Act, 1971

(xi) The Contract Labour (Regulation and Abolition) Act, 1976

(xii) The Equal Remuneration Act, 1976

(xiii) The Child Marriage Restraint (Amendment) Act, 1979

(xiv) The Criminal (Amendment) Act, 19086

(xv) The Factories (Amendment) Act, 1986

(xvi) Indecent Representation of Women (Prohibition) Act, 1986

(xvii) Commission of Sati (Prevention) Act, 1987

5.2.4 The detailed State/UT-wise statistics of these crimes are presented in the relevant chapters of report, while related analysis is discussed in the following paragraphs. Complete details pertaining to Child Marriage Restraint Act are discussed in Chapter on Crime Against Children which an exclusive Chapter on the Subject.

Incidence of Crimes Against Women – All India (1996-1998)

5.3.1 The Crime head-wise incidence of reported crimes during 1996 and 1998 along with percentage variation is presented below. It is observed that Crimes Against Women in 1998 reported an increase of 8.3 per cent and 4.8 per cent over previous year 1997 and 1996 respectively. In absolute numbers, an increase of 10,073 cases was reported at All-India level in 1998 over 1997.

Table 5.1

Sl No	Crime Head	Year 1996	1997	Percentage Variation in 1998 over 1997
		1998		
(1)	(2)	(4)	(5)	(7)
		(6)		
1.	Rape	14846	15330	-2.0
2.	Kidnapping & Abduction	15031		4.9
3.	Dowry Death	14877	15617	15.9
4.	Torture	16381		12.9
5.	Molestation	5513	6006	0.9
6.	Sexual Harassment	6917		40.1
7.	Importation of Girls	35246	36592	87.2
8.	Sati Prevention Act	41318		-100.0
9.	Immoral Traffic (P) act	28939	30764	4.5
10.	Indecent Rep. Of Women	31046		163.0
11.	(P) Act	5671	5796	29.9
	Dowry Prohibition Act	8123		
		182	78	
		146		
		0	1	
		0		
		7706	8323	
		8695		
		96	73	
		192		
		2647	2685	
		3489		
	Total	**115723**	**121265**	**8.3**
		131338		

5.3.2 The proportion of IPC crimes committed against women towards total IPC crimes remained around 6.0 per cent during the last 3 years.

Table 5.3

Proportion of crime against women (IPC) toward total IPC crimes.

Sl. No.	Year	Total IPC Crimes	Crime against Women (IPC Case)	Percentage to total IPC crimes
(1)	(2)	(3)	(4)	(5)
1	1996	1709576	115723	6.8
2	1997	1719820	110183	6.4
3	1998	1779111	118962	6.7

5.3.3 The available data indicates an increasing trend during the last three years in all the IPC crimes against women except "Rape", "Sati" (Prevention) Act" and "Importation of Girls" which reported a declining trend during this period. All crimes against women reported under Special & Local Laws also resulted increasing trends during 3 years except " Indecent Representation of Women (P) Act" which reported a declining trend.

Crime Right (States & UTs)

5.4.1 All India Crime rate i.e. no. of crimes per lakh population for crimes against women reported to the police worked out to be 13.5 during 1998. However, when estimated with reference to female population this rate almost doubles to 28.1 per lakh female population. This rate of crime which does not appear alarming at first sight may be viewed with caution, as a sizeable number of crimes against women go unreported due to social stigma attached to them.

5.4.2 Uttar Pradesh State reported highest incidence (13.3%) of these crimes followed by Madhya Pradesh (12.1%) and Maharastra (10.9%). In contrast, Delhi, which accounted for only 1.9 per cent of total crimes and shared only 1.3 % of the population in the country reported third high rate of such crime at 19.6 after Madhya Pradesh (20.5).

5.4.4 Incidence of rape cases (15,031) reported a decline of 2% during 1998 and 1997, Madhya Pradesh alone reported 22.3 per cent of total rape cases in the country, UT of Delhi, which represented only 2.9 per cent cases reported fourth highest rate at 3.4 after Mizoram (9.3) Madhya Pradesh (4.3) and D & N Haveli (3.9).

Rape Victims

5.4.5. At national level there were 15,033 rape victims compared to 15,336 in the previous year representing a decrease of nearly 2 per cent. Of these 8,414 (56%) were in the age group of 16-30 years, 3,433 (22.8%) in the age-group of 10-16 years and 626 (4.2%) of age 10 years & below. Similar to decrease (2%) in the number of Rape victims over previous year, the child victims (below 19 years) of age also reported decrease of 18.7% and the victims above 30 years of age reported an increase of 10.8 per cent signifying decrease of incidents relating to rape of Children.

Table 5.4

Victims of Rape by Age – Groups during 1996-1998 and percentage chagens during 1998 and 1997[161]

Sl. No.	Year	Below 10 years	10-16 years	16-39 years	30 years & above	Total of all age groups
(1)	(2)	(3)	(4)	(5)	(6)	(7)
1.	1996	608	3475	8281	2485	14849
2.	1997	770	3644	8612	2310	15336
3.	1998	626	3433	8414	2560	15033
4.	Percentage change in 1998 over 1997	-18.7	-5.8	-2.3	10.8	-2.0

[161] Judicial Colloquia on Gender and Law - 2001

THE PROTECTION OF WOMEN FROM DOMESTIC VIOLENCE ACT, 2005[162]

(Act No. 43 of 2005)

13th September, 2005

An Act to provide for more effective protection of the rights of women guaranteed under the Constitution who are victims of violence of any kind occurring within the family and for matters connected therewith or incidental thereto.

Be it enacted by Parliament in the Fifty-sixth Year of the Republic of India as follows:

CHAPTER 1

PRELIMINARY

1. Short title, extent and commencement - (1) This Act may be called the Protection of Women from Domestic Vilence Act, 2005.

2. It extends to the whole of India except the State of Jammu and Kashmir.

3. It shall come into force on such date (w.e.f. 13.9.2005) as the Central Government may, by notification in the Official Gazette, appoint.

[162] THE PROTECTION OF WOMEN FROM DOMESTIC VIOLENCE ACT, 2005.

2. Definitions : In this Act, unless the context otherwise requires -

a) "**aggrieved person**" means any woman who is, or has been, in a domestic relationship with the respondent and who alleges to have been subjected to any act of domestic violence by the respondent;

b) "**child**" means any person below the age of eighteen years and includes any adopted, step or foster child

c) "**compensation order**" means an order granted in terms of Section 22 ;

d) "**custody order**" means an order granted in terms of Section 21 ;

e) "**domestic incident report**" means a report made in the prescribed form on receipt of a complaint of domestic violence from an aggrieved person ;

f) "**domestic relationship**" means a relationship between two persons who live or have, at any point of time, lived together in a shared household, when they are related by consanguinity, marriage, or through a relationship in the nature of marriage, adoption or are family members living together as a joint .family

g) "**domestic violence**" has the same meaning as assigned to it in section 3 ;

h) "**dowry**" shall have the same meaning as assigned to it in Section 2 of the dowry Prohibition Act, 1961 (28 of 1961);

i) "**Magistrate**" means the Judicial Magistrate of the first class, or as the case may be the Metropolitan Magistrate, exercising jurisdiction under the Code of Criminal Procedure, 1973 (2 of 1974) in the area where the aggrieved person resides temporarily or otherwise or the respondent resides or the domestic violence is alleged to have taken place ; j) "medical facility" means such facility as may be notified by the State Government to be a medical facility for the purposes of this act;

k) "**monetary relief**" means the compensation which the Magistrate may order the respondent to pay to the aggrieved person, at any stage during the hearing " of an application seeking any relief under this Act, to meet the expenses incurred and the losses suffered by the aggrieved person as a result of the domestic violence;

l) "**notification**" means a notification published in the Official Gazette and the expression "notified" shall be construed accordingly ;

m) "**prescribed**" means prescribed by rules made under this Act;

n) "**Protection Officer**" means an officer appointed by the State Government under sub-section (1) of Section 8 ;

o) "**protection order**" means an order made in terms of Section 18 ;

p) "**residence order**" means an order granted in terms of sub-section (1) of Section 19 ;

q) "**respondent**" means any adult male person who is, or has been, in a domestic relationship with the aggrieved person and against whom the aggrieved person has sought any relief under this Act; Provided that an aggrieved wife or female living in a relationship in the nature of marriage may also file a complaint against a relative of the husband or the male partner.

r) "**service provider**" means an entity registered under sub-section (1) of Section 10,

s) "**shared household**" means a household where the person aggrieved lives or at any stage has lived in a domestic relationship either singly or along with the respondent and includes such a household whether owned or tenanted either jointly by the aggrieved person and the respondent, or owned or tenanted by either of them in respect of which either the aggrieved person or the respondent or both jointly or singly have any right, title, interest or equity and includes such a household which may belong to the joint family of which the respondent is a member, irrespective of whether the respondent or the aggrieved person has any right, title and interest in the shared household.

t) "**shelter home**" means any shelter home as may be notified by the state Government to be a shelter home for the purposes of this Act.

CHAPTER II

DOMESTIC VIOLENCE

3. Definition of domestic violence : For the purposes of this Act, any act, omission or commission or conduct of the respondent shall constitute domestic violence in case it-

a) harms or injures or endangers the health, safety, life limb on well-being, whether mental or physical, of the aggrieved person or tends to do so and includes causing physical abuse, sexual abuse, verbal and emotional abuse and economic abuse ; or

b) harasses, harms, injures or endangers the aggrieved person with a view to coerce her or any other person related to her to meet any unlawful demand for any dowry or other property or valuable security ; or

c) has the effect of threatening the aggrieved person or any person related to her by any conduct mentioned in clause (a) or clause (b) ; or

d) otherwise injures or causes harm, whether physical or mental, to the aggrieved person.

Explanation I - For the purposes of this section :

i) 'physical abuse' means any act or conduct which is of such a nature as to cause bodily pain , harm, or danger to life, limb, or health or impair the health or development of the aggrieved person and includes assault, criminal intimidation and criminal force ;

ii) 'sexual abuses' includes any conduct of a sexual nature that abuses, humiliates, degrades or otherwise violates the dignity of woman ;

iii) ' verbal and emotional abuse' includes -

a) insults, ridicule, humiliation,' name calling and insults or ridicule specially with regard to not having a child or a male child; and

b) repeated threats to cause physical pain to any person in whom the aggrieved person is interested, iv) 'economic abuse' includes -

a) deprivation of all or any economic or financial resources to which the aggrieve person is entitled under any law or custom whether payable under an order of a Court or otherwise or which the aggrieved person requires out of necessity including, but not limited to, household necessities for the aggrieved person and her children, if any, stridhan, property, jointly or separately owned by the aggrieved person, payment of rental related to the shared household and maintenance;

c)

b)disposal of household effects, any alienation of

assets whether movable or immovable, valuables, shares, securities, bonds and the like or other property in which the aggrieved person has an interest or is entitled to use by virtue of the domestic relationship or which may be reasonably required by the aggrieved person or her children or her stridhan or any other property jointly or separately held by the aggrieved per son; and prohibition or restriction to continued access to resources or facilities which the aggrieved person is entitled to use or enjoy by virtue of the domestic relationship including access to the shared household.

Explanation II - For the purpose of determining whether any act, omission, commission or conduct of the respondent constitutes "domestic violence" . under this section, the overall facts and circumstances of the case shall be taken into consideration.

CHAPTER HI POWERS AND DUTIES OF PROTECTION OFFICERS, SERVICE PROVIDERS, ETC.

4. Information to Protection Officer and exclusion of liability of informant: 1) Any person who has reason to believe that an act of domestic violence has been, or is being or is likely to be committed may ,

give information about it to the concerned Protection Officer, 2) No liability, civil or criminal, shall be incurred by any person for giving in good faith of information for the purpose of sub-section (1).

5. Duties of police officers, service providers and Magistrate A police Officer, Protection Officer, service provider or Magistrate who has received a complaint of domestic violence or is otherwise present at the place of an incident of domestic violence or when the incident of domestic violence is reported to him, shall inform the aggrieved person

a) of her right to make an application for obtaining a relief by way of a protection order, an order for monetary relief, a custody order, a residence order, a compensation order or more than one such order under this Act;

b) —-

c) Officers;

d) —

of the availability of services of service providers; of the availability of services of the Protection

of her right to free legal services under the Legal Services Authorities Act, 1987 (39 of 1987); e) of her right to file a complaint under Section 498-A

of the Indian Penal Code (45 of 1860), wherever

relevant;

Provided that nothing in this Act shall be construed in any manner as to relieve a police officer from his duty to proceed in accordance with law upon receipt of information as to the commission of a cognizable offence.

6. Duties of shelter homes : If an aggrieved person or on her behalf a Protection Officer or a-service provider requests the person in charge of a shelter home to provide shelter to her, such person in charge of the shelter home shall provide shelter to the aggrieved person in the shelter home.

7. Duties of medical facilities : If an aggrieved person or, on her behalf a Protection Officer or a service provider requests the person in charge of a medical facility to provide any medical aid to her, such person in charge of the medical facility shall provide medical aid to the aggrieved person in the medical facility.

8. Appointment of Protection Officers : 1) The State - Government shall, by notification^ appoint such number of Protection Officers in each district as it may consider necessary and shall also notify the area or areas within which a Protection Officer shall exercise the powers and perform the duties conferred on him by or under this Act.

2) The Protection Officers shall as far as possible be women and shall possess such qualifications and experience as may be prescribed.

3) The terms and conditions of service of the Protection Officer and the other officers subordinate to him shall be such as may be prescribed.

9. Duties and functions of Protection Officers :

1) It shall be the duty of the Protection Officer -

a) to assist the Magistrate in the discharge of his functions under this Act;

b) to make a domestic incident report to the Magistrate, in such form and in such manner as may be prescribed, upon receipt of a complaint of domestic violence and forward copies thereof to the police officer in charge of the police station within the local limits of whose jurisdiction domestic violence is alleged to have been committed and to the service providers in that area ;

c) to make an application in such form and in such manner as may be prescribed to the Magistrate, if the aggrieved person so desires, claiming relief for issuance of a protection order ;

d) to ensure that the aggrieved person is provided legal aid under the legal Services Authorities Act, 1987 (39 of 1987) and make available free of cost the prescribed form in which a complaint is to be made ;

e) to maintain a list of all service providers providing legal aid or counseling, shelter homes and medical facilities in a local area within the jurisdiction of the Magistrate ;

f) to make available a safe shelter home, if the aggrieved person so requires and forward a copy of his report of having lodged the aggrieved person in a shelter home to the police station and the Magistrate having jurisdiction in the area where the shelter home is situated ;

g) to get the aggrieved person medically examined, if she has sustained bodily injuries and forward a copy of the medical report to the police station and the Magistrate having jurisdiction in the area where the domestic violence is alleged to have been taken place ;

h) --

1) –

2) to ensure that the order for monetary relief under Section 20 is complied with and executed, in accordance with the procedure prescribed under the code of Criminal Procedure, 1973 (2 of 1974); to perform such other duties as may be prescribed. The

Protection Officer shall be under the control and supervision of the Magistrate, and shall perform the duties imposed on him by the Magistrate and the Government by, or under, this Act. 10. Service providers : 1) Subject to such rules as may be made in this behalf, any voluntary association registered under the Societies Registration act, 1860 (21 of 1860) or a company registered under the Companies Act, 1956 (1 of 1956) or any other law for the time being in force with the objective of protecting the rights and interests of women by any lawful means including providing of legal aid, medical, financial or other assistance shall register itself with the state Government as a service provider for the purposes of this Act. 2) A service provider registered under Sub-Section (1)

shall have the power to -

a) record the domestic incident report in the prescribed form if the aggrieved person so desires and forward a copy thereof to the Magistrate and the Protection officer having jurisdiction in the area where the domestic violence took place;

b) get the aggrieved person medically examined and forward a copy of the medical report to the Protection Officer and the police station within the local limits of which the domestic violence took place;

c) ensure that the aggrieved person is provided shelter in a shelter home, if she so requires and forward a report of the lodging of the aggrieved person in the shelter home to the police station within the local limits of which the domestic violence took place.

3) No suit, prosecution or other legal proceeding shall lie against any service provider or any member of the service provider who is, or who is deemed to be, acting or purporting to act under this Act, for anything which is in good faith done or intended to be done in the exercise of powers' or discharge of functions under this Act towards the prevention of the commission of domestic violence. 11) Duties of Government: The Central Government and every State Government, shall take all measures to ensure that -

a) the provisions of this Act are given wide publicity through public medical including the television, radio and the print media at regular intervals ;

b) the Central Government and State Government officers including the police officers and the members of the judicial services are given periodic sensitization and awareness training on the issues addressed by this Act;

c) effective co-ordination between the services provided by concerned Ministries and Departments dealing with law, home affairs including law and order, health and human resources to address issues of domestic violence is established and periodical review of the same is conducted;

d) protocols for the various Ministers concerned with the delivery of services to women under this Act including the courts are prepared and put in place.

CHAPTER IV

PROCEDURE FOR OBTAINING ORDERS OF RELIEFS

12. Application to Magistrate :- 1) An aggrieved person or a Protection Officer or any other person on behalf of the aggrieved person may present an application to the Magistrate seeking one or more relief's under this Act: Provided that before passing any order on such application, the Magistrate shall take into consideration any domestic incident report received by him from the Protection Officer or the service provider.

2) The relief sought for under sub-section (1) may include a relief for issuance of an order for payment of compensation or damages without prejudice to the right of such person to institute a suit for compensation or damages for the injuries caused by the

acts of domestic violence committed by the respondent ;

Provided that where a decree for any amount as compensation or damages has been passed by any Court in favour of the aggrieved person, the amount, if any, paid or payable in pursuance of the order made by the Magistrate under this Act shall be set off against the amount payable under such decree and the decree shall, notwithstanding anything contained in the Code of Civil Procedure, 1908 (5 of 1908), or any other law for the time being in force, be executable for the balance amount, if any, left after such set off.

3) Every application under sub-section (1) shall be in such form and contain such particulars as may be prescribed or as nearly as possible thereto.

4) The Magistrate shall fix the first date of hearing, which shall not ordinarily be beyond three days - from the date of receipt of the application by the Court.

5) The Magistrate shall endeavor to dispose of every application made under sub-section (1) within a period of sixty days from the date of its first hearing.

13. Service of notice : 1) A notice of the date of hearing fixed under Section 12 shall be given by the

Magistrate to the Protection Officer, who shall get it served by such means as may be prescribed on the respondent, and on any other person, as directed by the Magistrate within a maximum period of two days or such further reasonable time as may be allowed by the Magistrate from the date of its receipt.

2) A declaration of service of notice made by the Protection Officer in such form as may be prescribed shall be the proof that such notice was served upon the respondent and on any other person as directed by the Magistrate unless the contrary is proved.

14. Counseling : 1) The Magistrate may, at any stage of the proceedings, under this Act, direct the respondent or the aggrieved person, either singly or jointly, to undergo counseling with any member of a service provider who possess such qualifications and experience in counseling as may be prescribed. 2) Where the Magistrate has issued any direction under sub-section (1), he shall fix the next day of hearing of the case within a period not exceeding two months.

15. Assistance of welfare expert: In any proceeding under this Act, the Magistrate may secure the services of such person, preferably a woman, whether related to the aggrieved person or not, including a person engaged in promoting family welfare as he thinks fit, for the purpose of assisting him in discharging his functions.

16. Proceedings to be held in earner : If the Magistrate considers that the circumstances of the case so warrant, and if either party to the proceedings so desires, he may conduct the proceedings under this Act in camera.

17. Right to reside in a shared household : 1) Not with-

standing anything contained in any other law for the time being in force, every woman in a domestic relationship shall have the right to reside in the shared household, whether or not she has any right, title or beneficial interest in the same.

2) The aggrieved person shall not be evicted or excluded from the shared household or any part of it by the respondent save in accordance with the procedure established by law.

18. Protection orders : The Magistrate may, after giving the aggrieved person and the respondent an opportunity of being heard and on being prima facie satisfied that domestic violence has taken place or is likely to take place, pass a protection order in favour of the aggrieved person and prohibit the respondent from -

a) committing any act of domestic violence;

b) aiding or abetting in the commission of acts of domestic violence,

c) entering the place of employment of the aggrieved person or, if the person aggrieved is a child, its school or any other place frequently by the aggrieved person;

d) attempting to communicate in any form, whatsoever, with the aggrieved person, including personal, oral or written or electronic or telephonic contact;

e) alienating any assets, operating bank lockers or bank accounts used or held or enjoyed by both the parties, jointly by the aggrieved person and the respondent or singly by the respondent, including her stridhan or any other property held either jointly by the parties or separately by them without the leave of the Magistrate;

f) causing violence to the dependents, other relatives or any person who give the aggrieved person assistance from domestic violence;,

g) committing any other act as specified in the protection order.

19. Residence orders : 1) While disposing of an application under sub-section (1) of Section 12, the

Magistrate may, on being satisfied that domestic violence has taken place, pass a resident order-

a) restraining the respondent from dispossessing or in any other manner disturbing the possession of the aggrieved person from the shared household, whether or not the respondent has a legal or equitable interest in the shared household;

b) directing the respondent to remove himself from the shared household;

c) restraining the respondent or any of his relatives from entering any portion of the shared household in which the aggrieved person resides;

d) restraining the respondent from alienating or disposing off the shared household or encumbering the same;

e) restraining the respondent from renouncing his rights in the shared household except with the leave of the Magistrate; or

f) directing the Respondent to secure same level of alternate accommodation for the aggrieved person as enjoyed by her in the shared house hold or to pay rent for the same, if the circumstances so require:

Provided that no order under clause (b) shall be passed against any person who is a woman.

2) The Magistrate may impose any additional conditions or pass any other direction which he may deem reasonably necessary to protect or to provide for the safety of the aggrieved person or any child of such aggrieved person.

3) the Magistrate may require from the respondent to execute a bond, with or without sureties, for preventing the commission of domestic violence.

4) an order under sub-section (3) shall be deemed to be an order under Chapter VIII of the Code of Criminal Procedure, 1973 (2 of 1974) and shall be

2) the monetary relief granted under this section shall be adequate, fair and reasonable and consistent with the standard of living to which the aggrieved person is accustomed.

3) The Magistrate shall have the power to order an appropriate lump-sum payment or monthly payments of maintenance, as the nature and circumstances of the case may require.

4) the Magistrate shall send a copy of the order for monetary relief made under sub-section (1) to the parties to the application and to the in-charge of the police station within the local limits of whose jurisdiction the respondent resides.

5) The Respondent shall pay the monetary relief granted to the aggrieved person within the period specified in the order under sub-section (1).

6) Upon the failure on the part of the respondent to make payment in terms of the order under sub-section (1), the Magistrate may direct the employer or a debtor of the respondent, to directly pay to the aggrieved person or to deposit with the Court a portion of the wages or salaries or debt due to or accrued to the credit of the respondent, which amount may be adjusted towards the monetary relief payable by the respondent.

21. Custody orders : Notwithstanding anything contained in any other law for the time being in force. The Magistrate may, at any stage of hearing of the application for protection order or for any other relief under this Act grant temporary custody of any child or children to the aggrieved person or the person making an application on her behalf and specify, if necessary, the arrangements for visit of such child or children by the respondent; Provided that if the Magistrate is of the opinion that any visit of the respondent may be harmful to the interests of the child or children. The Magistrate shall refuse to allow such visit.

22. Compensation orders : In addition to other relief as may be granted under this Act, the Magistrate may on an application being made by the aggrieved person, pass an order dircting the respondent to pay compensation and damages for the injuries, including mental torture and emotional distress, caused by the acts of domestic violence committed by that respondent.

23. Power to grant interim and ex parte orders :

1) In any proceeding before him under this Act, the Magistrate may pass such interim order as he deems just and

proper.

2) If the Magistrate is satisfied that an appliction prima facie discloses that the respondent is committing, or has committed an act of domestic violence or that there is a likelihood that the Respondent may commit an act of domestic violence, he may grant an ex parte order on the basis of the affidavit in such form, as may be prescribed, of the aggrieved person under Section 18, Section 19, Section 20, Section 21 or, as the case may be, Section 22 against the respondent.

24. Court to give copies of order free of cost: The Magistrate shall, in all cases where he has passed any order under this Act, order that a copy fo such order,

shall be given free of cost, to the parties to the application, the police officer-in-charge of the police station in the jurisdiction of which the Magistrate has been approached, and any servie provider located within the local limits of the jurisdiction of the Court and if any service provider has registered a doemstic incident report, to that
service provider.

25. Duration and alteration of orders. - 1) A protection order made under Section 18 shall be in force till the aggrieved person applies for discharge.

2) If the Magistrate, on receipt of an application from the aggrieved person or the respondent, is satisfied that there is a change in the circumstances requiring alteration, modification or revocation of any order made under this Act, he may, for reasons to be recorded in writing pass such order, as he may deem appropriate.

26. Relief in other suits and legal proceedings. - (1) any relief available under Sections 18,19, 20, 21 and 22 may also be sought in any legal proceeding before a civil Court, family Court or a Criminal Court, affecting the aggrieved person and the respondent whether such proceeding was initiated before or after the commencement of this Act.

2) Any relief referred to in sub-section (1) may be sought for in addition to and along with any other relief that the aggrieved person may seek in such suit or legal proceeding before a Civil or Criminal Court.

3) In case any relief has been obtained by the aggrieved person in any proceedings other than a proceeding under this Act, she shall be bound to inform the Magistrate of the grant of such relief.

27. Jurisdiction : 1) The Court of Judicial Magistrate of the first class or the Metropolitan Magistrate, as the case may be, within the local limits of which -

a) the person aggrieved permanently or temporarily resides or carries on business or is employed; or

b) the respondent resides or carries on business is employed; or

c) the cause of action has arisen,

shall be the competent Court to grant a protection order and other orders under this Act and to try offences under this Act.

2) Any order made under this Act shall be enforceable throughout India.

28. Procedure : 1) Save as otherwise provided in this Act, all proceedings under Sections 12, 18, 19, 20, 21,22 and 23 and offences under Section 31 shall be governed by the provisions of the Code of Criminal Procedure, 1973 (2 of 1974)

2) Nothing in sub-section (1) shall prevent the Court from laying down its own procedure for disposal of an applciation under Section 12 or under Subsection (2) of Section 23.

29. Appeal: There shall lie an appeal to the Court of Session within thirty days from the date on which the order made by the Magistrate is served on the aggrieved person or the respondent, as the case may be, whichever is later.

CHAPTER V MISCELLANEOUS

30. Protection Officers and members of service provides to be public servants. - The Protection Officers and members of service providers, while acting or purporting to act in pursuance of any of the provisions of this Act or any rules or orders made there under shall be deemed to be public servants within the meaning of Section 21 of the Indian Penal Code (45 of 1860).

31. Penalty for breach of protection order by Respondent

1) A breach of protection order, or of any interim protection order, by the respondent shall be an offence under this Act and shall be punishable with imprisonment of

either description for a term which may extend to one year, or with fine which may extend to twenty thousand rupees, or with both.

2) The offence under sub-section (1) shall as far as practicable be tried by the Magistrate who had passed the order, the breach of which has been alleged to have been caused by the accused.

3) While framing charges under sub-section (1), the Magistrate may also frame charges under Section 498-A of the Indian Penal Code (45 of 1860) or any other provision of that Code or the Dowry Prohibition Act, 1961 (28 of 1961), as the case may be, if the facts disclose the commission of an offence under those provisions.

32. Cognizance and proof.: 1) Notwithstanding anything contained in the Code of Criminal Procedure, 1973 (2 of 1974), the offence under sub-section (1) of Section 31 shall be cognizable and non-bailable. 2) Upon the sole testimony of the aggrieved person, the court may conclude that an offence under subsection (1) of Section 31 has been committed by the accused.

33. Penalty for not discharging duty by Protrection Officer : If any Protectiion Officer fails or refuses to discharges his duties as directed by the Magistrate in the protection order without any sufficient cause, he shall be punished with imprisonment of either description for a term which may extend to one year, or with fine which may extend to twenty thousand rupees, or with both.

34. Cognizance of offence committed by Protection Officer : No prosecution or other legal proceeding shall lie against the Protection Officer unless a complaint is filed with the previous sanction of the State Government or an officer authorized by it in this behalf.

35. Protection of action taken in good faith. : No suit. prosecution or other legal proceeding shall lie against the Protection Officer for any damage caused or likely to be caused by anything which is in good faith done or intended to be done under this Act or any rule or order made thereunder.

36. Act not in derogation of any other law : The provisions of this Act Act shall be in addition to, and not in derogation of the provisions of any other law, for the time being in force.

37. Power of Central Government to make rules : 1) The Central Government may, by notification, make rules for carrying out the provisions of this Act. 2) In particular, and without prejudice to the generality of the foregoing power, such rules may provide for all or any of the following matters, namely:-a) the qualifications and experience which a Protection Officer shall posses under sub-section (2) of

Section 8;

b) the terms and conditions of service of the Protection Officers and the other officers subordinate to him, under sub-section (3) of Section 8;

c) the form and manner in which a domestic incident report may be made under clause (b) of sub-section (1) of Section 9;

d) the form and the manner in which an application for protection order may be made to the Magistrate under clause (c) of sub-section (1) of Section

9;

e) the form in which a complaint is to be filed under clause (d) of sub-section (1) of Section 9;

f) the other duties to be performed by the Protection Officer under clause (i) of sub-section (1) of Section 9;

g) the rules regulating registration of service providers under sub-section (1) of Section 10;

h) the form in which an application under sub-section (1) of Section 12 seeking relief's under this Act may be made and the particulars which such application shall contain under sub-section (2) of that

i)j)

k) 1)

section;

the means of serving notices under sub-section (1) of Section 13;

the form of declaration of service of notice to be made by the Protection Officer under Sub Section (2) of Section 13;

the qualifications and experience in counseling which a member of the service provider shall possess under sub-section (1) of Section 14;

the form in which an affidavit may be filed by the aggrieved person under sub-section (2) of Section 23; m) any other matter which has to be, or may be, pre-

scribed. 3) Every rule made under this Act shall be laid, as

soon as may be after it is made, before each House of Parliament, while it is in session for a total period of thirty days which may be comprised in one session or in two or more successive sessions, and if, before the expiry of the session immediately following the session or the successive sessions aforesaid, both Houses agree in making any modification in the rule or both Houses agree that the rule should not be made, the rule shall thereafter have effect only in such modified form or be of no effect, as the case may be; so, however, that any such modification or annulment shall be without prejudice to the validity of anything previously done under that rule dealt with accordingly.

5) While passing an order under sub-section (1), sub-section (2) or sub-section (3), the Court may also pass an order directing the officer-in charge of the nearest police station to give protection to the aggrieved person or to assist her or the person making an application on her behalf in the implementation of the order.

6) While making an order under sub-section (1), the Magistrate may impose on the respondent obligations relating to the discharge of rent and other payments, having regard to the financial needs and resources of the parties.

7) The Magistrate may direct the officer-in-charge of the police station in whose jurisdiction the Magistrate has been approached to assist in the implementation of the protecting order.

8) The Magistrate may direct the respondent to return to the possession of the aggrieved person her stridhan or any other property or valuable security to which she is entitled to.

20. Monetary reliefs. (1) While disposing of an application under sub-section (1) of Section 12, the Magistrate may direct the respondent to pay monetary relief to meet the expenses incurred and losses suffered by the aggrieved person and any child of the aggrieved person as a result of the domestic violence and such relief may include but is not limited to,-

a) the loss of earnings;

b) the medical expenses;

c) the loss caused due to the destruction, damage or removal of any property from the control-of the aggrieved person, and

d) the maintenance for the aggrieved person as well as her children, if any, including an order under or in addition to an order of maintenance under Section 125 of the Code of Criminal Procedure, 1973 (2 of 1974) or any other law for the time being in.

PROTECTION OF WOMEN FROM DOSMESTIC VIOLENCE ACT 2005

ACT

There has been a new enactment recently coverings topic of domestic viol even in fact no doubt there are other provisions in IPC which seeks to punish beating or violence in normal circumstances. However, the legislature rightly thought that these provisions are too general and cannot meet the special circumstances in which the house wife normally placed.

Domestic Violence is a kind of its own and therefore rightly needs a needed enactment . It is common knowledge that violence against women is mostly committed in four corners of residential houses,. Many a times witnesses are not available for such phelonail acts . It is very difficult to find a witness even amongst neighbours who can really an be eye witness with to such crimes unfortunately, Inspite of several matrimonial and Criminal Law the instances of Domestic Violence are ever increased . The offence naturally been committed inside the house cannot be witnessed by closest neigh. It is bounded to result the accused getting of the crime . It is for this reason the special enactment has now been passed to get punishment for Domestic Violence against women.

This enactment not only provide punish for D.V. against women. it contains other salutary provisions of law like appointment of protection officers, service providers, shelter homes of counselors. Domestic Violence is the worst of crime being naturally clandestinely committed without possibility of express, such enactment is no doubt the need of the hour.

In the said enactment the new terminology was introduced for example 'domestic' relationship, protection order, residence order, shared household etc.

This Act has invested jurisdiction with magi to entertain any application for compensation, damages. The magi can direct counseling at any stage of proceeding.

The right to rigid in a shared household is in fact a secured provision to give a right to have shelter even after matrimonial dispute. For this purpose the magi can pass residence orders, custody orders of child, protection orders etc.

If we evaluate these provisions are can see that the jurisdiction given to the magi is an add form for the aggrieved too men. However, I think that add may require them to move on toe from family court, Civil Court and Criminal Courts. The magi Courts and this add jurisdiction may metric the proceedings and also can be misused. So the very successful implementation will be at peril.

The Various Reports on Gender Equality[163]:-

The Universal Declaration of Human Rights (UDHR) adopted has formed the basis for the development of international human rights instruments.

Article 2 status that

"Everyone is entitled to all rights and freedoms set forth in the declaration, without distinction of any kind, such as race, colour, sex language, religious, political or other opinion national or social origin, property, birth or other status."

Article 3 status that,

"Everyone has the right to life, liberty and security of the persons."

According to article 5,

"No one shall be subjected to torture or to cruel, inhuman or degrading treatment and punishment."

Articles 2, 3, & 5 if taken together means that any form of violence against women which can be constructed as a threat to her life, liberty or security of person in which can constitutes torture for cruel,

[163] Violence against women by Dr. Poornima Advani.

inhuman or degrading treatment violates the principles of the universal Declaration and the international obligations of members states.

The International covenants on Civil & Political Rights (ICCPR) adopted in 1966 & the international covenant of economie, social & cultural Rights (ICESCR) also adopted in 1966, like wise prohibit violence against women.

In 1993, the united Nations, General assembly adopted the Declaration on Elimination of violence against women.

Of the declaration affirms that violence against women both violates & impairs or nullifies the enjoyment of women of their human rights & fundamental freedom & is concerned about the longstanding failure to protect & to promote those rights & freedoms in relation to violence against women.

Of the preamble to the Declaration clearly reacquires that –

Violence against women is an abstract to the achievement of equality, development & peace, "expressing alarm that opportunities for women to achieve legal, social, political & economical equality in society are limited by continuing & endemic violence."

The Empowerment of women – Indian respectivel[164]

The principle of gender equality is enshrined in the Indian constitution in its preamble, Fundamental Rights, Fundamental Duties & Directive principles. The constitution not only grants equality to women, but also empowers the State to adopt measures of positive discrimination in favour of women.

Within the framework of a democratic polity, our laws, development polices, plans & programmes have aimed at women's advancement in different spheres. From the fifth five year plan (1974-78) onwards to women's issues from welfare to development. In recent years, the empowerment of women has been recognized as the central issue in determining the status of women of the National Commission for women was set up by an Act of parliament to safeguard the rights & legal entitlements of women.

The Mexico plan of Action (1975) Nairobi Forward hooking strategies (1985) the Beijing Declaration as well as the platform for action (1995)

---

[164] A decade of women empowerment initiatives—Bejjing+5 and beyond—By Dr.Najama Heptulla

& the outcome Documents adopted by the UNGA session on Gender equality & Development & peace for the 21st Century, titled "Further actions & initiatives to implement for Action" have been unreservedly endorsed by India for appropriate follow up.

The policy also takes note of the commitments of the Ninth Five year plan & the other sectoral polices relating to empowerment of women.

The women's movements & a wide spread network of non-Government organizations which have strong grassroots presence & deep insight into women's concerns have contributed in inspiring initiatives for the empowerment of women.

However, there will exists a wide gap between the goals enunciated in the institution, legislation, policies, plans, programmes & related mechanisms on the one hand & the women in India on the other. This has been analyzed extensively in the Report of the committee on the status of Women in India, "Towards Equality". 1974 & highlighted in the national perspective plan for women 1988 & the platform for Action. Five years after an assessment.

Dr. Najma Heptulla in her article further writes that, Gender disparity manifests itself in various forms, the most obvious being the trend of continuously declining female ratio in the population in the last few decades. Social stereotyping & violence at the domestic & societal levels are some of the other manifestations. Discrimination against girl children, adolescent girls & women persists in parts of the country.

The goal of this policy is to bring about the advancement, development & empowerment of women. The policy will be widely disseminated so as to encourage active participation of all stakeholders for achieving its goals specifically, the objectives of this policy includes –

i) Creating an environment through positive economic & social policies for full development of women to enable them to realize their full potent.

ii) The de jure & de facto enjoyment of all human rights & fundamental freedom by women on equal basis with men in all spheres – political, economic, social, cultural & civil.

iii) Equal access to participation & decision making of women in social, political & economic life of the nation.

iv) Equal access to women to health case quality education at all levels, career & vocational guidance. Employment, equal remuneration, occupational health & softy social security & public office etc.

v) Strengthening legal system aimed at elimination of all forms of discrimination against women.

vi) Changing societal attitudes & community matrices by active participation & involvement of both men & women.

vii) Mainstreaming a gender perspective in the development process.

viii) Elimination of discrimination & all forms of violence against women & the girl child.

ix) Building & strengthening partnerships with civil society, particularly women's organizations.

Over the last 10 years gender sensitization of a traditionally make dominated society have been intensified sensitization of the law enforcement agencies, especially police and the judiciary through periodic training given both by government agencies & NGO's.

Positive & Negative Impact of Globalization –

Women have gained in new avenues, for example, in Information Technology, there are mainly urban & educated women. However, an adverse impact on women's livelihood, such as in agriculture has been reported from different parts of the country. key areas of concern include women in small subsistence farming households, women workers in government and textiles who will face increase competition after the phasing out of the Multi Fiber Agreement in 2005 & women displaced by new technologies in sectors such as construction, which have traditionally absorbed large numbers of women. Government, NGO & Civil society partnership have been crucial in the in march towards women's equality so far, and they will play a critical role in facing the new challenges that have emerged.

CEDAW (Convention on the Elimination of Discrimination Against Women)[165]

Legal movement towards equality for women has really come with the Convention on the Elimination of Discrimination Against Women (CEDAW). CEDAW contains wide-ranging and concrete equality guarantees including :

- State obligation to eliminate discrimination against women (art.2)
- Ensure women's full development and advancement (art.3)
- Eliminate discriminatory customs, practices, stereotypes and notions of superiority/inferiority of either sex (art.5)
- Suppress traffic in and exploitation of women (art.6)
- Promote equality in political and public life (art. 7)
- Eliminate educational discrimination (art. 10)
- Employment (art. 11-1)
- Health care (art. 12)
- Economics & social law (art. 15)

---

[165] Judicial Colloquia on Gender and Law - 2001

- Prohibits discrimination in marriage and family (art. 16)
- Maternity rights guaranteed (art. 11-2,3)

More specifically, Recommendation # 19 of CEDAW (1992) specifically declares Violence Against Women as discrimination and describes gender-based violence as "violence that is directed against a woman because she is a woman or that affects women disproportionately."

FACTS ABOUT GENDER :

Where gender equality exists, the gender development index and human development index will be the same. The greater the gender disparity in basic human development, the lower is a country's GDI (gender development index) compared with its HDI (human development Index). Across the board, all countries GDI was lower than HDI disclosing global gender inequality.

Gender empowerment measures (GEM) exposes inequality in economic and political opportunity areas i.e. political life, management, and technical areas

Trinidad and Tobago outperform Italy and Japan on the GEM

The Message-high income is not a prerequisite to creating opportunities for women.

(Source : Human Development Report 2001)

VIOLENCE AGAINST WOMEN :

- Around the world, at least one in every three women has been beaten, coerced into sex, or abused in some other way – most often by someone she knows, including by her husband or another made family member; one woman in four has been abused during preganancy.
- Psychological abuse almost always accompanies physical abuse. In addition, one third to one half of all cases involve sexual abuse. A high proportion of women who are beaten are subjected to violence repeatedly.
- At least 60 million girls who would otherwise be expected to be alive are "missing" from various populations, mostly in Asia, as a result of sex-selective abortions, infanticide or neglect;
- Studies suggest domestic violence is widespread in most societies and is a frequent cause of suicides among women;

- Rape and other forms of sexual violence are increasing. Many rapes go unreported because of the stigma and trauma associated with them and the lack of sympathetic treatment from legal systems. Estimates of the proportion of rapes reported to authorities very – from less than 3 per cent in South Africa 16 per cent in the United States;
- Two million girls between ages 5 and 15 are introduced into the commercial sex market each year;
- At least 130 million women have been forced to undergo female genital mutilation or cutting; another 2 million are at risk each year from this degrading and dangerous practice;
- So-called "honour" killings take the lives of thousands of young women every year, mainly in Western Asia, North Africa and parts of South Asia. At least 1,000 women were murdered in Pakistan in 1999.
- In the United States, a woman is battered usually by her intimate partner, every 15 seconds.

(Source : State of the World's Population : 2001)

NATIONAL POLICY FOR THE EMPOWERMENT OF WOMEN
(2001)

Introduction

The principle of gender equality is enshrined in the Indian Constitution in its Preamble, Fundamental Rights, Fundamental Duties and Directive Principles. The Constitution not only grants equality to women, but also empowers the State to adopt measures of positive discrimination in favour of women.

Within the framework of a democratic polity, our laws, development policies, Plans and programmes have aimed at women's advancement in different spheres. From the Fifth Five Year Plan (1974-78) onwards has been a marked shift in the approach to women's issues from welfare to development. In recent years, the empowerment of women has been recognized as the central issue in determining the status of women. The National Commission for Women was set up by an Act of Parliament in 1990 to safeguard the rights and legal entitlements of women. The 73rd and 74th Amendments (1993) to the Constitution of India have provided for reservation of seats in the local bodies of Panchayats and Municipalities for women, laying a strong foundation for their participation in decision making at the local levels.

1.3 India has also ratified various international conventions and human rights instruments committing to secure equal rights of women. Key among them is the ratification of the Convention on Elimination of All Forms of Discrimination Against Women (CEDAW) in 1993.

1.4 The Mexico Plan of Action (1975), the Nairobi Forward Looking Strategies (1985), the Beijing Declaration as well as the Platform for Action (1995) and the Outcome Document adopted by the UNGA Session on Gender Equality and Development & Peace for the 21st century, titled "Further actions and initiatives to implement the Beijing Declaration and the Platform for

Action" have been unreservedly endorsed by India for appropriate follow up.

1.5 The Policy also takes note of the commitments of the Ninth Five Year Plan and the other Sectoral Policies relating to empowerment of Women.

1.6 The women's movement and a wide-spread network of non-Government Organisations which have strong grass-roots presence and deep insight into women's concerns have contributed in inspiring initiatives for the empowerment of women.

1.7 However, there still exists a wide gap between the goals enunciated in the Constitution, legislation, policies, plans, programmes, and related mechanisms on the one hand and the situational reality of the status of women in India, on the other. This has been analyzed extensively in the Report of the Committee on the Status of Women in India, "Towards Equality", 1974 and highlighted in the National Perspective Plan for Women, 1988-2000, the Shramshakti Report, 1988 and the Platform for Action, Five Years After- An assessment"

1.8 Gender disparity manifests itself in various forms, the most obvious being the trend of continuously declining female ratio in the population in the last few decades. Social stereotyping and violence at the domestic and societal levels are some of the other manifestations. Discrimination against girl children, adolescent girls and women persists in parts of the country.

1.9 The underlying causes of gender inequality are related to social and economic structure, which is based on informal and formal norms, and practices.

1.10 Consequently, the access of women particularly those belonging to weaker sections including Scheduled Castes/Scheduled Tribes/ Other backward Classes and minorities, majority of whom are in the rural areas and in the informal, unorganized sector – to education, health and productive resources, among others, is inadequate. Therefore, they remain largely marginalized, poor and socially excluded.

Goal and Objectives

1.11 The goal of this Policy is to bring about the advancement, development and empowerment of women. The Policy will be widely disseminated so as to encourage active participation of all stakeholders for achieving its goals. Specifically, the objectives of this Policy include

(i) Creating an environment through positive economic and social policies for full development of women to enable them to realize their full potential

(ii) The *de-jure* and *de-facto* enjoyment of all human rights and fundamental freedom by women on equal basis with men in all spheres – political, economic, social, cultural and civil

(iii) Equal access to participation and decision making of women in social, political and economic life of the nation

(iv) Equal access to women to health care, quality education at all levels, career and vocational guidance, employment, equal remuneration, occupational health and safety, social security and public office etc.,

(v) Strengthening legal systems aimed at elimination of all forms of discrimination against women

(vi) Changing societal attitudes and community practices by active participation and involvement of both men and women.

(vii) Mainstreaming a gender perspective in the

development process.

(viii) Elimination of discrimination and all forms of violence against women and the girl child; and

(ix) Building and strengthening partnerships with civil society, particularly women's organizations.

Policy Prescriptions

Judicial Legal Systems

Legal-judicial system will be made more responsive and gender sensitive to women's needs, especially in cases of domestic violence and personal assault. New laws will be enacted and existing laws reviewed to ensure that justice is quick and the punishment meted out to the culprits is commensurate with the severity of the offence.

2.2 At the initiative of and with the full participation of all stakeholders including community and religious leaders, the Policy would aim to encourage changes in personal laws such as those related to marriage, divorce, maintenance and guardianship so as to eliminate discrimination against women.

2.3 The evolution of property rights in a patriarchal system has contributed to the subordinate status of women. The Policy would aim to encourage changes in laws relating to ownership of property and inheritance by evolving consensus in order to make them gender just.

Decision Making

3.1 Women's equality in power sharing and active participation in decision making, including decision making in political process at all levels will be ensured for the achievement of the goals of empowerment. All measures will be taken to guarantee women equal access to and full participation in decision making bodies at every level, including the legislative, executive, judicial, corporate, statutory bodies, as also the advisory Commissions, Committees, Boards, Trusts etc. Affirmative action such as reservations/quotas, including in higher legislative bodies, will be considered whenever necessary on a time bound basis. Women–friendly personnel policies will also be drawn up to encourage women to participate effectively in the developmental process.

Mainstreaming a Gender Perspective in the Development Process

4.1 Policies, programmes and systems will be established to ensure mainstreaming of women's perspectives in all developmental processes, as catalysts, participants and recipients. Wherever there are gaps in policies and programmes, women specific interventions would be undertaken to bridge these. Coordinating and monitoring mechanisms will also be devised to assess from time to time the progress of such mainstreaming mechanisms. Women's issues and concerns as a result will specially be addressed and reflected in all concerned laws, sectoral policies, plans and programmes of action.

Economic Empowerment of women

Poverty Eradication

5.1 Since women comprise the majority of the population below the poverty line and are very often in situations of extreme poverty, given the harsh realities of intra-household and social discrimination, macro economic policies and poverty eradication programmes will specifically address the needs and problems of such women. There will be improved implementation of programmes which are already women oriented with special targets for women. Steps will be taken for mobilization of poor women and convergence of services, by offering them a range of economic and social options, along with necessary support measures to enhance their capabilities

Micro Credit

5.2 In order to enhance women's access to credit for consumption and production, the establishment of new, and strengthening of existing micro-credit mechanisms and micro-finance institution will be undertaken so that the outreach of credit is enhanced. Other supportive measures would be taken to ensure adequate flow of credit through extant financial institutions and banks, so that all women below poverty line have easy access to credit.

Women and Economy

5.3 Women's perspectives will be included in designing and implementing macro-economic and social policies by institutionalizing their participation in such processes. Their contribution to socio-economic development as producers and workers will be recognized in the formal and informal sectors (including home based workers) and appropriate policies relating to employment and to her working conditions will be drawn up. Such measures could include:

Reinterpretation and redefinition of conventional concepts of work wherever necessary e.g. in the Census records, to reflect women's contribution as producers and workers.

Preparation of satellite and national accounts.

Development of appropriate methodologies for undertaking (i) and (ii) above.

Globalization

Globalization has presented new challenges for the realization of the goal of women's equality, the gender impact of which has not been systematically evaluated fully. However, from the micro-level studies that were commissioned by the Department of Women & Child Development, it is evident that there is a need for re-framing policies for access to employment and quality of employment. Benefits of the growing global economy have been unevenly distributed leading to wider economic disparities, the feminization of poverty, increased gender inequality through often deteriorating working conditions and unsafe working environment especially in the informal economy and rural areas. Strategies will be designed to enhance the capacity of women and empower them to meet the negative social and economic impacts, which may flow from the globalization process.

Women and Agriculture

5.5 In view of the critical role of women in the agriculture and allied sectors, as producers, concentrated efforts will be made to ensure that benefits of training, extension and various programmes will reach them in proportion to their numbers. The programmes for training women in soil conservation, social forestry, dairy development and other occupations allied to agriculture like horticulture, livestock including small animal husbandry, poultry, fisheries etc. will be expanded to benefit women workers in the agriculture sector.

Women and Industry

5.6 The important role played by women in electronics, information technology and food processing and agro industry and textiles has been crucial to the development of these sectors. They would be given comprehensive support in terms of labour legislation, social security and other support services to participate in various industrial sectors.

5.7 Women at present cannot work in night shift in

factories even if they wish to. Suitable measures will be taken to enable women to work on the night shift in factories. This will be accompanied with support services for security, transportation etc.

Support Services

5.8 The provision of support services for women, like child care facilities, including crèches at work places and educational institutions, homes for the aged and the disabled will be expanded and improved to create an enabling environment and to ensure their full cooperation in social, political and economic life. Women-friendly personnel policies will also be drawn up to encourage women to participate effectively in the developmental process.

Social Empowerment of Women

Education

6.1 Equal access to education for women and girls will be ensured. Special measures will be taken to eliminate discrimination, universalize education, eradicate illiteracy, create a gender-sensitive educational system, increase enrolment and retention rates of girls and improve the quality of education to facilitate life-long learning as well as development of occupation/vocation/technical skills by women. Reducing the gender gap in secondary and higher education would be a focus area. Sectoral time targets in existing policies will be achieved, with a special focus on girls and women, particularly those belonging to weaker sections including the Scheduled Castes / Scheduled Tribes / Other Backward Classes / Minorities. Gender sensitive curricula would be developed at all levels of educational system in order to address sex stereotyping as one of the causes of gender discrimination.

Health

6.2 A holistic approach to women's health which includes both nutrition and health services will be adopted and special attention will be given to the needs of women and the girl at all stages of the life cycle. The reduction of infant mortality and maternal mortality, which are sensitive indicators of human development, is a priority concern. This policy reiterates the national demographic goals for Infant Mortality Rate (IMR), Maternal Mortality Rate (MMR) set out in the National Population Policy 2000. Women should have access to comprehensive, affordable and quality health care. Measures will be adopted that take into account the reproductive rights of women to enable them to exercise informed choices, their vulnerability to sexual and health problems together with endemic, infectious and communicable diseases such as malaria, TB, and water borne diseases as well as hypertension and cardio-pulmonary diseases. The social, developmental and health consequences of HIV/AIDS and other sexually transmitted diseases will be tackled from a gender perspective.

6.3 To effectively meet problems of infant and maternal mortality, and early marriage the availability of good and accurate data at micro level on deaths, birth and marriages is required. Strict implementation of registration of births and deaths would be ensured and registration of marriages would be made compulsory.

6.4 In accordance with the commitment of the National Population Policy (2000) to population stabilization, this Policy recognizes the critical need of men and women to have access to safe, effective and affordable methods of family planning of their choice and the need to suitably address the issues of early marriages and spacing of children. Interventions such as spread of education, compulsory registration of marriage and special programmes like BSY should impact on delaying the age of marriage so that by 2010 child marriages are eliminated.

6.5 Women's traditional knowledge about health care and nutrition will be recognized through proper documentation and its use will be encouraged. The use of Indian and alternative systems of medicine will be enhanced within the framework of overall health infrastructure available for women.

Nutrition

6.6 In view of the high risk of malnutrition and disease that women face at all the three critical stages viz., infancy and childhood, adolescent and reproductive phase, focussed attention would be paid to meeting the nutritional needs of women at all stages of the life cycle. This is also important in view of the critical link between the health of adolescent girls, pregnant and lactating women with the health of infant and young children. Special efforts will be made to tackle the problem of macro and micro nutrient deficiencies especially amongst pregnant and lactating women as it leads to various diseases and disabilities.

6.7 Intra-household discrimination in nutritional matters vis-à-vis girls and women will be sought to be ended through appropriate strategies. Widespread use of nutrition education would be made to address the issues of intra-household imbalances in nutrition and the special needs of pregnant and lactating women. Women's participation will also be ensured in the planning, superintendence and delivery of the system.

Drinking Water and Sanitation

6.8 Special attention will be given to the needs of women in the provision of safe drinking water, sewage disposal, toilet facilities and sanitation within accessible reach of households, especially in rural areas and urban slums.

Women's participation will be ensured in the planning, delivery and maintenance of such services.

Housing and Shelter

6.9 Women's perspectives will be included in housing policies, planning of housing colonies and provision of shelter both in rural and urban areas. Special attention will be given for providing adequate and safe housing and accommodation for women including single women, heads of households, working women, students, apprentices and trainees.

Environment

6.10 Women will be involved and their perspectives reflected in the policies and programmes for environment, conservation and restoration. Considering the impact of environmental factors on their livelihoods, women's participation will be ensured in the conservation of the environment and control of environmental degradation. The vast majority of rural women still depend on the locally available non-commercial sources of energy such as animal dung, crop waste and fuel wood. In order to ensure the efficient use of these energy resources in an environmental friendly manner, the Policy will aim at promoting the programmes of non-conventional energy resources. Women will be involved in spreading the use of solar energy, biogas, smokeless chulahs and other rural application so as to have a visible impact of these measures in influencing eco system and in changing the life styles of rural women.

Science and Technology

6.11 Programmes will be strengthened to bring about a greater involvement of women in science and technology. These will include measures to motivate girls to take up science and technology for higher education and also ensure that development projects with scientific and technical inputs involve women fully. Efforts to develop a scientific temper and awareness will also be stepped up. Special measures would be taken for their training in areas where they have special skills like communication and information technology. Efforts to develop appropriate technologies suited to women's needs as well as to reduce their drudgery will be given a special focus too.

Women in Difficult Circumstances

6.12 In recognition of the diversity of women's situations and in acknowledgement of the needs of specially disadvantaged groups, measures and programmes will be undertaken to provide them with special assistance. These groups include women in extreme poverty, destitute women, women in conflict situations, women affected by natural calamities, women in less developed regions, the disabled widows, elderly women, single women in difficult circumstances, women heading households, those displaced from employment, migrants, women who are victims of marital violence, deserted women and prostitutes etc.

Violence against women

7.1 All forms of violence against women, physical and mental, whether at domestic or societal levels, including those arising from customs, traditions or accepted practices shall be dealt with effectively with a view to eliminate its incidence. Institutions and mechanisms/schemes for assistance will be created and strengthened for prevention of such violence , including sexual harassment at work place and customs like dowry; for the rehabilitation of the victims of violence and for taking effective action against the perpetrators of such violence. A special emphasis will also be laid on programmes and measures to deal with trafficking in women and girls.

Rights of the Girl Child

8.1 All forms of discrimination against the girl child and violation of her rights shall be eliminated by undertaking strong measures both preventive and punitive within and outside the family. These would relate specifically to strict enforcement of laws against prenatal sex selection and the practices of female feticide, female infanticide, child marriage, child abuse and child prostitution etc. Removal of discrimination in the treatment of the girl child within the family and outside and projection of a positive image of the girl child will be actively fostered. There will be special emphasis on the needs of the girl child and earmarking of substantial investments in the areas relating to food and nutrition, health and education, and in vocational education. In implementing programmes for eliminating child labour, there will be a special focus on girl children.

Mass Media

9.1 Media will be used to portray images consistent with human dignity of girls and women. The Policy will specifically strive to remove demeaning, degrading and negative conventional stereotypical images of women and violence against women. Private sector partners and media networks will be involved at all levels to ensure equal access for women particularly in the area of information and communication technologies. The media would be encouraged to develop codes of conduct, professional guidelines and other self regulatory mechanisms to remove gender stereotypes and promote balanced portrayals of women and men.

Operational Strategies

Action Plans

10.1 All Central and State Ministries will draw up time bound Action Plans for translating the Policy into a set of concrete actions, through a participatory process of consultation with Centre/State Departments of Women and Child Development and National /State Commissions for Women. The Plans will specifically including the following: -

i) Measurable goals to be achieved by 2010.

ii) Identification and commitment of resources.

iii) Responsibilities for implementation of action points.

iv) Structures and mechanisms to ensure efficient monitoring, review and gender impact assessment of action points and policies.

v) Introduction of a gender perspective in the budgeting process.

10.2 In order to support better planning and programme formulation and adequate allocation of resources, Gender Development Indices (GDI) will be developed by networking with specialized agencies. These could be analyzed and studied in depth. Gender auditing and development of evaluation mechanisms will also be undertaken along side.

10.3 Collection of gender disaggregated data by all primary data collecting agencies of the Central and State Governments as well as Research and Academic Institutions in the Public and Private Sectors will be undertaken. Data and information gaps in vital areas reflecting the status of women will be sought to be filled in by these immediately. All Ministries/Corporations/Banks and financial institutions etc will be advised to collect, collate, disseminate and maintain/publish data related to programmes and benefits on a gender disaggregated basis. This will help in meaningful planning and evaluation of policies.

Institutional Mechanisms

11.1 Institutional mechanisms, to promote the advancement of women, which exist at the Central and State levels, will be strengthened. These will be through interventions as may be appropriate and will relate to, among others, provision of adequate resources, training and advocacy skills to effectively influence macro-policies, legislation, programmes etc. to achieve the empowerment of women.

11.2 National and State Councils will be formed to oversee the operationalisation of the Policy on a regular basis. The National Council will be headed by the Prime Minister and the State Councils by the Chief Ministers and be broad in composition having representatives from the concerned Departments/Ministries, National and State Commissions for Women, Social Welfare Boards, representatives of Non-Government Organizations, Women's Organisations, Corporate Sector, Trade Unions, financing institutions, academics, experts and social activists etc. These bodies will review the progress made in implementing the Policy twice a year. The National Development Council will also be informed of the progress of the programme undertaken under the policy from time to time for advice and comments.

11.3 National and State Resource Centres on women will be established with mandates for collection and dissemination of information, undertaking research work, conducting surveys, implementing training and awareness generation programmes, etc. These Centers will link up with Women's Studies Centres and other research and academic institutions through suitable information networking systems.

11.4 While institutions at the district level will be strengthened, at the grass-roots, women will be helped by Government through its programmes to organize and strengthen into Self-Help Groups (SHGs) at the Anganwadi/Village/Town level. The women's groups will be helped to institutionalize themselves into registered societies and to federate at the Panchyat/Municipal level. These societies will bring about synergistic implementation of all the social and economic development programmes by drawing resources made available through Government and Non-Government channels, including banks and financial institutions and by establishing a close Interface with the Panchayats/ Municipalities.

Resource Management

12.1 Availability of adequate financial, human and market resources to implement the Policy will be managed by concerned Departments, financial credit institutions and banks, private sector, civil society and other connected institutions. This process will include:

(a) Assessment of benefits flowing to women and resource allocation to the programmes relating to them through an exercise of gender budgeting. Appropriate changes in policies will be made to optimize benefits to women under these schemes;

(b) Adequate resource allocation to develop and promote the policy outlined earlier based on (a) above by concerned Departments.

(c) Developing synergy between personnel of Health, Rural Development, Education and Women & Child Development Department at field level and other village level functionaries'

(d) Meeting credit needs by banks and financial credit institutions through suitable policy initiatives and development of new institutions in coordination with the Department of Women & Child Development.

12.2 The strategy of Women's Component Plan adopted in the Ninth Plan of ensuring that not less than 30% of benefits/funds flow to women from all Ministries and Departments will be implemented effectively so that the needs and interests of women and girls are addressed by all concerned sectors. The Department of Women and Child Development being the nodal Ministry will monitor and review the progress of the implementation of the Component Plan from time to time, in terms of both quality and quantity in collaboration with the Planning Commission.

12.3 Efforts will be made to channelize private sector investments too, to support programmes and projects for advancement of women

Legislation

13.1 The existing legislative structure will be reviewed and additional legislative measures taken by identified departments to implement the Policy. This will also involve a review of all existing laws including personal, customary and tribal laws, subordinate legislation, related rules as well as executive and administrative regulations to eliminate all gender discriminatory references. The process will be planned over a time period 2000-2003. The specific measures required would be evolved through a consultation process involving civil society, National Commission for Women and Department of Women and Child Development. In appropriate cases the consultation process would be widened to include other stakeholders too.

13.2 Effective implementation of legislation would be promoted by involving civil society and community. Appropriate changes in legislation will be undertaken, if necessary.

13.3 In addition, following other specific measures will be taken to implement the legislation effectively.

(a) Strict enforcement of all relevant legal provisions and speedy redressal of grievances will be ensured, with a special focus on violence and gender related atrocities.

(b) Measures to prevent and punish sexual harassment at the place of work, protection for women workers in the organized/ unorganized sector and strict enforcement of relevant laws such as Equal Remuneration Act and Minimum Wages Act will be undertaken,

(c) Crimes against women, their incidence, prevention, investigation, detection and prosecution will be regularly reviewed at all Crime Review fora and Conferences at the Central, State and District levels. Recognised, local, voluntary organizations will be authorized to lodge Complaints and facilitate registration, investigations and legal proceedings related to violence and atrocities against girls and women.

(d) Women's Cells in Police Stations, Encourage Women Police Stations Family Courts, Mahila Courts, Counselling Centers, Legal Aid Centers and Nyaya Panchayats will be strengthened and expanded to eliminate violence and atrocities against women.

(e) Widespread dissemination of information on all aspects of legal rights, human rights and other entitlements of women, through specially designed legal literacy programmes and rights information programmes will be

done.

Gender Sensitization

14.1 Training of personnel of executive, legislative and judicial wings of the State, with a special focus on policy and programme framers, implementation and development agencies, law enforcement machinery and the judiciary, as well as non-governmental organizations will be undertaken. Other measures will include:

(a) Promoting societal awareness to gender issues and women's human rights.

(b) Review of curriculum and educational materials to include gender education and human rights issues

(c) Removal of all references derogatory to the dignity of women from all public documents and legal instruments.

(d) Use of different forms of mass media to communicate social messages relating to women's equality and empowerment.

Panchayati Raj Institutions

15.1 The 73rd and 74th Amendments (1993) to the Indian Constitution have served as a breakthrough towards ensuring equal access and increased participation in political power structure for women. The PRIs will play a central role in the process of enhancing women's participation in public life. The PRIs and the local self Governments will be actively involved in the implementation and execution of the National Policy for Women at the grassroots level.

Partnership with the voluntary sector organizations

16.1 The involvement of voluntary organizations, associations, federations, trade unions, non-governmental organizations, women's organizations, as well as institutions dealing with education, training and research will be ensured in the formulation, implementation, monitoring and review of all policies and programmes affecting women. Towards this end, they will be provided with appropriate support related to resources and capacity building and facilitated to participate actively in the process of the empowerment of women.

International Cooperation

17.1 The Policy will aim at implementation of international obligations/commitments in all sectors on empowerment of women such as the Convention on All Forms of Discrimination Against Women (CEDAW), Convention on the Rights of the Child (CRC), International Conference on Population and Development (ICPD+5) and other such instruments. International, regional and sub-regional cooperation towards the empowerment of women will continue to be encouraged through sharing of experiences, exchange of ideas and technology, networking with institutions and organizations and through bilateral and multi-lateral partnerships.

www.oup.co.in [166]

[166] www.oup.co.in

List of relevant Indian laws relating to women[167] :

- Hindu Marriage Act, 1955
- The Special Marriage Act, 1954
- Hindu Succession Act, 1956
- Hindu Adoption and Maintenance Act, 1956
- The Child Marriage Restraint (Amendment) Act 1976
- The Factories Act, 1948, Mines act, 1952 and Plantation Labour Act, 1951
- The Employees State Insurance Act, 1948
- The Maternity Benefits Act, 1961
- The Factories (Amendment) Act 1976
- The Equal Remuneration Act, 1976
- The Contract Labour (Regulation and Abortion) Act, 1978
- The Dowry Prohibition Act, 1961
- The Immoral Trafic (Prevention) Act 1986
- Amendment to the Criminal Laws
- Family Courts
- Indecent Representation of Women (Prohibition) Act 1986
- The National Commission for Women Act, 1992

[167] Judicial colloquia on Gender and Law - 2001

The legal position thus effectively affirms and promotes the principles of equity and equality of women and takes care of their special needs.

The Department of Women & Child Development's major recent initiatives have aimed at ensuring better enforcement of all these laws as well as at amending them with the twin objectives of making them more stringent and therefore more effective in bridging the widely perceived gap between de facto and de jure status of woman and of removing any gender bias against women from these as well as other laws. Major new proposals have been made by the Department in respect of the following existing and new laws :

1. **Existing Laws**

- The Dowry Prohibition Act
- The Commission of Sati (Prevention) Act :
- The Indecent Representation of Women (Prohibition) Act; and
- The Immoral Traffic (Prevention) Act.

2. **New Laws concerning**

- Rape of Minor Girls
- Compulsory Registration of Marriages and
- Domestic Violence Against Women

CHAPTER VII

CONCLUSION AND SUGGESTIONS
(SPIRTUALLITY IN THE DOMAIN OF LAW)

CONCLUSION AND SUGGESTIONS

Woman is compassionate, courteous companion & complementary but not a commodity as she is being treated in this civilized era. It is said that, the civilization of the country is known by the fact, how woman in that country is being treated.

The preamble of our constitution unequivocally declares that, No more shall she be a dainty doll without her personality No more shall an unequal member barred from various pursuits because of her gender.

In order to achieve this goal, the gender equality & gender justice to women, the Government of India has initiated several programmes for empowering women. To this effect, the national commission for women was set up in 1990 by an act of parliament with the mandate to monitor the implementation of various programmers for women of having regard to the importance of education for women's equality, national policy on education 1986, the national communities on self employed women &

women in informal sector recommended in 1993 not only to impart mere literacy but to deliver education service which should lead the woman to deal with the question of equality, social justice & self confidence.

Even under the legal services Act 1987 Legal education seminar for women are organized in number of villages in districts in which the judges themselves deliver education service to rustic women. This is in fact a very innovative & effective step to make the woman cultured & civilized for empowering herself. We can see the importance of education in this shloka -

On circumspection the arena of my subject for thesis one may feel that what is in it as position of women in law is equal. However by this paper I want to conclude & suggest that the position of women in law is the result of changing social & economic scenario of society & only because of the judicial activism of our apex court & high courts, otherwise legislations would be dead letters.

Law & Public Opinion

'Law' is considered as reflection of public opinion in a changing society. India being a developing country due to globalization gives due regard to the public opinion in the form of law. Fortunately, the development in women's law in India is the reflection of the women's trait i.e. struggle. The anguish, agony, pathetic situation, mercilessness, domestic violence, cruelty, bride battering eve teasing molestative, prostitution, sexual harassment are unfortunately concerning female in patriarchal society. The women suffered, sacrificed & subjugated since years together at the hands of male dominated society. Of course, the course of law may have changed the nature of domination but it is there as everlasting.

Relief Through Public Interest litigation— PIL has played vital role in the development of women's law.

In early 1980's in Hussainara Vs. state of Bihar[168] the apex court has given a new facet

[168] AIR 1979 sc 1377

to directive principles by interpreting it in fundamental right under act 21.For example Equal pay for equal works, the rights of children & right to free legal aid as per Hussainara decision.

In Delhi Domestic workingwomen's forum vs. union of India[169] the Supreme Court has indicated the broad parameters in assisting the victims of rape. Which includes legal presentation to victims, legal assistance to victim at police station, direction was given to set up the criminal injuries compensation Board as contained under Act 38 CPI of constitution.

In Bodhi Satwa Gautam vs. Subhrato Chakrobarty[170] the apex court held,

"Rape is not only a crime against the person of a woman (victim) it is a crime against entire society. It is crime against basic human rights & is violative of the victims most cherished fundamental rights namely right to life."

---

[169] AIR 1993 sc 14

[170] AIR 1996 SC 922

The apex court in Chairman Railway Board VS Chandrima Das[171] referred the said decision.

Where Smt. Hanoofa Khatoon a Bangladeshi national was gang raped by many including employees of Railways in Yatri Niwas at Hawrah station. It was held; under Act 21 the state was under a constitutional libility to pay compensation to her & accord 10 lakhs compensation to this alive.

In Molai & Another's vs. state of M.P[172].

Accused raped a 16 years old girl when she was studying & causal sharp bodily injury on her private part & thrown away her body into septic tank. Held; it was rarest of rare case where capital punishment was rightly awarded.

The gap between equality as principle & equal treatment

The state has no doubt left no stone unturned to uplift the position of woman in domain of law. The principle of equality

[171] AIR 2000 988
[172] AIR 2000 sc 177

before law is accepted, enacted in all spheres of Law. But if we take a bird's eye view of all these Acts we have to say that there is gab between cup & tea. The state has given Armour to woman as to shield their rights but practically this Armour remains in the hands of man.

The development in woman's law is not due to sympathy or activism of the men in society but they have gained the same through constant struggle, after lot of humiliation & sufferings. The non-governmental organization (NGO's) played important role in it. And the foremost is that our horrible supreme court has stood firmly behind all these activities & incorporated the CEDAW treaty in Indian law as per Art 52 & 252 of the constitution.

The equality principles in scriptures :-

In Indian Mythology, the spiritual equality of man & woman is reflected during early stages of Srushti. Brahma expanded himself to the size of man & woman embracing each other & then his body split into two-satrupa-the woman & man. Brahma ordained that all future creates would be through twin forms of his own self.

Thus in Hindu Mythology women were considered equal in all respect. However their role is different. Shri Mataji[173] said, "women are potential & man is kynatic. The woman should stand behind man in any right decision. Both should respect each other & understand their roles. As two wheels are similar but left wheel cannot take place of right wheel women are creation of world."

Colonial law-

During colonial rule in India law was little responsive to the social needs. In fact with the advent of the British Rule the development of the native law came to half. So the custom of sati was allowed to perpetuate in society in the name of religion.

Women defiled & defamed in all ages—

The oppression of woman since ages together is a social phenomenon. However, in every ages the women were tortured & oppressed in different ways. Before

[173] www.adishakti.org

independence in 18th & 19th century Widows were at the receiving end. Due to child marriage many small girls were got married with a very old man of even 75 years. During that period epilogue of plague & other diseases made life dangerous. So the husband dies & the small wife (minor) became widow. The remarriage of widow were prohibited. So these small buds used to droop before they could flourish. There was a very disgusting custom of making baldness of hairs of widows. So these widows should not look good & were kept away from all materialist things & pleasure V.S.Khandekar in his novel has very pathetically elaborated all these things. In Marathi drama 'Sharda' the mismatch of minor bride with old bridegroom is depicted.

The widow had no right to adopt a child. The widow had right to keep properly for herself only for maintenance. Women's 'child-hood' was spoiled in the name of 'widowhood' in those days.

The doors of education were not opened to women so they were totally depended on their male counter part karta of family. In those days the women were not spoiled in society but in their own home by their in laws members. There were no platforms for the widows to cry for their spoiled chastity by their joint family members. The widows had a silence cry for their destiny & secondary position in their house & society.

During colonial days no doubt Britishers tried to stop such practices & the outcome was

1) Child marriage restraint Act 1929
2) Prevention of sati Act 1829
3) Widows remarriage Act 1856
4) Widows property Act 1937

During independence movement Maharshi Dhonde Keshav Karve, Mahatma Jyotiba Phule & Savitribai Phule took this cause on their shining agenda & the dawn has come in India for women's education movement. Savitribai took the cause of literacy of woman from this slavery for leading the march of women's liberation & empowerment. Thus position of woman in

Indian law during colonial period was very worst. The law had brought some social & economical changes in this period by enacting various laws relating to woman to lock the torturous custom by codifying laws.

Socio economic goal of the constitution :-

The independence of the country heralded a new era. The socio economic goal & the founding faiths of our nation were in corporate in the constitution. The family law in India was lagging behind social advancement. The British government did not take any substantial legislative measures in this regard for political reasons. So after independence Hindu marriage act 1956,Hindu succession Act 1956,Hindu minority & guardianship Act 1956,Special marriage Act 1954,were passed. Hindu marriage Act has been amended a number of times to meet the changing social outlook & requirements. These Acts without making complete break from the past introduce radical changes conforming to new ideas & requirements. Now the marriages are not inviolable. New matrimonial relief' have been provided. The female's rights in the matter of succession & proprietary rights have been made equal to that of males. Position of female has been improved in the matter of adoption to that of males. Dowry Prohibition (Amendment) Act 1986,to deal with social evil of dowry. Family courts Act 1884 have been enacted for the settiement of matrimonial disputes.

Moreover Andhra Pradesh, Maharashtra & Karnataka state brought amendment in Hindu succession Act 1956.This amendment confirms equal rights of inheritance to Hindu women along with men for achieving the constitutional mandate of equality. This important measure has eradicated the ills of dowry system. At the same time this piece of legislation ameliorating the condition of women in Hindu society.

For Christian women population, the ruling of Supreme Court in Marylyn's case is landmark. The ruling has brought the female Christian population of Kerala within the ambit of the Indian succession Act, applicable to all Christians. The Act provides for equality in succession to property.

For Muslim women the legal development march is in reverse direction because of passing of the Muslim women's (Protection of rights on Divorce) Act 1986.which denied divorced Muslim woman the protection under law that's available to woman of other communities in similar circumstances.

Socio Eco position of woman in Early 1980's :-

I have already discussed in detailed how early 1980's was the most pervasive theme of woman's liberation movement, in India. The in famous Mathura's rape case[174] ignited the issue & burst out of shadows to stand as symbol of woman's oppression The judicial approach on the factum of 'consent' moved the public opinion & ultimately the criminal law was amended in the shape of criminal law (second amendment) Act 1983 (anti rape amendment).

---

[174] State of Maharastra V/s. Tukaram AIR 1979 SC 185

National commission for women :-

National commission for women has been formed by national commission act 1990.The commission is engaged in the task of evaluating & suggesting reforms in woman concerning legislation & rehabilitation to ensure justice to victims of such crimes of violence. Some provision of the national commission for women (NCW) Act specifically requires the commission to-

Investigate & examine all matters relating to the safe guards provided for women under the constitution of India & other laws.

Present to the central government annually & at such other times as the
Commission may deem fit, reports upon the working of those safe guards.

Make in such reports, recommendations for the effective implementations of those safe guards for improving the conditions of women by the union or any state.

Review, from time to time. The existing provisions of the constitution & otter laws affecting women & recommend amendments there to so as to suggest remedial legislative measures to meet any lacunae, inadequacies or shortcomings in such legislation.

Take up the cases of violation of the provision of the constitution & of other laws relating to women with appropriate authors ties.

Accordingly since formation of NCW it has played vital role for the cause of women & the commission is in fact a milling stone in the development of women's law as to achieve their equal status in society & law.

The national commission for women proposed the following legal amendments[175].

To remove restriction on lodging of complaint in respect of offences under sections 494 and 494 of the Indian penal code.

---

[175] Criminal Procedure code, 1973 -amendment of sections 198 and 320

Amendment of section 320 so as to make the offences under section 498 of the Indian Penal Code as compoundable.

Indian Penal Code, 1860[176].

Strengthening of the laws to curb the incidence of sale of minor girls.

Dowry Prohibition Act, 1961.

To transfer the substantive provisions under the Indian Penal Code.

Dowry givers should be excluded from punishment.

Appointment of Dowry Prohibition Officers.

The marriage expenses should be limited to 20% of the annual income of the girl's parents/guardian.

Commission of Sati (Prevention) Act, 1987.

To transfer the substantive provisions under the Indian Penal Code.

The offence may be called as "Sati murder"

Hindu marriage Act, 1955.

Amendment of section 5 so as to omit epilepsy as a ground for divorce.

[176] www.nic.com

Child Marriage Restraint Act, 1929.

Amendment should not make to change the definition of kidnapping under section 359 of the IPC.

The marriage of a minor should be made void.

The offence should be made cognizable and non-boilable.

Indecent Representation of Women (Prohibition) Act, 1986.

The commission recommended for the amendment of Section 1 of the Act to make the definition of derogatory representation of women wider. Further provided for the increasing of punishment to the violators.

Immoral Traffic (Prevention) Act, 1956

(For elimination of child prostitution and devising a comprehensive package for rehabilitation.)

The commission recommended that the age of majority of the child under the Act might be raised to 18 years.

Further the government should take up correctional measures and also to rehabilitate the women and children in prostitution.

Medical Termination of Pregnancy Act, 1971

The women's consent must be obtained in every case.

To provide stringent punishment to the violators.

Family Courts Act, 1984

There shall be one or more family courts in every district.

Appeal under these matters will lie only to the High courts.

Foreign Marriage Act, 1969

The commission has recommended for the stipulation of conditions for the performance of Marriages under this Act.

The Family courts should deal the matters connected with this Act.

Guardians and Wards Act, 1890

The commission recommended that Section 15 and 16 or the Act should be amended so as to remove the compulsory linking of the wife's Domicile with that of the husband.

Further a testamentary guardian may be appointed only with the consent of the parent if alive and capable of acting.

Infant Milk Substitutes, Feeling Vittles and Infant Food (Regulation of Production, Supply and Distribution) Act, 1992

The commission recommended amendment of section 2(g), 3(g), 6,12,13,17,19(2), 21and 23 of the said Act, for strengthening the provision for better implementation.

More Powers to NCW through: NCW (Amendment) Bill 1998

Power to appoint its own staff.

Appointment of commissioner for women's rights.

Power of Prosecution in the lines of NHRC & Kerala State Commission for women.

Thus, a birds eye view of the attempts made by the legislators, executive judiciary see social workers unmistakably point that, the position of the women in domain of law has been theoretically accepted as unique & complementary to the advancement of women in society & culture. Great strides have been taken towards emancipation of women, stabilization of their status as acknowledged by religious & ethical tenets, and pieces of social legislations as & part of great movement as though.

Unfortunately, in spite of all these progressive legislation & change of outlook in the social approach towards women; these are steps in retrograde also out of political & patrochial consideration. Such steps thwart the progress already achieved & almost amount to abrogation of the entire progressive steps.

With great regret I am constrained to make a reference to a bill introduced in J & K assembly and even passed by one house of assembly where under the right of women marrying out side the state are sought to be forfeited. This piece of legislation though not brought on the statute books because of failure of other house to cause the same. And because of the mounting pressure the people in entire state & country is no doubt the matter of concern from the point of future position of women not only in that state but also in entire country. It may be a straw but it is likely to change the course of wind that blow. If we read this proposed bill one wonders whether all the lofty aim & object proclaimed in constitution & various pieces of legislators are set at naught.

It appears as though Art 15 of the constitution against discrimination on citizens on grounds of sex is not there at all in the constitution. Such discriminatory legislation makes one wonder whether all the salutary provisions of constitution & other laws were passed at all. It brings back the position of women at square one. These steps in retrogreat make one apprehensive of the future status of women in the country. In fact this piece of legislations should not have been introduced at all in the light of constitution & other provision of law. The very fact that such a legislation was to introduce makes not only apprehensive of future status of women but leads one irresistible conclusion that, all the progress made & sought to be is only theoretically achieved. The stork realities are likely to come to surface with the slightest move by any political party for its political convenience. The theoretical achievements need to be achieved in practical sphere & that is need of the hour.

But the one thousand doller questions are how can this to be achieved? Are all these pieces of legislation not strong enough to achieve this realistic goal? It is just like gift given by one hand and taking back by the other hand. This vicious circle has to come to an end. The practical achievement of force has to be by a natural & logical consequence of charge in outlook of the society as a whole. It is heartening however to note that attempts to fault the progress already made are stoutly opposed by the rational members of society. In fact this small incident also usefully proved that society & the country as a whole stoutly oppose such undesirable acts. And it is very & a healthy sign no doubt despite the discordant note struck by the authors of said legislation. But this is not all social.

Other factors & hurdles

Apart from those that are mentioned above these have been fresh inroads upon the theoretically accepted position of women in law. These are of course tainted with political consideration. For instance, the recent controversy, which is still simmering discontent, regarding introduction of reservation of women's Bill in parliament has thrown light on the inner contradiction despite of theoretical acceptance of position of women in law. Suffice is to say without elaborating on the causes of such abstraction by various political parties in parliament; even introduction of bill in parliament has not been so possible. Some kind of reservation is no doubt theoretically accepted but haggling's over the ratio, the applicability of the same to other cast & religion has created such insurmountable difficulties. This leads us to social complexities that hinder the implementation of the equality before law.

As rightly printed out by author of animal from -

"All are equal but something themselves to be equal. Thus this equality added to the superiority & inferiority complex of more equality & thus created paradoxical situation".

Women are equal on paper but the paper is as though spoiled by inks of other social considerations.

What is the way out?

The consideration of position of women in law has really been considered because of these innate contradictions. The society as a whole needs to be reorganized with the powerful benevolent arm of law. The ultimate object is to ushering in equality in life itself. It is not limited to legislative considerations. As pointed out by one scholar, "there is a cartload of legislation giving rights to women but I would like to add that this cart crumbles under its own weight. The harmonize reconstruction of theory & practice thus to be achieved. Law, has rightly pointed out by Veer Sawarkar from letter Andaman must be a righteous resolve of a free people.

One more natural limitation must be taken into conderation. Nature has created certainly certain physiological limitations in the body of men & women. Though no doubt women have achieved excellence in all walks of life including even in the military & air travels, the natural phenomenon cannot be altogether ignored. It is not possible to stress the principle of equality to its absurdity without taking into consideration limitations imposed by nature.

The principle of equality cannot be achieved to its logical absurdity. Exceptional achievement cannot be taken for granted in every normal individual & we have to take into consideration ground realities while considering principle of equality for law. But the principal of equality however, admits of no exception with natural phenomenal limitations.

In conclusion therefore law has no doubt guaranteed equality before law. The constitution as well as in very legislations. But the sabotaqous attempts on various pretext to nullify the same must be nipped in to bud. For that paradox if may require a vigilant force of enlightened citizens is necessary. This can only be done if the letter & spirit of very legal propositions have to be carried out by social awareness. The aim of law should be to create an ideal society. Where in injustice born out of inequality. Mania can be forbidden. The achievement of this ideal should be the real goal. There may be failures as are bound to be in all cases of attempts to achieve this ideal situation, but the same goal "not failure but low aim is crime". History of civilization is History of struggle of women in spite of these snags the chariot of revaluation that has started is going on its journey towards progressive humanity. Its result cannot be little if we look back, we realized that the fruits of evolution are not small & it is aftèr all continuing process.

As repeatedly stated, discussion of position of women in law is mainly the object of achieving the goal of kingdom of haven on earth as though. This kingdom in fact is one we have already biterring in as in garden. The permanent abodes though plant & articulated have yet to be constructed. In the words of Ravindranath Tagor, 'our object should be the world where the head is held high! This can only be achieved of course communize of minds of men & women."

The legal provisions are only handmaid to achieve that goal. The march of revaluation is unending & it has no doubt is very fruitful at every step. The snags referred above have to be guarded against by humanitarism, activism assisted by legal process. Had this evolution not taken place, the present revolution would not occur. The facts remain that today nobody can theoretically refused equality of women in any sphere. It has become a settled & principle reality under attempts to sabotage it, has to be frustrated by an iron hand & rosy fragrance. This rosy picture is not only imaginative now. It has achieved the state of reality may be on the screen now built no doubt a reality. No body has audacity to dispute this proposition. But the struggle is must. It is no doubt paradoxical that women we have been glorified as goddesses (shaktidevata) have to constantly struggle at every point to obtain, maintain & achieve equal rights. This struggle starts from our hearts & home & continuously has to go on in all walks of life.

Tragedy has to be treated as ornamental as in the case of Hardy's Novel "Tess"—she went to the gallows for indicating her honour & her own husband with his new wife saluted her memory.

Universal Law & Women

The universal law in fact is that men & women are not only complementary to each other but indispensably a part & parcel of natural phenomenon. Therefore, this evolution has no doubt elevated as ennobled the notion of feeling between men & women. They are not only physical. The irony of situation is that, while laudable principles are ensured in various religious provisions relating to women; the proposition of atrocities in women & dowry death are not lessened at all. It is curious that the more the safety guaranteed in such laws; the more are the incidents of sexual harassment & even abductions on women & rape. Sometimes one feels that, too much materializations of life itself are leading to increase in such incidents. The outlook in life itself is hedonistic. Therefore, material prosperity & money are the only goes after which people are hankering today. The outlook on life therefore has to be changed so as to values in a life. And then alone such madness would stop.

Place of women in law therefore has to be in consonance with the places of intrinsic values in life. Shakespeare had very aptly pointed at these degrading values in life in hamlet. Hamlet says "Father & mother means husband & wife". That technical description of relationship of father & mother is the very cause of degradation of moral standards in life. The evolution that has taken place & that will take place result in evolution has struck a balance between materialist & abrogation of all prosperity in life. Women therefore have to self reliant in spite of this danger of material degradation. Such proves like 125 CrPC have taken care of this stork reality of life namely that women have to be stand on there own legs. At the same time however, increasing pleasure seeking trend has to be cheated & regulations so to avoid excess greediness in life.

Dowry Death is the direct result of this perverted travel in life. Hankering after material prosperity regardless of moral values. Place of women therefore has to be sanctified in such a manner that entire outlook on life of which women are an integral part has to be elevated. This is the ideal situation. This is the dream that has to be cherished. Therefore the modern Shakespeare would not say, "frailty name is women", but he should say, "Morality thy name is life." The innate disposition of man should have mark linings towards human values. It may appear to be an ivory tower. But as on English author has rightly said,

"You should not live in an ivory tower but always write in it."

We in India do not want merry go lucky citizen. We want people who say we would make merry (woman) really lucky.

Last, but not the least one. Additional aspect has to be taken into consideration in this regard. We Indians have a philosophy way of a life at least in idealist sense & we value family ties & other related relationship as most dear to our life. This cultural background interwoven in our social fabric stands out distinctly from the rest of pleasure seeking societies in the worst of women. Sacrifice is the key word in our family life. Family life the very bad rock of our social existence though it is stoutly failed in these days because of the peculiar situation in modern era .Our family life cannot be compared with communes of other country. Because love & affections are very soul of our social structure. Place of women in law should not be aimed at deliberately disrupting this fiber of society. It may inevitably change its nature & form husband & wife living separately in different countries. Can still maintain that sacred tie because of, high cultured heritage. This aspect cannot be ignored & should not be ignored. Though, due to change in entire environment some inevitable changes are bound to be in structural forms. Basically however, love & affection should not only be the guiding principles in our family life but if should to be aspect we should increase its spiritual strength.

-Violence 1in any form is not caused has to be abhorred. Domestic violence is another demon that puts an end to family life. It is heartening to note that legal station or domestic violence or cards & it will soon find place in statute book. The credit of all these pieces of benevolent legislation goes to social workers, NGOs judiciary legislators & rulers. The responsibility of maintaining it in its sacred status manner is on the shoulder vigilant & enlightened citizens of country by increasing their moral values or spiritual strength.

The relation between law & morality

Definition of 'law' by legal philosophers[177]

The term 'law' means & includes different things in different societies. The corresponding word for the term 'law' in Hindu system is 'Dharma', in Islamic system it is 'Hukum' in Roman it is jus'. These words convey different meanings & ideas.

[177] Jurisprudence and Legal Theory – S.P. Dwivedi

The difference between the laws of two societies is not only that of stage of development but it is in characteristics also. Thus in all the societies from primitive to those which have reached the highest peak of civilization in one or the other from there is law. Law is a social science. To keep pace with the society, the function & scope of law remains always changing.

As per Hindu theory, origin of law is divine. Smritikars laid down four sources of law i.e. Veda, Smriti, Sadachar & self-satisfaction. The Hindu Dharmashastrakar believed in dynamics of law. The Smritikars adopted the more ancient law to progressive conditions. They brought about evolution, growth & expansion of the system. The commentators gave in genius interpretation to prevalent custom & usage in law & brought in harmony with prevailing motions of justice & enabled it to meet the requirements of the changing society, which we have experienced through the recent judicial exploration.

Manu defines law is an order of human behaviour. The rights and duties of man, established by this law, are innate or inborn in him, because they are implanted by nature & not imposed from outside. Briefly speaking Hindu legal philosophers think of law as a device to keep each man in his appointed groove in society & thus prevent friction with his fellows. The virtue indeed consists of knowing the limits which nature fixes for human conduct & keeping within them. The vice, which they denounce, is the willful transgression of the appointed bound.

Ancient theories of law

Socratis said that like natural physical law there is natural moral law. Man possesses 'insight' & this 'insight' revels to him the goodness & badness of things & makes him know the absolute & eternal moral values.

Aristotle said man is part of nature in two ways. First creature of god & second man's reason, which is part of nature. Aristotle defines 'Natural Justice' as "that which everywhere has the same force".

As per theory of stoics in Rome[178], the entire universe is governed by 'reason' Man's

[178] Jurisprudence and Legal Theory – S.P. Dwivedi

reason is a part of the 'universal reason'. Therefore when he lives according to reason, he lives according to nature or lives 'naturally. It is moral duty of man to subject himself to the 'law of nature'. Positive law must conform to the 'natural law'. Natural law principle is 'justice', equity & good conscience. Which has exercised a great formative influence on the English law is founded on natural law ideas.

In America the power of legislation is limited by the principles of natural justice and the Supreme Court has the power of judicial review of the legislation.

India[179] --

In India, a number of legal principles & concepts have been borrowed from England, many of them based on natural law. The Indian constitution embodies a number of principles 'natural law' it guarantees certain basic liberties i.e. fundamental rights to citizens. It empowers the high courts & Supreme Court to exercise control over the administrative & quasi. Judicial tribunals.

---

[179] Jurisprudence and Legal Theory – S.P. Dwivedi

The idea of natural law & justice is based on moral or religious grounds. The idea of natural law found in Greek, Rome & Hindu legal thought. Natural law rules and positive law acted & reacted upon each other & brought about development of law. Natural law has given a great support to International law & gives solid grounds to stand upon the backdrop of all these legal principles, one can see that for real development of law the positive law has to be conciled with divine law. For the development of women law in particular, I would say that we have achieved the natural law, principle of equity, & justice (legal justice) but not good consciousness. It will be achieved through spiritual evolution, only we can work it out.

The legislation & precedents by the apex court & various High Court have brought the Indian women at par. with principle of equality & justice, but if we peep into their social & family status; We will say still the position of women in domestic & social atmosphere is secondary & not equal.

Why this happened? Because we have forgotten our richest culture where the women worshiped as goddess Shakti. The women chastity is spoiled & she treated as commodity.

In Hindu scripture goddess 'Adishakti' is known as "Ma Shakti, Devi etc. & is worshiped, In Christians Merry Mata is worshiped. Russian author Maxim Gorky writes a book 'mother'. The all religion & nations worshiped motherhood –and spiritual mother. But they do not respect their personal mother, motherhood in society. When the motherhood is spoiled in its image, when mother are no more mothers, when they are not respectable, then they are not respected. When children don't respect mothers, they have no respect for anything else whatsoever. The first and last thing is the respect for the mother. Shri Mataji Nirmaladevi said, to be a mother is a greater responsibility than that of a king because a king can only go up to material level or physical level. But the spiritual level you can only achieve from your mother.

Women & Shakti Principles as per Scriptures[180]

'Ya Devi Sarva Bhuteshu, Shakti Rupen Sansthita, Namastasye, Namastasye, Namastasye, Namo Namah!

Goddess Devi, we bow before you in the form of goddess Shakti!

'Shakti' means creative energy and Shaktism means "Doctrine of the creative Energy. Shaktism visualizes the ultimate reality as having two as aspects, transcendent & immanent. Shiva is the transcendent aspect, the supreme cosmic consciousness and Shakti is the supreme creative energy. Shiva & shakti are goddess and god's creative energy inseparably connected divine couple, representing the male & female principle in creation.

The god of Shaktism is to unite with Shiva such unity is possible only with the grace of the Divine Mother, who unfolds as Iccha Shakti (the power of desire, will & love) i.e. Mahakali, Kriyashakti (power of

180 www.adishakti.com

action i.e. Mahasaraswati), and Jhana Shakti (the power of knowledge & wisdom i.e. Mahalaxmi.) Through a spiritual discipline, Shakti is awakened & it rises through the spine and unites with Shiva in sahasrar. When this energy transformation occurs, the individual attains cosmic consciousness and is said to have realized the self.

Within Shaktism, Shiva is the unmanifest absolute & Shakti is the Divine Mother of the manifest creation. The Divine Mother is worshipped in both the fierce & benign forms. The fierce forms of goddess includes Kali, Durga, Chandi, Chamundi, Bhadrakali, & Bhairavi. The benign forms of goddess include Uma, Gauri, Ambika, Parvati, Maheshwri, Lalita, Lakshmi, Saraswati & Annapurna.[181]

Since this primordial power of the ultimate is the creature of everything we experience, she is worshipped as Mother from time immemorial. In fact Shakti worship in India is as old as man. She is Mahasaraswati aspect of Shakti who by presenting to the

---

181 .- www.hindubooks .org.

sadhaka the knowledge of the ultimate reality –Atmajnana.[182]

Cause & occasion of Her Manifestation[183]

When there is decline of righteousness and a rise of unrighteousness, she manifests for destruction of the wicked & the establishment of true righteousness. In Treta age the decline begins and becomes rapid in Dvapara Age. In Kali age, the most evil of the ages, unrighteousness or Adhorma prevails. In this age the godhead, the divine mother, manifest herself for the establishment of righteousness or Dharma.

Adharma or unrighteousness

When the righteous, innocent, weak, pious & spiritual people are exploited by unrighteous cruel, strong, wicked & mundane people & and when moral values are lost & immorality prevails, that state is the state of decline of righteousness & the rise of unrighteousness then Adhiparshakti manifest Herself.

---

[182] C.Suryanarayan Merthy, Shri Lalita Sahasranama

[183] www.adishakti.com

The Prophecies of Nostradomus for Women[184]

Manuela Dunn & Peter Lori in their book. Nostradamus, prophecies for women wrote that, the message of the Holy Spirit that Homo Sapiens have to transform themselves into higher beings will be different to be accepted & imbibed by the aggressive, macho, ego- oriented male dominated societies even as they stand on the brink of spiritual anolihilation. The global race & greed for material wealth has reached satanic proportions with little regard for existing resources, environment or humans-everything is a commodity. Human relationship are being stripped of all warmth, love & compassion as wars, drugs crimes, violence, divorces, unwed mothers, poverty, racism, media immorality, untruth religions, corruption, politics, litigation, homelessness and hopelessness take their daily toll. Humans are being dehumanized and devoured by the very society they have built for themselves.

[184] www.adishakti.com

Any community that does not put the spirit of humans first doomed to fail. Thus includes all Eastern societies now seduced into embracing the virtues of materialism with a vulgar display of wantonness & abandon, forgetting & realizing their ancient spiritual roots that had nourished their inner self & kept the fabric of humanity intact.

The false fears of poverty (or "lack" of wealth) keep human minds trapped in a vicious illusion & permanent population. They are mentally shackled in a male dominated culture of power, greed & consumerism. They will find it difficult even to listen to the voices of wisdom, let alone transform. Enlighten takes some time to be understood. Few really believe that their spirit within exist and is eternal. Without the comfort faith & security of this knowledge life continues to be a one-night stand of wild abandon, devoid of decorum, direction or destiny. <u>The only hope lies in the awakening and empowerment of women and the reversal of patriarchal personalities.</u>

Further more in this book. 'Nostradamus prophesies for women' in century 2:12 it is mentioned- the body without soul no longer to be sacrificed. Self-realization is rebirth of the physical human into the spirit being. Once this takes place the Holy Spirit (Mother Kundalini) within begins to nurse, nourish, cleanse & guide her child. The lunar consciousness will reveal that all religious, rituals, fasts, sacrifices, celibacy, penance, confessions, vegetarianism, caste, kosher foods Shari at laws – are to be discarded like old garments. There will be no more religious austerities of the external physical body but nourishment of the inner spiritual soul, with inward growth, meditation, peace, joy, happiness, joy, happiness, bliss, love, compassion, humility, tenderness, tranquility and truth and truth. All the false ministers of external idols will be abandoned as they suffocate the human spirit with layer upon layer of rules, regulations, laws, dogmas, theologies, interpretations, falsehood and lies.

Those are the false prophets who have worked diligently over the centuries, devising ingenious ways to divide & rule his children.

A Unique Discovery of Kundalini awakening by Shri Mataji Nirmaladevi[185].

All evolution of the manifestation of material energy is guided by the supreme energy of Divine Love. We do not know how powerful & thoughtful this unknown energy is! After self-realization this energy appears to us as silent throbbing vibrations flowing through our being. But we have been unable to achieve self-realization because we cannot fix our attention on something that looks form (abstract being). Instead our attention wonders outside on forms. Now there is a method to tap the Divine power—Sahaja Yoga[186].

'Sahaja' means born with you or inborn. What ever is an inborn manifest without any effort? Hence, Sahaja Yoga is the name given to this system, which is effortless, easy & spontaneous. It is a part of Nature; we may call it life's source, the vitality of the Divine.

---

185 www.adishakti.org
186 www.sahajayoga.org

How to achieve spiritual strength

We may have organized series of lectures workshops, seminars, conferences etc. on the problems of women & at every such academic functions. We come to the conclusion of increasing moral values of society or charge in attitude of man or a society as a whole towards women, or for sensitization of the gender justice issue. However, have we experienced the change in attitude of society due to enactment of law? A particular law may had executed its operation on offender or wrong doer. But this action on account of law in no way changes the person from his insight. The law could only restrict his physical activities like confining him in prison, or payment of fine etc. But after completing his punishment he again enters in the same world with same mental setup to do crime, so what is the way out to achieve the inner wisdom?

The spiritual references of position of women in society

We have already taken a detailed account of the socio, eco, physiological & number of other reasons for the present position of women in society. However, all these reasons are the by-product of one main reason i.e. the moral degradation of women by the society first & secondly by themselves. We are not adhered to our high culture of maintaining the dignity & honour of women in our society. This position is affirmed by the Hon'ble Supreme Court in Vishaha's & Apparel's cases we have forgotten that in our Indian mythology power of Sada- Shiv is the Adishakti Primordial power) who is his feminine counter part or spouse. It is she who does all things. She created the universe and the gods who attend over it (for example triune Shiva, Bramha & Vishnu, the Adishakti is the mother of all things. She gave birth to the universe and she is the feminine power of every deity and celestial being. Classic poetry such as' the Saundarya lahari'. Shankaracharya said ,

"all glory unto the current of Divine Bliss which, brimming from the river of The Holy Stories, flows into the lake of my mind through the canals of intellect, subduing the dust of sin and cooling the heat of memory."

Consider this text from the book of[187] - "I have reached the inner vision and through They spirit in me I have heard the wondrous secret, though the mystic insight. Thou hast caused a spring of knowledge to well up within me, a fountain of power pouring forth living waters, a flood of love and of all embracing wisdom like the splendor light."

Vedams Books from India[188] –

"This book offers a variety of scholarly studies in the idea, situation, and definition-including the self-definition-of women in Indian society, form the earliest historical period up to the present day. Both in its range of topics and depth of research, this volume creates a sustained focus that is not presently available in the literature on women in India.

"In ancient times, women in India were revered as Goddess and she occupied a great position in the family and society. But this position of woman degraded as time passed in the name of religious and socio-political practices and they were denied opportunities of growth. Since then many attempts

---

[187] Hymens of the Dead Sea scrolls

[188] www.vedamsbooks.com

were made to ameliorate and emancipate the woman but much result could not be obtained due to hard core religious practices and superstitions prevalent in the society and her position remained more or less the same.

The movement for the improvement of legal status of women was an integral part of the general movement for the emancipation of women. The social reformers from the very beginning held the view that one of the principal means of improving the status of women was legislation. The study of history of social legislation in India thus becomes necessary to ascertain and evaluate the progress made and empowerment gained by Indian womanhood."

"Twentieth century has brought a great change in the lives of women all over the world influencing their attitudes, values, aspirations, ways of feeling, standards of behaviour and actions for effective participation in all walks of life. Women's quest for equality and emancipation has become global phenomenon. Yet, gender gap is not diminished and more complex types of problems are arising out of application of modern and sophisticated technology in all fields. A large number of gender issues continue to determine the nature and shape of our society like most traditional societies where women do not/can not enjoy an average quality of life equal to that of men in terms of life expectancy, health, morality, access to education, access to employment, access to lawful freedoms, and the meaningful exercise of civil and political rights. There has been a tremendous concern on these issues during the last few decades as reflected in the number of studies on the construction and representation of gender roles and gender identities in South Asia.

Gender Issues in India : Some reflections/Sushma Yadav and Anil Dutta Mishra.

"Women constitute almost half of the human population have been suffering social and economic deprivation and oppression through millennium all over the world. Improvement in the status of movement has been accepted by the founding fathers of the constitution and subsequently by the government from the very beginning of independent India. Over the year number of social legislations have been passed in favour of women but still we find that the status of women in our society has not achieved the desired standard of course law is one of the most effective modern made for tackling social issues, discrimination and exploitation in society including those, operating against women but law alone is not sufficient to achieve the desired results. The book entitles "Status of Women in India" analyses and discussed the constitution obligation of providing legal aid to the women, consequent to sex determination test status of women on one hand, and on the other equal remuneration for equal work and better working conditions for female workers.

Supreme Court and High Court Judgments Relating to Women and Children/edited by Charu Walikhanna and Nandita Rao.[189]

"This book is an effort to handover women an instrument to understand and use the law. The principles of fairness and equity are enshrined in the constitution of India, that unequivocally mandates gender equality. Such equality-truly in fact and deed – is a national imperative for no nation can hope to attain its full potential of development if it were to underutilize or suppress half its human resource that women represent. Discrimination and violence against women do not just victimize the individual women, but do indeed hold back whole sections of society. Guaranteeing rights to women and enabling them to effectively access these rights and

[189] www.vedamsbook.com

entitlements is an investment in making the whole nation stronger and self-reliant.

India is a multi-linguistic, multi-cultural and multi-religious country of more that a billion people, of which almost half comprise females. For the vast mass of these women it is particularly the personal law that principally governs their lives, though to many the exact dimension and how it controls the lives of each one of us may not be very clear. Simply stated, women in India though common in need and circumstance are divided by caste, religion, social and regional customs and are therefore unable to agitate or ensure a humane and equitable entitlement for themselves on issues which are fundamental to all women, such as, maintenance, custody, physical and mental security in marriage, fair and equal divorce entitlements. It is in this context that a book like this become important in bringing together in a single text all the laws that effect women.

Role of women in society – the reasons of their present position - with brief reference of Shri Mataji Nirmala Devi's speech before Beijing women conference 1995[190]

In a Beijing women's conference 1995 Shri Adishakti Mataji Nirmaladevi has thrown light on the pathetic position of women in society, the role of women for society, their duties towards family and society and suggestion for their upgrade ness only through spiritual evolution awakening Kundalini by self-realization.

I am referring the important points of the speech of Divine Mother which relates to my subject in hand and one and the only suggestion which can only change the attitude of the society towards women and for giving them equal position not only as per the positive law but it has to be given through Divine law by awakening of Kundalini.

[190] www.adishakti.org

Shri Mataji Nirmala Devi's speech before Beijing women conference 1995[191]

Brothers and Sisters of the World, It is a great honour for me to talk about global problems of women in front of this distinguished assembly. First of all I would like to offer my profound gratitude to the government and the people of our host country, the People's Republic of China. I have had the privilege of visiting China on two previous occasions and I am a great admirer of the wisdom and culture of this great nation that I have visited.

Shri (Dr.) Shri Mataji Nirmala Devi

This is, beyond my imagination, the most glorious time in the history of the world that at this time we are so much aware of the problems of women. Women as a whole have definitely suffered over the ages because we have not realized what their importance is and what their proper role is in human society. Society itself, which

[191] www.adishakti.org

is her creation, tries to control or put down the womanhood. In the East, we can say, that due to fundamentalist influence women have been under great pressure and their morality is based on fear rather than freedom. In the West they have fought for their freedom, but what they have attained is spurious freedom. The women in the West have the freedom to abandon all social and moral values. Thus in the East, we can say, that most of the women are timid, oppressed and cannot express themselves, while in the West we find most of the women are reduced to a sex symbol. They are keen to expose their body; their anxiety is to appear in fashion advertisement s and very cheap popularity. Most of them accepted this position because otherwise they could not have survived in that chaotic world of the West. What most of the women in the East would regard as very humiliating and degrading is regarded as something very glorifying in the West. I have seen both the worlds very deeply and I feel that unless and until you bring a new culture by which women from the East and women from the

West can both rise in their own esteem and express themselves in such a way that they create high moral standards for their society, women neither in the East nor in the West will rise to their full stature of feminine speciality. The speciality is that if women are respected for their womanhood, understanding what they are capable of and how they can empower themselves with all the education needed, all the security will be provided to them and they will provide security to the society.

All the fundamentalists who talk of religion expect women to be absolutely moral and the men can do whatever they like. I feel we have to educate men more than women. I must admit it is not difficult to collect money for poor women in the developing countries and help them to get out of their poverty, but unfortunately, my knowledge is that the money we are collecting may not reach the poor women but may end up into the pockets of the corrupt ministers, bureaucrats and other people in charge.

One has to have a very good network of people, specially women, who are involved and who are honest, compassionate and who would like to make the best out of this money, helping the women to achieve social equality. The main work of womanhood is to create a good society.

Immorality and corruption are the two horrible monsters which are eating up our society. I would blame the mothers of these immoral and corrupt persons because they failed in their duty as mothers in their childhood. The loving training of the mother is the first and most effective influence in shaping the children into beautiful citizens. Mothers who have never tried to guide with great concern and love, or the wives or the daughters who are falling into the fear of the men or of the destructive culture, have not done their duty as integral members of the family to strengthen the moral fibre of the men. It is important also to see how children are treated in these two cultures of East and West. What we see in the East is that children would listen to their mothers if they were not under fundamentalist culture. This culture relegates women to the level of an inferior human being, fit to be dominated by men and children. In the West also the same thing happens. Children don't respect their mothers neither do they listen to them. I feel this is because, generally, the Western women spend more time looking after their body and looks than on looking after and loving their children. The nexus between the mother and children weakens and breaks. It is for this reason that many children become street urchins. Fortunately there are still many families in the East and some in the West who deeply defy the corrupting trends of today and look after their children and bring them up properly.

But still I must say that the children in the East are not that much ruined as they are in the West. The reason, also, is that in the East there are many people who have not taken to fundamentalist culture or to the Western culture and have a very good society and produce children who are exceptionally good although this number may not be very great. But whatever culture they have inherited, since long, traditionally, is very much ingrained in them and to them the moral value system is the highest, more than money or power.

The West is now full of problems. Though they have money, they don't have peace within and without. The truth is that women are the potential power of every civilization and every country. It is evident that women are the creators and the preservers of the entire humankind. This is the role that the almighty God has assigned to them. Seeds cannot create anything by themselves. It is the Mother Earth which provides the flowers and the fruits and other bounties. Similarly, it is the woman who creates the child, who nurtures the baby and eventually brings up the citizen of tomorrow. Women must therefore rank with Mother Earth as the edifice of the entire humanity. Unfortunately, men have utilized muscle power to gain a dominating position over women. They have not recognized that women are complementary and equal but not similar partners in human endeavors. A society that does recognize this fundamental truth and does not given to women their rightful role is not a civilized society.

In my own country there is a saying in Sanskrit, "Yatra nayra pujyante tatra ramante devata" , which means that "Where the women are respected and respectable, there resides the Gods of our well-being". So it is for us, at this moment, to recognize the value of this great power that is given to us by our Creator. But what do we find? Whether in the East or in the West, women have not been able to give a full manifestation of their greatness. I am not suggesting at all that the only role of women in society is that of the Mother, the pro-creator and preserver of children, or that of a wife, or a sister. Women have a full right to participate as equal partners in every aspect of life; social, cultural, educational, political, economical, administrative and the rest. In order to prepare themselves for this all-pervading role, they must have the right to education in all branches of knowledge. But if they are mothers, they have a great responsibility towards their children as well as their society. Men are responsible for the politics and economics of the country but women are responsible for the society. Women can also support men and they can take leading part, of course, in any position but, it is very important that they should not forget that they are women who have to manifest deep motherly concern and love. If they become manly and aggressive the balance of society cannot be maintained.

At the same time I must submit that while we ask for the rights of women we must also stress the fundamental duties of women to the human society. The women in the West, or those who are educated in the West, have gone to the other extreme when they are taking to political, economical or administrative role. To compete with men they have become much too self-willed, self-centered and ambitious. They have no more their soothing and pleasing qualities which can keep the balance. On the contrary, they become dominating, pleasure-seeking individuals. They are far more worried about their physical attractions than having a pleasing, sweet and dignified personality. They give into their baser self much faster than men, wittingly or unwittingly. All this leads to chaotic societies and children grow up into street urchins, thieves and even murderers as we read everyday in the paper. What we need is a balance between the two extremes. We need women as equal but not similar partners wit h men, but with a subtle understanding of the nature of men and how to bring them into the centre with inner balance. We need balanced women in order to have a balanced human race with peace within itself. You might say all this is excellent in thought, but how do we achieve this state of balance? How do we stem the tide of diseases, corruption, immorality and immaturity. How do we end the present state of conflict and conf usion? How do we bring about peace within every mind and heart? I very humbly submit that there is an answer to these questions. There is a new way.

Whatever I am going to tell you now is not be taken for granted. You should, of course, have your minds open like scientists and treat whatever I am stating as a hypothesis. If this hypothesis can be proved, then you have to accept it as honest persons as the absolute truth because it is for your benevolence. It is for the benevolence of your family, it is for the benevolence of your country and for the benevolence of the whole world.

I am here to tell you about the last breakthrough of our evolution. This breakthrough of our evolution in our awareness has to happen in these modern times and has been, moreover, recorded in the writings of many seers. These are the times called as the "Decadent Times" last called by the great saint Vyasa who has written the Gita, and it is the decadence of humanity that we see around in every way possible.

Now I would like to tell the secret knowledge of our inner being which was known in India thousands of years back. For our evolution and spiritual ascent there is a residual power within us which is located in the triangular bone at the base of our spine. This residual power is known as Kundalini. Though the knowledge of this power was available thousands of years back in India, the awakening of the Kundalini was done, traditionally, on an individual basis only. One guru would given awakening to one disciple. As a result of that awakening, what happens is that you achieve your self-realization, your self-hood. Secondly, when this power is awakened, it rises and passes through six subtle energy centres in your body, nourishing them and integrating them. Ultimately, this power breaks through the fontanel bone area called as the Talu or the Brahmarandra and connects you to the all-pervading power of Divine love, which is described in the bible also as the "cool breeze of the Holy Ghost" also in the Koran as "Ruh" and also in the Indian scriptures as "Paramchaitanya". Patanjali has called it as "Ritambhara Pragya". Whatever the name, this is a power which is all-pervading, which does all the subtle works of living process, of evolutionary process. The existence of this all-pervading energy is not felt before realisation but after self-realisation you can feel it on your finger tips or at the centre of your palm or above the fontanel bone area. Moreover, this process has to be spontaneous, "Sahaja". "Saha" means "with" and "ja" means "born". That means the right to get this union with the all-pervading power of Divine love is the birth right of every human being. Our mental energies are limited. Our limited mental energy, which is linear in movement and has not sustenance of reality, reaches a point and stops. From there it boomerangs and all that mental, linear movement comes back to us as a punishment sometimes. So now we need more energy, higher energy, deeper energy and for that this happening has to take place.

I must say that in the West, I have met many people who are true seekers of Truth and are fed up of artificiality of the Western life. Also they didn't know what they were seeking sometimes and they have made lots of mistakes. They have gone to false gurus who have taken lots of money and the people have become bankrupts and mentally and physically handicapped. The one thing you must note is that the awakening of the Kundalini and thus achieving self-realisation is a living process of evolution for which we cannot pay anything. It is like putting a seed in the Mother Earth. It sprouts because Mother Earth has the power to sprout it and the seed has an in-built germinating quality within it. In the same way we have this germinating power in the triangular bone which Greeks called as Sacrum. Actually in some people you can see this triangular bone pulsating and the Kundalini very slowly rising, but where there are no obstructions and if the person is a balance being, the Kundalini rises form the Sacrum just like a jet and passes through the fontanel bone area to become one with the all-pervading power. This Kundalini is the spiritual mother of every individual and She knows or has recorded all the past aspirations of Her child. She is anxious to give second birth to Her child and during Her ascent, She nourishes six energy centres. When a person is not connected to the all pervading power, he is like an instrument which is not connected to the mains and has no identity, has no meaning, has no purpose. As soon as it is connected, all that is built in inside this instrument starts working and manifesting itself. When this Kundalini rises it connects you to the all pervading power, which is vital and which is an ocean of knowledge as well as an ocean of bliss. After the awakening of Kundalini, you experience many coincidences which are miraculous and extremely blissful. Above all Kundalini is the ocean of forgiveness. So what ever mistakes you have committed in the past are forgiven and instead you get your self-realisation as a blessing.

The consequences of the awakening of the Kundalini and thereby the attainment of self-realisation are numerous. First and foremost, such a person is constantly in contact with or is in fact a part of the all pervading Divine power. He seeks the truth by using his new awareness. And truth is one, all self-realised persons see this same truth. Thus conflicts are avoided. Purely mental activity without self-realisation, leads to conflicting ideas and even wars. All this is avoided after self-realisation. Now, let us see how many other things happen in a person who gets realisation. Firstly you start feeling the cool breeze of the Holy Ghost on your fingertips, which represent the subtle energy centres. Thus you know the truth on your finger tips. You transcend all the limitations of race, religion and other ideas and you go beyond your mind to see and feel the reality and understand it. The next thing that happens is that you become thoughtlessly aware. We live in the future and the past through our thoughts. They come to us from these two areas of time but we cannot be in the present. While these thoughts are rising and falling we are jumping on the cusp of these thoughts. But when Kundalini rises She elongates these thoughts and thereby creates some space in-between which is the present, which is the reality. So the past is over and the future doesn't exist. At that time you have no thoughts. You reach a new state as you become thoughtlessly aware about which Jung has written clearly. At this moment whatsoever happens is recorded in your memory well and you enjoy every moment of this in reality. When you become thoughtlessly aware then you become completely peaceful within yourself.

A person who has achieved this peace also emits peace and creates a peaceful atmosphere around himself. This peace is very important. Unless and until we have this peace we will never truly understand whatever our ideas are, whether universal or just limited. You can feel your own seven centres on your fingertips. Also you can feel the centres of others because you develop a new level of awareness which is called as collective consciousness. When such new awareness is established into you, you start feeling also the centres of others. I must tell you that these centres are responsible for our physical, mental, emotional and spiritual well being and when they are affected or they are in jeopardy, people suffer from one disease or another. As a result of the awakening of the Kundalini and the nourishment of these centres, an important development would be that you will feel an inner balance and you will enjoy good health. Many diseases, even some incurable ones, have been cured by the awakening of the Kundalini. Even the data base of the inherited genes may be restructured after self-realisation through the awakening of the Kundalini. As a result, a person who might have inherited genes indicating criminal tendency might become a good man.

Our attention also becomes very pure. In the light of the spirit we can see things much more clearly than when we were blind. For example, a person who goes with his blind eyes and feels an elephant and then another comes in and a third comes in, all of them have different ideas about the elephant, depending on whichever part of the elephant they have touched. But if they open their eyes then they can all see the same thing, the reality and there will be no quarrel and fights. A self-realised person can feel the absolute knowledge on the fingertips. Supposing someone doesn't believe in God. A self-realised person can suggest to the non-believer that he should ask the question: "Is there God?" The questioner will get, you will find, a very nice cool breeze coming into his being. He may not believe in God but there is God. Unfortunately, so many of those who believe in God are also absurd, hypocritical, cruel, weird and so immoral that people have lost faith in God, But while those who represent God may be wrong, God himself exists and his power also exists which we call as the all-pervading power of Divine love. This is the power of love and compassion and not of aggression and destruction when it is imbibed in a yogi or in a self-realised person, it works in a very different way like an angel. Such people can cure others and cure themselves. Even mental cases have been cured. Not only that. Even those who have been to wrong gurus in their search of truth have achieved their spiritual stability after leaving false gurus and coming to the path of self-realisation.

In the next stage, you become thoughtlessly aware, when your Kundalini is stabilised and you know undoubtedly that you have achieved your self-realisation, that you have attained all the powers that can be utilised. You become very powerful because you can raise the Kundalini of others. You become very active and you don't feel tired easily. For example, I am seventy three years of age and I am traveling about every third day, but I am quite alright. This energy flows into you and fills you up with vitality. You become extremely dynamic and at the same time extremely compassionate, kind and mild. You feel that you are protected and thus you are confident but not egotistical. Your whole personality changes. This is the kind of global transformation which is taking place with such a speed all over that I, myself, am surprised at how it is working out so fast.

Actually, this knowledge existed a long time back but my contribution, if there is any, is that we can now achieve en-masse realisation. Thousands can achieve mass realisation. It is a gift of this time where it was predicted that such global transformation will take place. In as many as 65 countries, thousands of people have attained their self-realisation through Sahaja Yoga.

The power of Kundalini is the pure desire of attaining your selfhood. If someone doesn't want to have it, you cannot force him because the Divine respects the freedom of that person. If he wants to go to heaven, he can go there, or if he wants to go to hell, he can go to hell. Self-realisation can be attained easily if the people have a sincere and pure desire to get their self-realisation. But if they stick to some of their ideas, which are fixed, the Kundalini won't rise. Also it cannot work for idiots or for immature people. It works for people who are wise, who are more in the centre, and it works very fast. I was amazed to see that it has worked even on people who were drug addicts , who were alcoholics and who were very immoral. But they all had an intense and pure desire to secure self-improvement, self-realisation. So many of such people achieved their goal of self-realisation. Overnight, they gave up their drugs, their alcoholism . Thus you become very powerful and at the same time you understand that yo u are now glorified and you start behaving in a very dignified and a very sensible manner. This is how a new culture is born and this new culture takes you , in a way, into a new style of life where you become innately, I say innately, righteous. Nobody has to tell you: "Don't do this" and "Don't do that". It is all achieved through your enlightened attention. This enlightened attention is also full of power. Wherever you put your attention it works, it creates peace, it creates harmony and also it creates a new dimension of collective consciousness.

So to blame your genes for your mistakes is not going to work out anymore because these genes can be changed in their database and can be brought to the level of a very righteous, angelic personality. The ego and the conditioning of a person gets dissolved by the ascent of the Kundalini and he becomes really a free bird. Absolute freedom is achieved in reality and his behavior changes tremendously with great faith in himself. He becomes a witness of the whole drama of life. When you are in the water you are afraid of getting drowned, but supposing you get into a boat, you can watch the same waters with enjoyment. But if you learn how to jump in the water and save others then it is even a higher situation and so we have a higher awareness which we call as doubtless awareness. Above all, we fall into the ocean of joy. Joy is absolute. It doesn't have duality. It is not like happiness and unhappiness. It is a singular thing and once you jump into it you learn easily how to enjoy everything, whether it is beautiful or ridiculous. In one case you see the beauty; in the other you see the humour as to how people are ridiculous. The remarkable thing is that Sahaja Yogis have become great musicians, great writers, great speakers, great administrators. In every way they have rise very high, specially in their attitude toward others. They respect everyone and they know what is wrong with other people so that they can approach them carefully, gently to see that this person who has these problems can be easily evolved and become a self-realised soul. It is like one candle lighting another candle. This work is going on all over the world and there is great hope that it will also start in China. Before this, somehow, I could not start my work but the Divine coincidence has given a chance to me by this conference to talk to Chinese people, who I find very wise and sensitive, about the great treasure of spirituality. This is not a coincidence. It was inevitable and has been brought about by this all-pervading power. In your life also you will notice lots of coincidences but you will not know how to connect them to something that is Divine unless and until you get connected to the Divine power.

Confucius has taught the humanity how we can improve our relations with other human beings. But Lao Tse in China has very beautifully described Tao, meaning the Kundalini. And I have had a voyage through the Yangtze River through which Lao Tse had gone many times. I know he was trying to show that this river which is the Kundalini, is flowing towards the sea and one should not be tempted by the nature that is around. The nature around the Yangtze River is very, very beautiful, no doubt, but one has to go through the river. Also there are lots of currents which flow and can be quite dangerous and we need a good navigator who should take his ship across to the point where it is nearer the sea. At that stage it becomes very silent and extremely simple in its flow.

This country has been endowed with great philosophers, I would say the greatest was Lao Tse, because humanism was for the preparation of human beings for their ascent about which Lao Tse had spoken. But because of the subtle subject it was not described in such a clear-cut manner as I am talking to you. It is such a pleasure for me to talk to this august gathering here. After traveling all over the world, I realise that China is one of the best countries as far as spirituality is concerned.

CPSIA information can be obtained
at www.ICGtesting.com
Printed in the USA
LVHW031117050423
743446LV00001B/23